# THE NEXT
# SOCIAL CONTRACT

WAYNE GABARDI

# THE NEXT
# SOCIAL CONTRACT

ANIMALS, THE ANTHROPOCENE,
AND BIOPOLITICS

TEMPLE UNIVERSITY PRESS
*Philadelphia • Rome • Tokyo*

TEMPLE UNIVERSITY PRESS
Philadelphia, Pennsylvania 19122
*www.temple.edu/tempress*

*Page iii photograph: Franz Marc,* The Fox *(1913). (Public domain image.)*

Library of Congress Cataloging-in-Publication Data

Names: Gabardi, Wayne, 1955– author.
Title: The next social contract : animals, the Anthropocene, and biopolitics
   / Wayne Gabardi.
Description: Philadelphia : Temple University Press, 2017. | Includes
   bibliographical references and index.
Identifiers: LCCN 2016049913 (print) | LCCN 2017011430 (ebook)
   | ISBN 9781439914113 (cloth : alk. paper) | ISBN 9781439914120 (pbk. : alk. paper)
   | ISBN 9781439914137 (E-Book)
Subjects: LCSH: Animals and civilization. | Animals—Effect of human beings on.
   | Bioethics. | Biopolitics.
Classification: LCC QL85 .G27 2017 (print) | LCC QL85 (ebook)
   | DDC 591.5—dc23
LC record available at https://lccn.loc.gov/2016049913

∞ The paper used in this publication meets the requirements of the American National
Standard for Information Sciences—Permanence of Paper for Printed Library Materials,
ANSI Z39.48-1992

Printed in the United States of America

9  8  7  6  5  4  3  2  1

*For Jamie*

*and*

*Little Big Man*

# CONTENTS

# THE NEXT
# SOCIAL CONTRACT

# INTRODUCTION

———

# THE ARGUMENT AND STRUCTURE
# OF THE BOOK

———

Animals consider man as a being like themselves
that has lost in a most dangerous way
its sound animal common sense.

—Friedrich Nietzsche,
*The Gay Science*, Book Three, Aphorism 224

This book concerns itself with the fate of animals in the Anthropocene. It is conceptualized and argued from a postanthropocentric standpoint. The argument consists of a set of interrelated propositions or theses that build on one another. Together, they yield an ethos and politics commensurate with the principles and practices of posthumanist ethics and justice.

The first proposition advanced is the Anthropocene hypothesis. The impact of *Homo sapiens* on Earth over the past two centuries has been so significant that our species has become a change agent equal to or greater than the planet's biophysical forces. There is a growing belief that Earth is in the early stages of an epochal shift. A number of scientists and concerned citizens have proposed identifying a new period in planetary history distinct from the Holocene epoch. The key drivers of this new era in planetary evolution are the human-population proliferation; the globalization of modernity in the form of fossil-fueled, high-tech, consumption-based, capitalist-growth economies; terrestrial re-engineering; mega-urbanization; the rise of a global middle class; and big industrial, monoculture farming. The effects of this civilizational juggernaut are global climate change, the disruption of ecosystems and social environments, and species extinction significant enough to be characterized as a potential mass extinction event. All of these global trends are interconnected.

The term "Anthropocene" was first introduced at the turn of the twenty-first century as a new scientific marker in evaluating the planet's current geological condition. It has since rapidly developed to become a major framing concept, discourse, interdisciplinary field of study, and ethical and political point of reference. Initially related to issues of anthropogenic climate change and global warming, population growth, and geological time-scale and "golden spike" debates, Anthropocene has expanded its range to include "the animal question" and the future of nonhuman life on the planet; the trajectory and legitimacy of late modern civilization; and the critical re-evaluation of the historical, political, and philosophical foundations of Western cultural anthropocentrism and modern humanism. This second wave of issues—anthropocentric planetization, the fate of animals in the twenty-first century, and the social contract of late modernity—is this book's principal concern.

It will take one to two centuries to fully verify or falsify the Anthropocene hypothesis. Nonetheless, humans need to act as though we have moved beyond the tipping point with regard to climate change, systematic environmental disruption, and species extinction. We need to think in terms of the conviction that this is our future: we are locked into a long cycle of planetary and evolutionary change that will result in the creation of a different Earth from the one we currently inhabit. I submit that we should adopt this mindset as a rational and prudent judgment and moral and political imperative. Chapter 1 therefore makes the case for three interrelated propositions. First, the Anthropocene is a valid framing hypothesis in evaluating the challenges facing the biosphere and its inhabitants in the twenty-first century. Second, we should think and act as though we have gone beyond a critical tipping point with respect to those global forces driving the Anthropocene. Third, from a posthumanist perspective, late-modern civilization lacks the resources to effectively mitigate or reverse those forces systematically displacing and eradicating animal life today at unprecedented rates.

In Chapter 2, I examine the plight of animals in the twenty-first century under conditions of accelerated anthropocentric planetization by focusing on four major challenges: (1) wild animals that are on the path to extinction by the twenty-first century's end, (2) the crisis of oceanic animals, (3) the fate of industrialized farm animals and the future of industrial agriculture, and (4) the trend of contact zone animals increasingly moving into human-occupied habitats. These are the principal battlegrounds of animal ethics and politics in the twenty-first century. I arrive at the proposition that what is required is nothing less than a culture shift in human-animal relations toward posthumanism and an ethical and political prioritization of animal life on par with that of humans' well-being.

These propositions require moral and political justification, which is the focus of Chapters 3 and 4. In Chapter 3, I make the case for a posthumanist ethics that draws on work done in coevolutionary neo-Darwinism, biocentric ethics, animal *umwelt* phenomenology, and nonanthropocentric animal ethics. Posthumanism rests on several core assumptions. First, the origin and purpose of morality lies in evolution. Morality is a biological and sociocultural adaptation designed to increase individual and group fitness through the regulation of social life and promotion of social cooperation. Second, morality arose before hominids arrived on the evolutionary scene and expresses itself biologically, socially, and culturally in many species. Third, one can develop a normative ethics based on evolutionary thinking.

My idea of "evolution as coevolution" underpins my conception of posthumanism. I employ it in a threefold sense. Coevolution, or a relationship between two or more species that reciprocally alters their evolutionary development, is an undervalued factor in biological evolution whose status needs to be upgraded. Second, the term explains cultural evolution and how sociocultural change evolves in a Darwinian-like way. Here, I am particularly influenced by the coevolution theory of Robert Boyd, Peter Richerson, and Kim Sterelny. Third, coevolution describes an ethical orientation and ethos with respect to how we ought to relate to, treat, and live with animals.

Adopting a coevolutionary, cultural Darwinian worldview is necessary but not sufficient for posthumanist ethics. It is equally a biocentric and life-world-based ideal. The biocentric ethical outlook pioneered by Paul Taylor in *Respect for Nature* (1986) provides another key foundation for posthumanism. It locates value in life itself, in the intrinsic worth of individual life-forms as "teleological centers" of their own good. The recent life philosophy of Roberto Esposito frames the question of the *bios* as one of biocentric ethics and biopolitics. I equally draw on *umwelt* phenomenology, the interspecies ethics of Ralph Acampora and Cynthia Willett, and J. M. Coetzee's ethic of connecting with animals through sympathetic-poetic imagination presented in the modern classic *The Lives of Animals* (1999). Modern empiricism and rationalism (science and philosophy) formally define ethics, but they do not primarily shape morality, because relating to others is equally subjective and intersubjective.

The predominant way of thinking in animal ethics is anthropocentric. One starts with a conception of human nature and evaluates how animals measure up using human capacities as the yardstick. Much of animal ethics consists of an ongoing war of position around revising the definition of personhood to uphold some version of modern humanism. Posthumanism travels down an alternative path. It strives to decenter anthropocentric humanism and relocate it as part of a larger evolutionary, biocentric worldview. Its life-centered perspective places humans as one species among many, all of which have intrinsic value as sentient beings and members of biological and biopolitical communities. Posthumanism views human-animal differences in terms of degree rather than kind. It further resists incorporating animals within the framework of conventional modern liberal humanism. In this sense, it is more than the extension of humanism to a new class of beings. Posthumanism is neohumanist in that it concerns itself with the ways by which human beings develop and justify ethical values and norms—that is, it is concerned with the human means (types of reasoning, discourses, theories, and models) by which animals and nonhuman nature are evaluated. Humans are the means and animals are the ends of ethical thought and action. In this sense, posthumanism reverses the logic of anthropocentric ethics.

Not only does posthumanism yield a set of core ethical propositions and principles; it also gives us a methodology. Here, I contend that a credible ethic must effectively triangulate three essential criteria and clusters of variables that should be factored in when coming to a moral and political judgment. Consistent with this approach in evaluating animal issues, posthumanist ethics triangulates (1) determinate ethical principles; (2) lifeworld context, relations, and affect; and (3) *phronesis*, or practical wisdom, which includes consideration of causality and consequences. It relies on what I refer to as a three-legged "ethical stool" whereby morality is conceived in terms of three essential inputs—objectivity, subjectivity, and intersubjectivity—that inform, check, and balance each other.

Posthumanism as a coevolutionary, biocentric, lifeworld-based ethics is the infrastructure of a more prescriptive animal ethic. It explains the *how* and *why* of morality, which I believe is critical if we are to arrive at the *who* and *what* of a credible normative ideal. Posthumanism also broadens and deepens the scope of animal ethics beyond the animal welfarist versus rights abolitionist frame to include all sentient life that inhabits the biosphere in the twenty-first-century Anthropocene. As a more determinate, prescriptive ethic, I develop an approach called "posthumanist communitarianism" and "*humanimal* coevolutionary communitarianism." This approach builds on yet differs from what I regard as the most influential positions in contemporary animal ethics: (1) universal rights–based vegan abolitionism, best represented in the philosophies of Gary Francione and Gary Steiner; (2) the utilitarian new animal welfarism of Peter Singer; (3) Kathy Rudy's ethics of care and affective connection narrative of "loving animals"; and (4) the postmodern posthumanism of Cary Wolfe and Matthew Calarco.

Chapter 4 translates posthumanist ethics into a political theory. I propose that the existing legitimizing narrative and social contract of late modernity needs to be fundamentally reconceived. At the theoretical level, this shift entails rethinking the very idea of the social contract construct. At the political level, this shift requires a twofold move that at first glance seems contradictory. On the one hand, the case needs to be made for the greater inclusion of animals in what is, in reality, a biopolitical contract that considers them to be our kin and sentient subjects of justice. At the same time, the current civilizational model of late modernity needs to be called into question. My use of the phrase "the next social contract" refers to the threefold task of (1) redefining the idea of the social contract as a biosocial reality evident in animals and humans, (2) calling into question the legitimacy of the modern social contract as a liberal humanist construct and judging its late-modern institutional expression as functionally obsolete, and (3) recasting the social contract as a human–nonhuman animal (*humanimal*) compact that is posthumanist, postmodern, postliberal, biopolitical, and communitarian.

The logic of modern social contract theory follows a basic three-step process: (1) an imagined or ideal "state of nature," "original position," or "communication community" of free and equal human agents; (2) a process of consent to a mutually binding normative agreement; and (3) the construction of a corresponding institutional reality. My idea of the contract is not based on the traditional premise of a counterfactual thought experiment, nor do I endorse the implicit belief that rational consensus should be the basis of legitimation. Our contemporary world is far more pluralistic, driven by diverse substantive conceptions of the good, and more incommensurable than either Rawlsians or Habermasians are willing to admit. My "original position" begins with the real "state of nature" today, the biosphere and the condition of life (particularly animal life) on this planet under globalized human sovereignty and informed by the Anthropocene hypothesis. Two fundamental questions frame my starting point: (1) What is our current state of nature? (2) What ought to be our place in it? The key word in both of these questions, "our," pertains to animals, of which humans are one species among millions. The purpose of the contractual reasoning process should be to elucidate a moral and political good that problematizes the current order of things and renders actionable (in theory) an alternative model.

Three key presuppositions inform my thinking about the next social contract. First, all animals that live in social groups—and I would add that most animals are social in the sense of inhabiting and conducting their lives within biosocial networks—operate within implicit social contracts. Second, animals have always been a part of human society since the Great Domestication and therefore have been members of our social contract, coevolving with us for millennia. Their fate has risen and fallen in the course of human social and cultural evolution, the result of ever-shifting power logics of inclusion and exclusion as well as status designations from privileged to product to pariah. Third, justice should be understood as something more than an ethical or political idea or theory. It is a biological, social, and cultural trait evident in human and nonhuman animals, the product of literally millions of years of evolution. Justice is an evolutionary adaptation for the purpose of regulating group life and maintaining social cooperation. As Frans de Waal and Marc Bekoff have empirically verified, many social and political animals have a sense of justice expressed in moral behaviors and emotions.

Traditionally, the pivotal moment in modern social contract theory has been the legitimation of sovereign consent. I reverse this logic and call into question the paradigm of modern sovereignty. For me, the pivotal moment is *dis*sent not *con*sent, the questioning of our hypermodern civilizational order that has delivered us into the Anthropocene conundrum we find ourselves in. The *us* I am speaking about here are the human and nonhuman inhabitants of the biosphere. To paraphrase Jürgen Habermas, the legitimation crisis of our time is one of system and lifeworld—yet it runs deeper than Habermas's analysis. It is not simply a crisis of institutions as well as human identity, meaning, and intersubjective life (i.e., culture). It is a crisis involving the mutual sustainability of the biosphere and human civilization. I submit that the social contract of late modernity, from a humanist and a posthumanist perspective, is an exhausted artifice. It sustains its hegemony and counteracts normative deficits through sheer technological power over human and animal bodies.

I also question attempts to fit animals and human-animal relations within the modern liberal tradition, conventional or radicalized, and the discourses and logics of personhood, human and citizenship rights, and humane treatment through legal and regulatory reform. Rather than attempting to fit nonhuman animals into rights, welfare, cosmopolitan, or even postmodern difference models of justice, I contend that communitarianism better reflects the real lives of animals. Rather than drawing inspiration from Benedict de Spinoza, David Hume, Jeremy Bentham, Friedrich Nietzsche, Emmanuel Levinas, Michel Foucault, or Jacques Derrida, perhaps we need to view the anarcho-communitarianism of Petr Kropotkin and Gary Snyder as our model of animal politics.

What, then, does justice for animals mean in a posthumanist world? I submit that we share a biological, ecological, social, affective, and moral kinship with animals based on our common evolutionary heritage; our sharing of habitats, communities, and households; our lifeworld connections as sentient beings; and our coevolutionary relationships. This kinship bond makes animals members of our moral community and social contract. They are neither persons nor property; rather, their status should be that of sentient moral subjects of justice and members of the posthumanist contract with varying degrees of biopolitical community identity, residency, and protection. In the short term, official justice for animals will operate within the confines of existing legal and biopolitical categories and classifications. However, in the everyday lifeworld and across countless communities and biosocial networks, posthumanist justice operates very differently. The long-term goal is the dismantlement and reconstruction of today's prevailing institutional and cultural reality, to the point that it becomes a topic of history. The ultimate goal is to replace the Anthropocene with a new chapter in planetary and human history.

My idea of justice for animals relies on six guiding principles, which I call the "six Rs"—recognition, reconciliation, responsibility to intervene, rehabilitation, restitution, and reinhabitation. The next social contract differs from the modern "zoopolis" of Sue Donaldson and Will Kymlicka, which represents the most ambitious and comprehensive animal political theory to date. It takes the form of a posthumanist "archipelago" that does not conform to the modern political-juridical paradigm of state sovereignty. It nurtures and protects human-animal relations within decentralized networks comprising diverse cultural niches; communities; corridors; and local, regional, and global nodal points connected by the ethos and politics of *humanimal* coevolutionary communitarianism. The archipelago is a cultural and political alternative to anthropocentric late modernity. It spatially (through biosocial networks) and temporally (through social deceleration) challenges prevailing institutions and norms of fast capitalism and late-modern sovereign power. Its citizens inhabit a social and political space that straddles old modernity and the posthumanist world, building new social networks and communities within the shell of old modernity. What they have in common is that they have taken their stand with animals under pressure from the forces of the Anthropocene.

The idea of a posthumanist archipelago draws on the anarcho-communitarian thinking of Kropotkin, the bioregional reinhabitory vision of the Buddhist deep-ecology poet Snyder, and the ecocommunitarianism of Bill McKibben. To paraphrase Snyder and McKibben, we need to "hunker down," "dig in," "reinhabit," and build new communities. New communities need to be developed over time, in which animals are more integrated as coresidents and, in some cases, co-laborers and co-citizens. Among these new communities are those that prioritize *humanimal* coevolution and coexistence. New models of sanctuary and rescue communities; postmodern farming; expanding, redefining, and fully legitimizing the contact zone; and rewilding and reinhabitory projects are just a few examples of posthumanist communitarianism.

A key recurring term that helps define my ideal of a posthumanist coevolutionary communitarian ethics and politics in the twenty-first-century Anthropocene is "*humanimal*." This relational concept expresses our connection to our fellow animals as coinhabitants and members of the social contract. It also stands for the process of forging relationships between humans and nonhuman animals. At the same time, it seeks to replace the old human-animal and human–nonhuman animal terminology and false distinction, as if humans are somehow categorically different from all other animals. It also expresses the primacy of our animal nature. We are animals and products of larger evolutionary processes, first and foremost. Our kinship with other animals is not simply a cultural invention or normative imperative but a biological and social reality. Finally, this concept expresses the leveling of the playing field between humans and other animals. Although we cannot absolutely overcome anthropocentrism and some form of humanism—for all species are, to some degree, species-ist—we should possess the awareness that this is an adaptive strategy and not some grandiose, separate, and superior level of being. The next social contract is *humanimal* for these reasons.

Another term that appears throughout this book is "biopolitics." Originally coined by Foucault to explain the modern state's policy shift toward defining and controlling biological life and life processes, biopolitics has increasingly been used to make sense of the plight of animals in today's world. Broadly defined, it represents the triumph of the modern sovereign civilizational system over all aspects of planetary life human and nonhuman. This victory includes the power to define and redefine life itself; to classify, categorize, and manage it; to declare exceptions to these designations; to distinguish "human" from "animal" life; and to systematically render human and nonhuman living beings as measurable quantities to be confined, sequestered, micromanaged, bred, worked, killed, and eaten.

Evident in the works of Giorgio Agamben, Esposito, Wolfe, and Dinesh Joseph Wadiwel, all of whom are indebted to Foucault, the use of the term "biopolitics" reflects an increasing understanding that animal ethics and politics are integrally intertwined. Animal ethics without biopolitics are not ethics at all. Indeed, biopolitics largely precedes and frames ethics rather than the other way around. I also regard biopolitics as a major defining and driving force of the Anthropocene. In the works of Foucault, Agamben, and Wadiwel, biopolitics is largely a sovereign totalitarian (hard and soft) force, a state-centered "anthropological machine" reducing life to "bare life"; maintaining arbitrary distinctions between human life, humans as animals, and animal life; and conducting an all-out "war against animals." I do not deny the existence of this type of biopolitics, yet I also draw on the more affirmative approaches of Esposito, Donna Haraway, and Jamie Lorimer.

I define *human biopolitics* in the Anthropocene as a complex assemblage of power that involves (1) the sovereign biopolitical institutional machinery of life classification and management organized around the state; (2) the capillary, microdisciplinary technologies of biopower operating on individual bodies; and (3) networks and nodal points of bioresistance and transformative change working within the spaces of macro- and microbiopolitics. As a more affirmative politics of resistance, ethos, and reconstructive political agency, I argue in favor of a posthumanist communitarianism that acknowledges the influence of Foucault's idea of resistance, Esposito's concept of *bios communitas*, Haraway's practices of "becoming companion species" and contact zone politics, and Lorimer's idea of a new paradigm for conservation in the Anthropocene built around a "wildlife ontology" for a multinatural, hybridized world of novel ecosystems and their inhabitants.

I conclude on a pessimistic note, for I believe that we have gone beyond a critical tipping point and that the biosphere and its inhabitants are in for a very rough road in this and the next century. I see the juggernaut of late-modern civilization rolling forward largely unchecked and, in many respects, on autopilot, programmed to deliver more and more high-end modernity to more and more people. Reforms will likely be minimal and largely to fine-tune an even more efficient and accelerated project of anthropocentric planetization. I see before us a tale of two planets: one ultramodern, technotopian, well protected, and well provided for the few, and the other increasingly Hobbesian for the many, which includes the overwhelming majority of animals. From a posthumanist ethical and political standpoint, the task ahead is nothing less than a labor of Sisyphus.

# 1

## THE ANTHROPOCENE HYPOTHESIS

The planet on which our civilization evolved no longer exits. The
stability that produced that civilization has vanished; epic changes have
begun. . . . We may, with commitment and luck, yet be able to maintain
a planet that will sustain some kind of civilization, but it won't be the
same planet, and hence it can't be the same civilization. The earth that
we knew—the only earth that we ever knew—is gone.

—BILL MCKIBBEN, *Eaarth: Making a Life on a Tough New Planet*

### The Idea of the Anthropocene

The idea of a new epoch in the history of planet Earth known as the Anthropocene—*anthropos* ("human") and *cene* ("new")—was proposed by
the biologist Eugene F. Stoermer and the Nobel Prize–winning atmospheric chemist Paul Jozef Crutzen in 2000.[1] Our most recent epoch, the
Holocene, began 11,700 years ago following the last Pleistocene Ice Age and
inaugurated Earth's current interglacial period. In this time span—a brief
event geologically—our species has become a global change agent equal to or
greater than Earth's biophysical systems. A growing number of geologists,
climatologists, biologists, and environmentalists are of the opinion that the
human impact on Earth over the past two centuries has been so significant
that identifying a new period in planetary history warrants examination. A
group of geologists led by Jan Zalasiewicz has proposed to the International
Commission on Stratigraphy, a body within the International Union of Geological Sciences, that the Anthropocene be recognized as a formal designation
in the geologic time scale.[2]

Geologic periodization depends on how scientists interpret sedimentary
rock layers and glacial ice and formally agree on a Global Stratotype Section
and Point (GSSP) known as the "golden spike."[3] Stratigraphic significance is
a factor of climate change and major shifts in evolutionary patterns. Evidence
verifying the hypothesis that we have entered a new period of Earth's history

will come not from the remains of humanity's civilization but rather from its effects, from climate change, species extinction, and changes in oceanic bio-chemistry. All of these events are currently occurring and at ever-increasing rates. The Anthropocene remains a hypothesis, not a scientific theory. Yet for many, the real question is not geoscience consensus but whether our current global environmental transition will be moderate or catastrophic. Here, the Anthropocene has a powerful framing effect.

The Anthropocene goes by other names, including the Anthropozoic, the Androcene, the Age of Man, the Homogocene, the New Pangea, and the Great Acceleration. Many proponents place its dawning around 1800 with the advent of the Industrial Revolution. Others cite the explosion in human population and consumption after World War II.[4] Simon Lewis and Mark Maslin identify 1610 and 1964 as more promising start dates for the Anthropocene: 1610 marks the global integration of the Old and New Worlds with respect to biotic homogenization (also known as "the Colombian Exchange" and "Orbis hypothesis"), while 1964 marks changes in the atmosphere due to nuclear test-ing.[5] Adrian Franklin writes:

> The most recent phase of the Anthropocene, in the last 50 years, is distinguished by two unprecedented types of change. The first involved unparalleled levels of impact from new technologies, market expansion, unprecedented levels of population growth, settlement, consumption, and mobility. The second, a cultural change, involved the arrival of audacious projects (often multiple and contradictory) to take control of entire environments, to order and reorder entire land-scapes, on national and international scales, often dedicated to revers-ing damaging levels of anthropogenic impact and restoring them to the imagined natures of earlier timelines.[6]

Niles Eldredge characterizes humans "as the first species in the 3.5-billion-year history of life to live outside the confines of the local ecosystem."[7] In this sense, the Anthropocene has been with us for a long time, emerging in tandem with the global diffusion of agricultural and civilizational modes of society and culture. Over the course of social evolution, the power elites of our species declared their independence from the world of nature and asserted their dominion over it in the name of their gods. Anthropocentrism historically has defined what it means to be fully "human" to justify dominion over those less than human. One can reconstruct a genealogy of Nietzschean-like "big men" who have re-engineered humanity and the planet. The Anthropocene repre-sents the most recent wave of this human biopolitical will-to-power over life.

As an ideological doctrine, anthropocentrism places the human animal ontologically, epistemologically, and politically at the center of moral evaluation as the only known "God species" in existence. This exclusive and hierarchical prioritization of the human species is justified by invoking the factually constructed belief in our unique and overpowering mental traits. Animals and lesser humans are either excluded or occluded from the privileged center of moral consideration. The practical consequence of this is the conviction that fully human needs and interests should have priority over those of lesser humans and the nonhuman world. Furthermore, lesser and nonhuman lives have utility value as objects of use and means for the greater ends of those who are fully human. Anthropocentrism is not monolithic. There have been weak and strong, benign and malignant, and other variants in all historical cultures. These beliefs have historically justified the great dualisms and binary logics of sovereign power and authority—master/slave, human/animal, civilized/barbarian, culture/nature, soul/body, patrician/plebian, civilized/primitive, people of God/pagan, political life/bare life.

While this worldview has been with us since the advent of civilization, it is through the globalization of industrial modernity and changes in the planet's biosphere in real time that the Anthropocene has become a full-blown empirical reality. The influence of Western culture and civilization on other societies, species, and the planet reached its apex during the modern age. To speak of modernity is to make reference to the era of Western dominance that can trace its origins back to the fifteenth century and the discovery, conquest, and colonization of the Americas. Thanks to the Industrial Revolution, the West was able to successfully solidify its cultural, economic, political, and technological domination of the world. Earth has been under Western management for the past two hundred years. Today, we are witnessing the resurgence of non-Western societies under conditions of accelerated modernization. The key drivers of globalization today are fossil-fueled, consumption-based, high-tech, capitalist-growth economies; terrestrial re-engineering; population growth; mega-urbanization; the rise of a global middle class; and big industrial, monoculture farming.

Major works on the Anthropocene have already begun to appear, among them Jedediah Purdy's *After Nature: A Politics for the Anthropocene*, Jamie Lorimer's *Wildlife in the Anthropocene: Conservation after Nature*, and *Animals in the Anthropocene: Critical Perspectives on Non-human Futures* by the Human Animal Research Network (HARN) at the University of Sydney. Purdy approaches the Anthropocene from the perspective of American environmental history and law, defining it as a "threefold crisis" of ecology (the end of the Holocene honeymoon), economics (the twilight of modern economics), and politics (the limits of the modern Western liberal-democratic, nation-state system).[8] He argues that we need a new "environmental imagination" and model of democracy ("a democratic Anthropocene") capable of solving the three main challenges of the twenty-first century—food and industrial agriculture, the treatment of animals, and climate change.[9]

Lorimer addresses the challenges facing wildlife in the Anthropocene from the vantage point of conservation biology and geography. The triumph and tragedy of modern Enlightenment sci-tech has resulted in the proliferation of novel ecosystems all across the planet characterized by destabilization, hybridization, territorial fragmentation, life on the move and on the run, and radical spatial transformation, all of which point to a "multinatural" biosphere. Traditional science and conservation biology are ill-equipped to deal with this new Earth in the making. What is required is a new "wildlife ontology" and paradigm shift in conservation practices commensurate with the Anthropocene's "multiple, fluid natures." We need a new conceptual approach as well as a new biopolitics.[10]

The essays in *Animals in the Anthropocene* are as much about the idea of the Anthropocene as they are about the future of animals. The Anthropocene enjoys a multiplicity of uses, intersecting, revitalizing, and problematizing many contemporary ideological and political positions. It reinforces and calls into question "humanity" as a Promethean-like force of evolutionary triumphalism and exceptionalism. It marks a new milestone for *Homo sapiens* as a planetary geological agent and, at the same time, the primary causal agent of a possible sixth mass extinction in Earth's evolutionary history. In one essay, Richie Nimmo comments that with the coming of the Anthropocene, "humans are finally unmasked as earthlings."[11]

## The Planetization of Modernity

The planetization of modernity largely defines the Anthropocene. At the beginning of the Industrial Revolution, the human population was 1 billion. By 1930, it had reached 2 billion. By 1960, it had reached 3 billion; by 1974, 4 billion; by 1987, 5 billion; by 1999, 6 billion; and by 2015, 7.3 billion. By 2050, it is projected to reach 9.6 billion. The most recent study from the United Nations Population Division concludes there is an 80 percent chance that in 2100, 11 billion humans will inhabit Earth.[12] The twentieth century alone witnessed a population explosion from 1.6 billion to 6.1 billion. Thanks to modern advances in technology, energy, medical science, and food production, our species has managed to avoid a global Malthusian crisis, containing outbreaks of mass starvation, pandemic diseases, and mortality to local and regional levels. Of course, these advances come at the expense of other species, as we invade, overcrowd, and alter habitats everywhere on the planet.

Some experts contend that the problem is not simply human population in the aggregate but rather its geographic distribution, density, and composition—the modernity of this population. Jack Goldstone has identified four demographic megatrends he believes will define human development in the twenty-first century.[13] One is the demographic and economic slowdown of the developed world (Europe, the United States, Canada, Japan, South Korea, Australia, New Zealand), with low fertility rates, aging and declining working-age populations, shrinking consumer markets, and rising medical and public-pension costs. In the developing world (Asia, Africa, and Muslim countries), we see the exact opposite trend: rapid population and economic growth, youthful populations, weak governments, and high levels of social and political conflict. The third trend is mega-urbanization. The fourth trend is the globalization of the consumer middle class driven by the developing world, particularly Asia.

Fertility rates in Europe and East Asia (Japan and South Korea) are below the steady state replacement rate of 2.1 children per woman. Canada, the United States, Australia, New Zealand, and most recently China and Brazil are at or just below the replacement rate. The rest of the world is above this rate. With fertility rates from 5 to 7 in many sub-Saharan countries, Africa's population is expected to quadruple by the end of this century to 4 billion. South Asia is expected to add a billion people by midcentury.[14] By 2050, the population of the West (Europe, the United States, Canada, and Oceania) will constitute 18 percent of the world's population; in 1913, it accounted for 35 percent of the world's population.[15]

By the middle of the twenty-first century, 70 percent of humanity will live in cities; in 1950, less than 30 percent of the world's population was urban. Two dominant trends of the twenty-first century will be rapid urbanization and the growth of megacities with populations greater than ten million in the developing world. China will jump from seeing 40 percent of its population urbanized to 74 percent by 2050, India from 30 to 55 percent, and sub-Saharan Africa from 40 to 67 percent. In the 1960s, there were two megacities: New York and Tokyo. In 2011, there were twenty-one. By 2030, there will be thirty. The majority of these megacities are in India (Mumbai, Delhi, Calcutta, and Chennai), China (Shanghai, Beijing, Guangzhou, and Shenzhen), Pakistan (Karachi and Lahore), Brazil (Sao Paulo and Rio de Janeiro), Mexico (Mexico City), and Africa (Kinshasa, Lagos, and Cairo).[16]

One billion people are urban outskirt dwellers, a number that is expected to triple by midcentury. Mega-urban outskirts are the key economic hubs of the developing world. The global "slum economy" generates ten trillion dollars in economic flows per year.[17] Another trend is the convergence of megacities into "megaregions." Rio de Janeiro and Sao Paulo are on target to merge into a region of around forty-three million. Massive infrastructural projects are in the works to connect several Chinese cities in the Guangdong province and Pearl River delta economic zone (Guangzhou, Shenzhen, Dongguan, Foshan, Zhuhai, and Jiangmen) and link them to Hong Kong and Macao, thereby creating a region the size of Switzerland inhabited by more than fifty million people.[18]

Mega-urbanization is different from suburban sprawl in that it spatially concentrates humans and sends development upward in the form of super-skyscrapers rather than simply outward. Nonetheless, it facilitates population growth and intensifies human consumption, thus putting more pressure on agricultural and energy production and therefore opening up even more land and water habitats to human development. At the center of this trend is an exploding, global, high-consumption middle class.

The gross world product (GWP) in 2012 was $72.44 trillion (in U.S. dollars). It is expected to increase fourfold by midcentury as the Emerging 7 (E7) economies (China, India, Brazil, Russia, Indonesia, Mexico, and Turkey) surpass the Group of 7 (G7) economies (the United States, Japan, Germany, the United Kingdom, France, Italy, and Canada). Before 2020, China will overtake the United States as the world's largest economy. By 2050, the world's largest economies will be China followed by the United States, India, the European Union, and Brazil. Europe and the United States will constitute 30 percent of GWP; in 1950, it accounted for 68 percent.[19]

Driven by the E7 and other emerging market economies, the world's middle class will mushroom by midcentury. Global middle-class status is defined by the United Nations and the Organization for Economic Co-operation and Development (OECD) as a person who earns $10 to $100 per day (in U.S. dollars) and has enough discretionary income to purchase durable consumer goods, such as automobiles, appliances, and telecommunication technologies. As of 2009, 1.845 billion people in the world were classified as "middle class." The global middle class is expected to increase to 3.249 billion by 2020 and 4.884 by 2030. In the case of Asia, the middle class is expected to explode from 525 million to 3.2 billion by 2030. One billion people in China will be middle class.[20]

Ecological footprint analysis, which measures the rate and scope of how humans consume resources and generate waste compared to nature's ability to absorb it and generate new resources, indicates that humanity currently uses the equivalent of 1.5 Earths; in other words, it takes Earth one year and six months to replenish what we use in a year. At our current rate, by 2050, the human race will be using the equivalent of three Earths. If all of humanity were to live like the average American currently lives, our species footprint would require five Earths,[21] This estimate is precisely where Earth is headed in the twenty-first century, in the hands of a global civilization dedicated to American-style, high levels of consumption. The sustainability of the biosphere will be severely challenged, yet modern neoliberalism is confident in the ability of technology and institutional capacity to produce the equivalent of five Earths to keep pace with anthropocentric planetization. One could define the twenty-first century in terms of two forces headed for a reckoning—human technological systems and planetary biology.

Significant increases in human population and consumption will require equally robust increases in global energy production. Current global energy sources are roughly 32 percent oil; 28 percent coal; 22 percent natural gas; 5.7 percent nuclear; 2.3 percent hydropower; and 1 percent solar, wind, geothermal, and biofuels. On the basis of current known reserves and consumption patterns, oil and natural gas will be significantly exhausted by the end of this century. Coal is the world's most abundant energy source. Six countries—the United States, Russia, India, China, Australia, and South Africa—account for 80 percent of coal reserves, and these reserves are expected to last for two centuries. Nonrenewable fossil fuels account for 80 percent of global electricity generation, with 50 percent coming from coal. Worldwide energy demand is predicted to increase 25 percent by 2030 and up to 56 percent by 2040, largely driven by Asian economies. The highest projected annual growth rate for energy consumption over the next twenty years is 3.7 percent for Asia, and the lowest is 0.7 percent for Europe. If energy consumption in the United States, China, and India continues to grow at its current rates, by 2050 these three countries will consume close to 50 percent of the world's energy.[22]

The renewable-energy sector—nuclear, hydropower, solar, and wind—is predicted to grow in this century. Currently, nuclear energy and hydropower account for 20 percent of global electricity generation. Wind, solar, and geothermal energy account for 1 percent of the world's electricity production. With most of the world's major rivers dammed, hydroelectric power is at capacity. The nuclear industry continues to face challenges of high start-up costs, costly delays, waste disposal, and risks of human error and natural disasters whose consequences last for thousands of years. Wind has a promising future, with Europe leading the way. Large-scale solar-energy plants are already underway, with the goal of turning the world's deserts into vast solar farms—yet they can pose serious threats to desert environments, which are home to fragile ecosystems and many rare and endangered species. Building solar farms requires stripping the landscape of vegetation and fencing it in. It has taken thousands of years for plants and animals to carefully adapt to desert conditions, so sudden changes can spell doom for desert species, such as tortoises and cacti. Solar-thermal plants require substantial groundwater for cooling, and the hotter temperature of the surrounding air poses threats to birds, whose feathers are literally burned in this environment.[23]

Yet despite growth in these energy sectors, by midcentury, fossil fuels will still account for 80 percent of world energy use. Human civilization remains committed to fossil-fuel economics, offshore and deep-water drilling, the exploitation of the melting Arctic, the mining and processing of oil sands, the hydraulic fracturing ("fracking") of rock veins to release natural gas and petroleum, and coal- and gas-fired power plants. The United States is in the midst of a fossil-fuel renaissance and is now the leading producer of oil and natural gas. The extraction of shale oil and gas in the upper Appalachian (the Marcellus deposit), Texas-Oklahoma-Louisiana (the Haynesville, Eagle Ford, and Woodford deposits), North Dakota (the Bakken deposit), and Wyoming accounts for one-third of natural gas production in the United States. The shale revolution has gone global, with major basins identified in Russia, Poland, Ukraine, China, Argentina, South Africa, Australia, Mexico, Libya, and Algeria. Fracking is at the center of the energy debate in America, with advocates stressing its potential for energy independence, jobs, wealth creation, tax revenues, and fewer carbon emissions than coal. Critics point out that fracking increases methane emissions; requires huge amounts of fresh water, which drawdown aquifers; creates huge, leaky wastewater ponds; increases the frequency of earthquakes as rock layers are weakened; has led to numerous railroad transportation accidents and explosions; and creates short-term boom-and-bust economies.[24]

Two key global effects of these powerful forces of anthropocentric planetization are habitat re-engineering and climate change. Combined, they threaten many species of life. A key indicator of the Anthropocene is the anthromization of the biosphere, which is the transformation of Earth's terrestrial landscape from mostly wild and seminatural territory to now largely anthropogenically re-engineered and human-occupied spaces. Most of Earth's natural ecosystems, or "biomes," have been transformed into anthropocentric biomes, or "anthromes." Using geographic information system (GIS) technology and vegetation, population density, and agricultural and urban land-use data sets and maps, a team of researchers has mapped the planet's biosphere over century-long intervals from 1700 to 2000.[25] The study identifies twenty-one anthrome classifications under six major groupings—dense settlements (urban, suburban, and towns), villages (rice, irrigated, rainfed, and pastoral), croplands (residential, irrigated, rainfed, and remote), rangelands (residential, populated, and remote), seminatural lands (woodlands and forests), and wildlands (forests and savanna, treeless and barren tundra and desert). "Used lands" refers to the sum of all crop, pasture, and human settlements. Those lands designated as "unused" do, however, have significant areas under human management, such as parks and forests.

In 1700, 6 percent of the biosphere consisted of used anthromes, 45 percent of Earth's ice free land was seminatural with relatively low levels of human impact, and 49 percent of the biosphere was wildlands. By 2000, 40 percent of the biosphere consisted of used anthromes, 37 percent was classified as "novel ecosystems" (a mosaic of used and seminatural lands), and 23 percent of Earth's surface was wildlands primarily located in the coldest and driest regions of tundra and desert. In other words, 55 percent of the terrestrial biosphere was fundamentally transformed by humans in the twentieth century. Today, agriculture accounts for 39 percent of the world's ice free land use. Human agriculture is the largest contributor to global warming, the largest user of fresh water, the primary cause of biodiversity loss, and a major contributor to species extinction.

Biologist Michael L. Rosenzweig has popularized the terms "Homogocene" and "New Pangea" to describe how anthromization has resulted in the fundamental breakdown of barriers between biogeographical regions, the rapid introduction of new invasive species into established habitats, and the resulting homogenization of the world's ecosystems into one single province. The speed and scope of global biotic homogenization decrease biodiversity and speciation rates while increasing extinction rates. Eventually, a new equilibrium or "steady-state global diversity" will be achieved, but in the short term, we can expect significant turbulence in ecosystems. While species diversity will increase in some local and isolated areas, globally "the real damage to diversity will come from shrinking areas of the Earth that harbor wild species."[26] George Newcombe and Frank M. Dugan contend that with regard to plants, the Homogocene began around 1500, which coincides with the genesis of early modernity.[27]

Climate change will likely be the defining event of the twenty-first century. Changes in atmospheric greenhouse-gas concentrations and global temperatures have occurred throughout Earth's history as a result of volcanic activity, changes in the planet's axis and orbit, tectonic plate movement, changes in solar brightness, and shifts in the movement of global oceanic currents known as the "thermohaline circulation." Climate scientists are convinced that current global warming levels and significant increases in atmospheric carbon dioxide, methane, and nitrous oxide are mainly due to industrial modernization. In the four hundred thousand years leading up to the Industrial Revolution, carbon-dioxide levels fluctuated between 180 and 280 parts per million (ppm), and only once did they reach 300 ppm. In the eight thousand years prior to 1750, carbon-dioxide levels varied between 260 and 280 ppm. By the mid-nineteenth century, levels were at 295 ppm. By 2005, they were at 379 ppm. The level in 2013 reached 400 ppm. The last time carbon-dioxide levels were this high was three million years ago.[28]

The foremost authority on climate change is the United Nations Intergovernmental Panel on Climate Change (IPCC). It comprises more than six hundred climatologists from more than one hundred countries organized into three major working groups—physical science; impacts, adaptation, and vulnerability assessment; and mitigation. The IPCC has issued major reports in 1990, 1995, 2001, 2007, and 2013–2014.[29] Earth's average temperature rose one degree Fahrenheit during the twentieth century. The IPCC, the National Oceanic and Atmospheric Administration (NOAA), and the U.S. Army Corps of Engineers all estimate a global temperature increase of three to four degrees and a rise in global sea levels of three to five feet by the end of the twenty-first century. Add to this an extra five to ten feet of storm surge. A 2014 IPCC time series analysis of atmospheric carbon-dioxide concentration estimates a conservative stabilization scenario of 550 ppm to a high of 950 ppm by the end of the century.[30] The Environmental Protection Agency (EPA) estimates a 450 ppm stabilization scenario to a high of 850 to 950 by 2100.[31]

The last time the planet experienced carbon-dioxide levels close to 1,000 ppm was fifty-six million years ago during the Paleocene-Eocene Thermal Maximum (PETM). This global warming event played out over two hundred thousand years, with its most intense period in the first ten thousand to thirty thousand years, and kept Earth in warm greenhouse conditions for roughly seven million years. It was caused by major volcanic eruptions that accompanied the final stages of the breakup of the Pangea supercontinent. Not only the atmosphere but also the oceans were warmed, and the warming of the oceans resulted in the release of frozen methane locked in the seabed, which caused acidification and shut down and reversed ocean current circulation belts.[32]

The effects of climate change today are already underway in the warming of the polar ice caps, melting glaciers, the collapse of massive ice sheets, and the increased incidence of extreme weather events and patterns. Scientists predict that by century's end, the great mountain glaciers in the Rockies, Andes, Alps, and Himalayas will disappear, causing sea levels to rise by one foot.

Increased oceanic thermal expansion, the melting of Greenland, and the now-inevitable collapse of the two-mile-thick Pine Island and Thwaites glacier basins in West Antarctica will result in another two- to three-foot rise in sea levels. Researchers have concluded that several major glaciers in West Antarctica are beyond the point of no return,[33] thus threatening heavily populated coastal areas around the world, where many megaport cities sit on giant artificially created deltas. Those hardest hit will be Bangladesh, Indonesia, the Mekong Delta, the Chinese coast, the Amazon River basin, the Gulf and East Atlantic coasts (Louisiana and Florida), Cuba, Denmark, the Netherlands, and the Adriatic coast. The "Venicization" of many of the world's major coastal cities—New Orleans, Miami, Mumbai, Dhaka, New York, Shanghai, Guangzhou, and Ho Chi Minh City—has already begun.[34]

Earth's warming has accelerated incidents of not only extreme weather but also prolonged extreme-weather patterns. The warming of the Arctic has slowed down the jet stream, resulting in blocked weather systems, meaning that weather patterns become stuck or locked into place, which leads to much longer and colder winters, longer and hotter summers, and shortened spring and autumn seasons. Several areas of the world are in the midst of transitioning from persistent drought to "megadrought" conditions lasting several decades to more than one hundred years. The cause of this change is ongoing global warming combined with continued, multiyear La Niña conditions. Megadroughts are underway in southern Europe, North Africa, East Africa (the Sahel region), Australia, and the American Southwest and Great Plains.[35]

Another critical consequence of anthropocentric climate change is the thawing of permafrost, or permanently frozen soil found throughout the higher latitudes of the Northern Hemisphere in northern Alaska, Canada, Greenland, and Siberia. Permafrost soils consist of thick layers of dead vegetation that freezing temperatures do not allow to fully decompose. The top "active layer" thaws in the summer, but the lower frozen layer can extend several hundred feet down. Most of the Arctic is a vast compost heap that is thousands of years old. This vast expanse of frozen organic mulch is rich in carbon and methane. Half of the planet's soil carbon is found in the Arctic permafrost, which composes roughly 21 percent of the planet's landmass. Climate models estimate that by the mid-twenty-first century, the northern planetary permafrost will be reduced by 25 percent, and by 2080 up to 50 percent could be thawed. A recent United Nations Environment Program report predicts that if current rates of climate change continue, we could see as many as 135 gigatons (a gigaton equals a billion metric tons) of carbon dioxide and methane released.[36] Methane is a much more powerful greenhouse gas than carbon dioxide and has 25 percent more warming power.

Permafrost melting affects millions of animals living in the tundra and bore-al forests as well as thousands of indigenous peoples, most of whom are nomadic reindeer herders.

All of these forces in the planetization of late modernity—exploding population growth; terrestrial re-engineering; mega-urbanization; a global, consumption-driven middle class; fossil-fuel economics; biogeographical homogenization; climate change; and big, corporate monoculture farming—have accelerated and converged to the point that the fates of many animals now hang in the balance. The obliteration and transformation of vast spaces of wild habitats have weakened and fragmented many established ecosystems to the point that many species find themselves on the path to extinction.

More than this, many scientists believe we could be in the early stages of a mass extinction event, a large-scale collapse in the diversity and abundance of plant and animal species in a geologically short time frame. There have been five known mass extinctions in planetary history in which 75 percent or more of all known species were wiped out in a few hundred thousand to fewer than 2 million years: the end of the Ordovician Period (440 million years ago), the end of the Devonian Period (370 million years ago), the end of the Permian Period (251 million years ago), the end of the Triassic Period (210 million years ago), and the Cretaceous Period or "K-T Extinction" (65.5 million years ago), which ended the great age of the dinosaurs. Signs indicate that we may be in the early stages of a big sixth. If this is the case, it would be the first mass extinction principally caused by a living species rather than physical processes, such as supervolcanoes, rapid glaciation, or an asteroid.[37]

Species extinction is a normal part of evolution—all species eventually become extinct. Catastrophic collapses are rare but natural occurrences, and there have been many "lesser extinction" events as well as major or mass events. Calculating extinction rates is not an exact science. One general yard-stick is the "background" or "natural" extinction rate, which is a mathematical estimate of how fast species have disappeared before human activity domi-nated the planet (pre-*Homo*) and not under catastrophic or mass-extinction conditions. This formula is derived from the study of marine fossils and pos-tulates that on average, a species of life tends to last about one million years before it goes extinct. As a general rule, if there were a million species on Earth, one species would go extinct every year. If there were only one species of life on the planet, it would likely go extinct in one million years, assuming relative environmental stability (1E/MSY).[38] A different calculation known as the "ecological extinction rate" occurs when a species drops to such a low number of individuals that it no longer has an input or function in the ecosys-tem it inhabits. It is on its way to extinction.[39]

Of course, the overall current extinction rate is calculated against the number of identified species, which most biologists regard as a small percentage of all life on the planet. Scientists have named 1.25 million species, yet the most recent scientific estimate of the total number of species on Earth is roughly 8.7 million—6.5 million on land and 2.2 million in the oceans.[40] Scientists believe they have accounted for most of all mammal, bird, and reptile species, yet they have cataloged only an estimated 45 percent of amphibians, 20 percent of insects, 17 percent of arachnids, around 15 percent of aquatic species, and only 7 percent of fungi.

The estimated number of species believed to be on the path to extinction ranges from a conservative low of five hundred to a high of thirty-six thousand.[41] Of the 5,501 known mammal species in the world today, 1,199 (22 percent) are listed as threatened with extinction. A staggering 41 percent of amphibians have been designated as vulnerable to extinction. Many species have been listed as "likely extinct" because they have not been seen for decades. A recent study of the world's seventy-four largest terrestrial herbivore species— among them, the elephant, rhinoceros, hippopotamus, giraffe, camel, tapir, zebra, wildebeest, moose, elk, gorilla, and orangutan—concluded that forty-four can be categorized as threatened with extinction.[42] The main causes of the rapid decline in animal populations and species extinction are human— 43 percent related to habitat loss and degradation, 37 percent due to exploitation (hunting, fishing, and extermination), 7 percent due to climate change, 5 percent due to invasive species, 4 percent due to pollution, and 2 percent due to disease.[43] Scientists estimate that 30 percent of all known plants and animals will be on their way to extinction by century's end. They further estimate that if trends continue, a sixth mass extinction will be fully underway by 2200.

The Brave New World that we face in the twenty-first century is not a science-fiction novel but a rapidly unfolding empirical reality. The biosphere and its inhabitants, who have lived under the ten-thousand-year dominion of a clever, handy, aggressive, prolific, globalizing, agricultural, civilized, and high-tech great ape, are at a crossroads. It is therefore not an exaggeration to hypothesize that the consequences of the Anthropocene will likely define the twenty-first century and beyond.

## Beyond the Tipping Point

How does one respond to the Anthropocene hypothesis? The question is as much normative as it is empirical. It is also a function of how one assigns meaning and value to the biosphere and to late modern civilization. The way

I see it, there are three main options: (1) one could dispute the empirical evidence, saying it is not occurring as described and/or at the scope and rate portrayed; (2) one could accept the validity of the hypothesis (with some reservations) but remain confident that we have not reached the tipping point and possess the civilizational resources to mitigate and reverse late-modern anthropocentric planetization; and (3) one could accept the Anthropocene hypothesis, believe we have gone beyond the tipping point (or act as though we have, even if we cannot conclusively validate it), and lack confidence in the ability of late-modern civilization to effectively mitigate or reverse these current trends.

I endorse the third option and work through the logic of its operating premise. My reasons for adopting a strong empirical, ethical, and political reading of the Anthropocene hypothesis are posthumanist. My priority concern is the fate of animals under looming conditions of anthropocentric planetization. My standpoint is one of nonanthropocentric, posthumanist ethics and politics. I am convinced that the late-modern social contract can no longer underwrite the kind of society and world many humans and most animals would want to live in.

In disputing the empirical evidence for the Anthropocene, one could make the following argument. Many demographers project that while Earth will likely reach eleven billion by century's end, this number will be our peak and then the world's population will level off. All modernizing countries go through a demographic transition that involves a population boom followed by a stabilization period when birth rates decline, life expectancy increases, and the population ages to where the birthrate drops below the replacement level. This was the case with modern Western civilization in the twentieth century and will be the case with Asia, Latin America, Africa, and the Middle East in the twenty-first century. Europe and Japan are in a fertility decline, while China and Brazil are now slightly below replacement fertility. Demographers also contend that it is not the world's population in the aggregate that is the problem but rather its location and distribution across the planet, which is uneven. World population density is the major challenge.

All of this speculation, of course, comes from a human-centered perspective. Earth may be able to support eleven billion people thanks to the technology and ingenuity of late-modern civilization, but it will not be able to support current levels of biodiversity. Habitat loss will accelerate, as will species extinctions. Most animals, which require larger and more stable habitats, will not be able to survive.[44] Furthermore, the problem is not simply total population but its modernity. The consumption patterns of an exploding global middle class pose a major threat to the biosphere and its inhabitants.

Levels modeled on the world's wealthiest nations will be difficult to sustain globally. Given these variables, what *is* the preferred human population? From the perspective of anthropocentric late modernity, eleven billion people is doable. Yet for posthumanists, the outlook is very different. Human over-population is a problem and a legitimate line of evidence in support of the Anthropocene hypothesis.

One could accept some or most of the Anthropocene hypothesis and still believe that a more progressive humanist and sci-tech reform program can alter the path of late modernity and reclaim the damage done to the biosphere and its inhabitants. This position has been articulated by advocates of neo-liberalism, technotopian engineering, ecomodernism, sustainable development, and transhumanism.

The dominant civilizational worldview and institutional reality today, especially in the West, is late-modern, big sci-tech, corporate-market global-ism. Neoliberals believe that the intensification of high-tech innovation and free-market capitalism is the optimal formula in meeting the challenges of the Anthropocene. The central driving institution of late modernity is and should be the transnational corporation.[45] Furthermore, we should not abdi-cate our unique species ability to radically re-engineer reality itself. The capa-bility of late-modern civilization to achieve ever-higher levels of growth and deliver consumable goods to more people is largely unquestioned. Human population growth, mega-urbanization, an exploding global middle class, and the current fossil-fuel renaissance are all proof of the success of neolib-eral globalization. As for the plight of animals, endangered species, and a possible sixth mass extinction, these costs can be more than made up for by corporate-backed conservation efforts and more efficient means of animal production for an even greater variety of human uses.

Another approach to the Anthropocene is big sci-tech, which continues to be a pillar of late-modern civilization. Ultramodern, mega-engineering solutions—such as mass producing genetically engineered carbon-eating trees, as proposed by Freeman Dyson, and geoengineering Earth's atmo-sphere, as advocated by Crutzen and David Keith—are two such examples. Both proposals are presented as relatively low cost and low risk. Since plants are good at absorbing carbon dioxide, we can manufacture special super-plants that would not only absorb most of the excess carbon dioxide in the atmosphere but also convert it into a chemical compound that could either be safely stored underground or converted into something useful, such as a new liquid fuel.[46] Geoengineering involves putting several million tons of sulfur dioxide into the upper atmosphere via a fleet of planes or balloons; this substance would turn into sulfate aerosol particles that reflect sunlight. Since these particles would remain in the air for only two years, the process would be ongoing until the planet cooled.[47]

Advocates of sustainable development, also known as ecological or reflexive modernization, seek a balance between neoliberalism and environmental protection in "green capitalism." Sustainable development zeroes in on the central doctrine of justification that underpins modern civilization—modern economics. It calls into question the conventional principles and models of micro- and macroeconomics, such as rational-choice cost-benefit analysis, how gross domestic product (GDP) is calculated, how businesses externalize the environmental and social costs of production, and how short-term return on investment drives contemporary capitalism. It equally questions technocratic policy making, wherein the near-exclusive emphasis is placed on technical solutions to all problems.[48]

The ecological modernization of our technocratic corporate civilization is pursued through a variety of means, including a shift from fossil fuels to cleaner, renewable energy; steady-state economics; appropriate technologies; and a new model of ecological citizenship. Sustainable development emphasizes the need for a balanced triangulation of economic growth, environmental protection, and social justice. Its long-range goal is to preserve the carrying capacity of a finite planet for future societies. It is a benign form of anthropocentric humanism that is dedicated to modernity lite, one that is ecological rather than Newtonian and industrial. It is more accepted in northern European countries and Japan, in part because these societies have already slowed down in terms of population growth, production, and consumption, thus making them more amenable to a steady-state economy and society. By contrast, neoliberalism is an Anglo-American ideology that largely rejects the idea of a finite biosphere in favor of technological triumphalism and a view of a human-centered world without limits.

Transhumanism is similar to posthumanism in that it seeks to fundamentally redefine the human condition and human nature, but the similarity ends there. Transhumanists, such as computer engineer, entrepreneur, and futurist Ray Kurzweil, envision the twenty-first century as the time of "technological singularity." A firm believer in "the law of accelerating returns," which is currently driving high-tech innovation, Kurzweil envisions major breakthroughs in biotechology, nanotechnology, robotics, and artificial intelligence (AI) converging around midcentury to produce "human enhancement" technologies that will literally liberate us from the confines of our biologically retrograde bodies and minds. Kurzweil predicts that the coming transhumanist supertech revolution will be greater than the Neolithic, civilizational, and Industrial Revolutions and send history into hyperdrive.[49]

Transhumanism takes neoliberalism and technological triumphalism to a new level. Just as industrial machinery, mass production, plastic, penicillin, and petroleum facilitated the unprecedented expansion of human population and civilization in the twentieth century, so too will nanotechnology, robotics, AI, whole-brain emulation or "mind uploading," synthetic biology, and geoengineering propel humanity to new heights of progress in the twenty-first century. We will enter a new post-Darwinian era of evolution where the physical world and biological organisms can be redesigned as biology and technology become one seamless reality. This will be a world of high-tech megacities; bio-reengineered plant, animal, and human DNA; new drugs, life-forms, and bioweapons; robots everywhere; life extension well beyond one hundred years; and a superintelligent cyborg elite.

Despite their different outlooks on the Anthropocene, the prevailing ideologies of our time—neoliberalism, neo-Keynesianism, technotopian mega-engineering, ecological modernization, reflexive modernization, sustainable development, and transhumanism—all share a common commitment to the central concern of human progress in the twenty-first century. They are all anthropocentric, neohumanist ideologies committed to various models of the next modernity. What is in the best interests of humanity—individually, collectively, and as a species—in the twenty-first-century Anthropocene? How should we re-engineer the biosphere, society, and human nature so that our species can extend the promise of modernity even further and maintain planetary dominion and stewardship?

This question is not the focus of this book or the ethics and politics of posthumanism. The principal question here asks how animals will fare under conditions of accelerating anthropocentric planetization. What is the fate of animals in the age of man? What does a world look like that ethically and politically prioritizes nonhuman life and places it on par with human life? What might a paradigm shift in human culture and politics from modern humanism to posthumanism look like? These are the driving concerns of a social and biopolitical compact very different from the one that underwrites globalized late modernity.

Like posthumanists, transhumanists speak of a postmodern civilization in the sense of moving beyond outdated modern humanist norms, ways of life, and institutional structures. Yet they diverge in locating the heart and soul of the next social contract: one is an ultramodern technological vision where humans transcend biology, and the other is a coevolutionary vision where humans reconnect to the biosphere and its inhabitants. While posthumanists emphasize the importance of new human-animal or *humanimal* social and cultural practices, transhumanists see most problems and solutions in terms of organism-machine (i.e., cyborg) re-engineering. Furthermore, the primary infrastructure that will deliver a transhumanist future is corporate capitalism, while for posthumanists, it is new communities.

Modern humanists, posthumanists, and transhumanists agree that animals should not live under conditions of suffering and extermination. Modern liberal humanists and animal welfarists recommend continued reforms of existing institutional practices to further lessen pain and suffering and to conserve more habitats. Posthumanists advocate a culture shift away from utilitarian anthropocentrism and the incremental abolition of animal exploitation, which implies the dismantling and reinventing of many existing institutions. Transhumanists recommend genetically engineering new animals designed to not experience pain and suffering, eliminating their "wildness," bringing online new strains of domesticated or tame animals, and creating new synthetic meat products grown from stem cells.

I am opposed to neoliberalism on the grounds that it is an extremely aggressive, unequitable, narrowly self-maximizing, environmentally damaging, and animal-exploiting form of anthropocentric modernity. However, I admit that it has a strong hold on the minds and bodies of modern humans in the West and across the world. As for mega-engineering and transhumanism, I regard them as narrowly and excessively technotopian. They have a nearly unreflective, secular faith in technology as the solution to all problems. While not a neo-Luddite, I am concerned about the establishment of one-dimensional technocultures where efficiency trumps all other values and interests and humans are happy adjuncts to and nearly completely dependent on high-tech and biotech assemblages.

My worldview shares much with that of sustainable development but, unfortunately, not its ecomodern optimism. The 2014 IPCC report concludes that anthropogenic climate change is unequivocal and that unless there is a massive shift in our civilizational paradigm within the next twenty to thirty years, the planet will be locked into a warming pattern for the next several centuries. Nothing less than major structural and cultural changes will reverse this trend. A major global agreement among nations that results in major shifts in energy, consumption, population, and neoliberal economics is not a realistic possibility, in my opinion.

As a posthumanist, I endorse the Anthropocene hypothesis and regard our current civilization being on the wrong track with no signs of a serious course correction. I believe it is reasonable and prudent to think and act as though we have gone beyond a critical tipping point. Posthumanism places human civilization on an equal footing with the biosphere and nonhuman species and prioritizes the plight of animals. It also calls into question the deeper logic of late-modern civilization and the ontology of late modernity—its framing of reality; radical anthropocentrism; corporate-controlled, high-consumption culture; and treatment of animals as inferior objects of propertied use. It equally questions the logic of modern-growth economics, the nation-state, and transnational corporation as the sovereign containers and delivery systems of high-end modernity and of technology as an end rather than a means.

The fates of Earth and its inhabitants lie in the hands of the human animal. I see modern humans as contented captives of a high-tech, global juggernaut largely run by machines programmed to deliver more high-end modernity and neutralize all systemic-level challenges. It is as though we are passengers on a high-speed train, watching the scenery of "nature" and "animals" passing us by as artifacts of a soon-to-be-bygone era. Without a significant cultural shift and institutional reforms, we will continue to accelerate our current practices of pushing ecosystems to the limits of collapse, sentencing thousands of species to extinction, exploiting and killing animals under conditions of institutionalized normalcy, and stretching the limits of civilization to the point of systemic overload. If we truly are a wise ape, then the social contract we negotiate over the next century or two may put the planet and its inhabitants on a trajectory of biosphere recovery. If not, then we will fulfill the Hobbesian vision of not only the state of nature but also the state of civilization, as a condition of life increasingly "poor, nasty, brutish, and short." As mentioned, it is no exaggeration to admit that the task before us is nothing less than a labor of Sisyphus.

## 2

## THE PLIGHT OF ANIMALS
## IN THE TWENTY-FIRST CENTURY

Anyone who says that life matters less to animals than it does to us
has not held in his hands an animal fighting for its life.

—JOHN COETZEE, *The Lives of Animals*

### The Anthropocene: An Age of Extinction?

Many scientists are convinced that building evidence supports the hypothesis that Earth is in the early stages of a mass extinction event, whereby the majority of species will be wiped out in a relatively short time, by geological standards. The generally accepted definition of a "mass extinction" is a loss of more than 75 percent of known species in fewer than 2 million years. Scientists have identified five such periods (the "Big Five"—the Ordovician, Devonian, Permian, Triassic, and Cretaceous) over the past 540 million years, when such catastrophic events as global glaciation, warming, supervolcanism, ocean acidification, and asteroid impact have resulted in the elimination of most species across the spectrum of life. Mass extinctions wipe the evolutionary slate clean, and it takes millions of years for life to recover.[1]

What is unique about Anthropocene extinction rates is that their primary cause is a single species, *Homo sapiens*, rather than a physical event. Furthermore, this event could take place in a few centuries to two thousand years rather than over several thousand years. More importantly, this species has the capacity and resources to reverse its magnitude and rate. Others remind us that extinction, even a mass extinction, is a normal part of evolution. All species are potential destroyers of worlds. Dominant species outcompete other species, transform environments, and go global. The logic of evolution is basic—species keep breeding and adapting until they dominate, find their niche, or die out.

A scientific study by paleontologist Anthony D. Barnosky's research team indicates that if species in eleven major groupings designated as "critically endangered" and "threatened" were to go extinct by the end of this century and if current trends were to continue unabated, then mammals, birds, and amphibians would be in the middle of a mass extinction 240 to 540 years from now. Most remaining species would reach their tipping point in 890 to 2,270 years. The planet Earth would qualify as being in its sixth mass extinction. Using current categories and extinction rates from the International Union for Conservation of Nature (IUCN) Red List, Barnosky's team estimates that by the end of this century, we could witness the following extinction levels: mammals (22 percent extinct, 1 in 5), birds (14 percent, 1 in 7.5), reptiles (29 percent, 1 in 3.4), amphibians (31–45 percent, 1 in 3), bony fish (25 percent, 1 in 4), gastropods (56 percent, 1 in 2), seed plants (64 percent, 1 in 1.65), bivalves (47 percent, 1 in 2), conifers (29 percent, 1 in 3.4), chondrichthyes (sharks and rays—17 percent, 1 in 6), and crustaceans (19 percent, 1 in 5). They conclude that "the recent loss of species is dramatic and serious but does not yet qualify as a mass extinction in the paleontological sense of the Big Five," but "taking into account the difficulties of comparing the fossil and modern records, and applying conservative comparative methods that favor minimizing the differences between fossil and modern extinction metrics, there are clear indications that losing species now in the 'critically endangered' category would propel the world to a state of mass extinction that has previously been seen only five times in about 540 million years."[2]

If we are in the early stages of a mass extinction event, then we need to remind ourselves that we are in the midst of its second act. The first act occurred at the end of the Pleistocene and beginning of the Holocene, some 50,000 to 10,000 years ago. Its principal casualties were "megafauna," giant mammals and birds weighing several hundred pounds to several tons, apex predators and dominant species that were the ancestors of many animals now facing extinction. Dominating Australia was the 7-foot-tall giant short-faced kangaroo and giant wombat *Diprotodon*, which weighed up to 3 tons and had a shoulder height of 6 feet. Northern Eurasia lost the woolly mammoth; woolly rhinoceros; Irish elk; scimitar cat; and cave lion, bear, and hyena. In the Americas, the mastodon, saber-toothed *Smilodon*, short-faced bear, *Glyptodon* armadillo, giant *Daeodon* pig, and *Megatherium* ground sloth disappeared. Madagascar had giant lemurs the size of gorillas, elephant bird species whose eggs were the size of basketballs, and giant fossa the size of cougars. More than 150 known genera of megafauna existed 50,000 years ago. Current data indicate that 10,000 years ago, at least 97 genera (66 percent) had disappeared.[3]

The late Pleistocene megafauna extinction is of such interest because its main suspect is *Homo sapiens*. Several hypotheses have been developed: (1) the human hunting or "overkill" hypothesis; (2) the "sitzkrieg" hypothesis, which emphasizes a slower extinction event caused by secondary human impacts, such as fire, deforestation, and habitat fragmentation; (3) the climate-change hypothesis; (4) the hyperdisease hypothesis; (5) the keystone-herbivore hypothesis; (6) the second-order predation hypothesis; and (7) the Clovis comet hypothesis. Most of these theories are associated with human colonization and hunting.[4]

The hunting/first-contact hypothesis was developed by Paul Martin in the 1960s. It contends that the primary cause of late Pleistocene megafauna extinctions was human overhunting. Its main explanatory focus is the Americas. Two derivative hypotheses stem from it—"blitzkrieg" and "Clovis first." The blitzkrieg theory, developed by James Mosimann as a computer simulation, estimates that it took 1,000 years (from 13,500 to 12,500) for humans to colonize the Americas in multiple waves, with each wave followed by an extinction event (i.e., a rolling extinction). It is closely associated with the appearance of Clovis culture, spear-point technology, and evidence of big-game hunting 13,200 to 12,800 years ago.

Today, this theory of a single Siberian people migrating across the Bering Land Bridge and colonizing the Americas through an ice-free corridor in western Canada has been challenged. Recent archaeological, genetic, and environmental evidence indicates the existence of two, possibly four, migration waves and cultures dating as far back as fifteen thousand years ago and occurring along the Pacific coastline with several inland dispersals. Others have questioned to what extent Paleo-Indians were principally big-game hunters. Ethnographic studies indicate that most hunter-gatherer cultures are involved in general rather than specialized resource acquisition. Evidence of a "Western-Stemmed" material culture (WST) and a maritime, coastal people who ate fish, shellfish, and plants has called into question the Clovis-first theory.[5]

Jared Diamond's sitzkrieg hypothesis emphasizes the secondary effects of human colonization and hunting, which include deforestation, the use of fire, and the introduction of nonnative species. Rather than stemming directly from hunting, megafauna extinctions occurred more from slower, indirect human impacts. Ross MacPhee's and Preston Marx's hyperdisease theory asserts that with the arrival of humans, new strains of diseases were introduced that the immune systems of a number of species could not combat. Norman

Owen-Smith's hypothesis focuses on the impact of the extinction of large herbivores on plant ecosystems, resulting in a cascading effect across the entire food chain. The second-order predation hypothesis is a modification of the overkill and herbivore theories. It proposes that humans killed key apex carnivores, which resulted in ecosystem disruptions in predator-prey relations. With most key predators thinned out or eliminated, prey populations were no longer under control, which most likely led to dramatic population increases, overgrazing, and boom-and-bust cycles in prey populations.

Climate-change theories remind us that the Pleistocene had twenty glacial cycles and extreme climate shifts, including a period of global warming that came to an abrupt end with the Younger Dryas mini–Ice Age 12,900 to 11,500 years ago. The most controversial and disputed theory, developed by geologists James Wittke and James Kennett and nuclear chemist Richard Firestone, correlates the great megafauna extinction with a likely comet impact, which unleashed the Younger Dryas and led to the end of Clovis culture and many big animals. They point to evidence of a layer of "black mat" in the sediment record that consists of charcoal, soot, fossil bones, tool remains, and microdiamonds.[6]

Recent analysis indicates that causality is more continent-dependent. Africa, Central Eurasia, and South Asia experienced relatively few extinctions. Megafauna and hominids coevolved over several hundred thousand years in these regions, and animals learned how to deal with humans. Humans were a new, invasive species in Australia, Siberia, the Americas, Madagascar, and New Zealand, and animals were naïve in their dealings with this strange creature. In addition, large Pleistocene animals had very slow and low reproductive and population-growth rates. It took them much longer to reach sexual maturity, and they had long gestation periods and few offspring. They also had few natural predators. When a clever and resourceful killer suddenly arrived on the scene, they could not rapidly adapt.

The hardest-hit continent was Australia; experts estimate that 88 percent of megafauna genera went extinct.[7] Human colonization occurred sixty thousand to forty-five thousand years ago, and the peak extinction period was between fifty thousand and forty thousand years ago. There is no evidence of significant climate change, but environmental change can be attributed to humans. No clear evidence thus far shows kill sites, cut marks, and broken fossil bones, but human-megafauna encounters and clashes appear in cave and rock art.[8]

In the case of northern Europe, Greenland, Siberia, and Alaska, 36 percent of megafauna went extinct in two periods—45,000 to 20,000 and 12,000 to 9,000 years ago.[9] The first period coincided with the arrival of

*Homo sapiens* in Europe. With regard to the second period, the Younger Dryas is viewed as a key causal factor. Its sudden onset, believed to have been caused by a shutdown in the North Atlantic thermohaline conveyor belt, affected the higher latitudes of the Northern Hemisphere. Most forests became glacial tundra, and the atmosphere became windier, colder, and filled with dust. It was followed by an equally sudden warming trend. Ample evidence suggests that giant mammoths (the famous woolly mammoth was one of a dozen *Mammuthus* species) were hunted by Neanderthals and modern humans. They were in significant decline by 11,300 and went extinct on the mainland by 9,650. An isolated population survived on Wrangel Island until around 4,000 years ago.

Megafauna extinction rates in the Americas were nearly as high as in Australia—72 percent in North America (33 genera) and 83 percent (50 genera) in South America—but occurred 30,000 years later.[10] Human colonization and climate change both figure into the equation, with human hunting leading the way. Several possible causal forces as well as overlapping time lines fit into several hypotheses. They include when humans first arrived; the influence of Clovis culture; the onset, duration, and impact of the Younger Dryas 12,900 to 11,500 years ago; and the peak period of megafauna extinctions, which is estimated to have been between 11,500 and 10,000 years ago.

Given the available evidence, three likely scenarios present themselves, all of which involve human causality. The human first-contact/overkill theory best fits the plight of megafauna on islands from Australia to Madagascar to New Zealand. Human overkill with climate change fits North America. Climate change followed by human overkill fits Eurasia. South America requires more study. Second-order predation and sitzkrieg can be plugged into all the above scenarios as reasonable possibilities. Only time will tell as research continues. What has made the late Pleistocene–early Holocene extinction a front-burner issue among many geoscientists, paleoanthropologists, and paleoecologists is the rapidly unfolding reality of our current Anthropocene extinction event.

What distinguishes the late Pleistocene–early Holocene extinction from the late Holocene–modern Anthropocene extinction is that the latter affects all classes of animals and plants, not just megafauna. It is a planetary event that is pervasive on every continent and in every ocean. Just as the first anthropogenic extinction occurred in tandem with the globalization of early *Homo sapiens*, our current event has occurred in tandem with the globalization of modern civilization. Holocene extinctions principally manifested themselves as island events in the Pacific and Indian oceans, on Madagascar,

Hawaii, New Zealand, and Mauritius. The most recent wave coincides with the globalization of Western modernity.

The earliest casualties of what is now an impending Anthropocene extinction include the auroch; thylacine ("Tasmanian tiger"); Atlas bear; tarpan; moa; Haast's eagle; dodo bird; Steller's sea cow; quagga (Plains zebra); passenger pigeon; great auk; Pyrenean ibex; Bali, Caspian, and Javan tigers; Caribbean monk seal; golden toad; Western black rhinoceros; and Baiji River dolphin, among others. The significance of many of these extinctions lies not in the animals' physical disappearance, which is a natural feature of evolution, but in the "unnatural" way (rate and magnitude) their particular extinctions took place at the hands of humans.

Nine species of the flightless moa bird thrived as the dominant herbivore in New Zealand until the arrival of the eastern Polynesian Maori people in the thirteenth century. Their only natural predator before humans was the Haast's eagle. DNA analysis of moa fossils concludes that the principal cause of their extinction was human overhunting and deforestation, which occurred within one hundred years of colonization.[11] Moa populations were strong and stable for four thousand years before human arrival. The Haast's eagle also went extinct with the moa, which was its principal food source. The legendary "dodo bird" faced a similar fate at the hands of Dutch settlers on the island of Mauritius in the seventeenth century. A descendant of pigeons that landed on the island during the Pleistocene, it evolved into a large, three-foot-tall, fifty-pound flightless bird. With no natural predators, it did not need to fly to survive, and it laid one egg. Named from the Dutch "dodoor," meaning sluggard, and "dowdo," meaning foolish, it wobbled right up to humans, who clubbed it to death for food. It was extinct fifty years following the Dutch settlement.

The passenger pigeon was the most abundant bird in North America, numbering in the billions when Europeans first arrived. It lived in large migratory flocks whose flight space could be up to one mile wide and three hundred miles long and would take several hours to pass by. Although nomadic, they were social animals who lived in large nesting colonies. Native Americans ate passenger pigeons but were careful to limit their kills to ensure their sustainability. Europeans hunted them indiscriminately, firing into flocks as they passed for sport. The nineteenth century spelled doom for them when they became a mass-marketed cheap meat source ("pigeon pie"), being sold for literally "a dime a dozen." Deforestation was another key contributing factor, but the main cause of the pigeons' extinction was slaughter at the hands of humans. From 1800 to 1870, their numbers declined, and from 1870 to 1900, they collapsed. The last passenger pigeon, Martha, died in the Cincinnati Zoo in 1914. The sad irony is that one year earlier, the U.S. Congress had passed a law regulating the hunting of migratory birds.[12]

Today, we are in the middle of the second great megafauna extinction. While other classes of animals are in worse shape—amphibians, corals, gastropods, and bivalves—attention is focused on our closest relatives, mammals, and in particular charismatic megafauna, such as great apes, big cats, rhinos, bears, elephants, giraffes, buffalo, wolves, and whales. Several species of rhinos are doomed to extinction thanks to poachers. A rhino horn can sell for several hundred thousand dollars on the black market in China and Vietnam. The Javan rhino is down to 30 remaining, the Sumatran rhino to between 150 and 250, and the geographic range of the white and black rhinos is now reduced to southeastern Africa. The Western black rhino was declared extinct in 2011, and the northern white rhino is ecologically or functionally extinct.[13] All of our closest evolutionary relatives, the great apes, are critically endangered. The Cross River and mountain gorillas will be extinct in the wild by midcentury, and the Eastern lowland gorilla likely by century's end. So, too, will the Sumatran orangutan.

Of the big cats, the tiger is the most critically endangered, with only around 3,000 left in the wild. The Javan, Bali, and Caspian tigers were driven to extinction by rapid human population growth, deforestation, plantation agriculture, and deliberate hunting and poisoning. The most recent subspecies to go extinct, the Javan tiger, was common on the island of Java until the beginning of the twentieth century, but it went extinct in the 1970s. The population of Java was 28 million at the beginning of the twentieth century; now, a little more than 100 years later, it is 143 million. The South China tiger is considered extinct in the wild, and the Amur or Far East Siberian tiger as well as the Sumatran tiger are down to between 300 and 400 adults. All 6 remaining tiger subspecies will likely be extinct in the wild by century's end.[14]

One of the most seriously threatened classes of species today is amphibians. A 2012 study relying on IUCN Red List data estimates that 40 percent of all known species (5,915) are "threatened with extinction" by century's end.[15] The current extinction rate of amphibians is estimated by some scientific accounts to be 45,000 times greater than the background extinction rate. Frogs have lost an estimated 200 species since the 1980s, and amphibians overall are disappearing by the dozens every year. Why should we care about frogs, salamanders, toads, newts, and caecilians? Not only do they have inherent worth as living beings; they are also integral to ecosystem sustainability. Amphibians are key indicator species in assessing habitat health and viability. They live in the most complex and diverse ecosystems, mostly tropical rainforests. They, therefore, are the canary in the coal mine. Amphibians have semipermeable skin that easily absorbs pollutants and toxins, complex reproductive systems, and few defenses against predators, and they occupy land and water habitats. In addition, amphibians are a major consumer of insects. Their decline opens the floodgates for insect population explosions and infestations.

The causes of amphibian population collapses implicate humans.[16] The most serious threat is habitat destruction and fragmentation, which affects more than 60 percent of all species and close to 90 percent of threatened species. Most amphibians occupy tropical microhabitats, and South America and Southeast Asia have been the center of recent clear cutting, logging, plantation agriculture, and rapid urbanization. Amphibians typically live in a particular terrestrial habitat and migrate to breed in a different place, usually a freshwater environment. Habitat collapse has disrupted this breeding migration. The second major threat is human environmental toxins (such as mercury, herbicides, pesticides, and fertilizer). Human colonization has also resulted in the introduction of invasive species that outcompete indigenous species for food and space, prey on them, and spread diseases and parasites. Amphibians, mostly frogs, are also killed for food and used in medicines, in research, and as pets. Climate change is another factor, as rising sea levels saturate wetlands, extreme weather disrupts the sensitive microhabitats, and the loss of Earth's ozone layer results in greater ultraviolet (UV) radiation, which has a damaging effect on their skin.

A key cause of the rapid collapse and sudden extinction of many frog species is the infectious disease *chytridiomycosis* spread by the chytrid fungus *Batrachochytrium dendrobatidis* (Bd).[17] It infects the wet, semipermeable skin of many amphibians, spreads, and then penetrates the deeper layers of the skin. It releases a toxin that short-circuits the immune system. Biologists also believe that the disease enters the circulatory system and its neurotoxic effects disable motor functions. Amphibian skin turns red, and the animal sheds excessively, with dead and diseased skin accumulating on its body. Animals become weak and lethargic, fail to move or flee potential predator threats, lose their ability to right themselves, and go into convulsions. Many scientists believe that amphibians had weakened immune systems before they came into contact with the fungus due to human alteration of their sensitive microhabitats and pesticides and pollutants. They are therefore highly susceptible to the chyrid pathogen.

All of this evidence can be evaluated in different ways, depending on one's normative framework and commitments. From a standard evolutionary perspective, for most of these species, their time has come. All species eventually go extinct, and nature does not care about extinction rates. Others, like me, acknowledge that extinction is a fact of evolution. However, what makes this situation a crisis that lends itself to intervention is a cluster of relevant variables. One is the "unnatural" and too often genocidal way in which humans have accelerated the extinction rate and scope of so many animals. Another key variable is the damage to biodiversity and ecosystem resilience. Yet another concern is the growing imbalance between rates of extinction and speciation. Then there is the important question concerning the value that we place on animals. All of these issues speak to the underlying problem of anthropocentric overextension. Bottom line: the fates of thousands of critically endangered species are in the hands of an excessively imperious and destructive species who should know better.

## Waterworld in Devolution

Earth is a blue planet, with 71 percent of its surface water. Oceans are the principal regulators of planetary climate and ecology, absorbing most of its carbon dioxide and producing most of its oxygen. More than 60 percent of humanity's population lives on or near coastlines. Oceans are the primary food source for more than a billion humans, yet today they are at an evolutionary crossroads. Waterworld is facing what has been dubbed "the great marine defaunation" and "Brave New Ocean."[18] Global warming, overfishing, pollution runoff, coastal development, garbage and plastic soup gyres, fish farming, seabed mining, container port traffic, and "seasteading," or the construction of artificial islands, have had systemic-level habitat and species effects. Habitat effects include ocean warming and acidification, an increase in the number and size of dead zones, the loss of mangrove areas, the degradation of continental shelf habitats, the collapse of coral reefs, the disruption of predator-prey food chains, and mass fields of mucilage. Species effects include significant contractions of geographic range; a decline in the number, size, and reproduction rate of numerous species; and a significant increase in extinction rates. Much of this change coincides with global oceanic industrialization over the past fifty years.[19] If current trends continue, we are looking at the real possibility of a reversal of oceanic evolution back to what life was like during the late Edicaran and Cambrian geological periods, 550 million to 485 million years ago.

Coral reefs are complex, diverse, stunningly beautiful, and fragile ecosystems that provide a viable habitat for thousands of different species of marine life. They are often described as the ocean's rainforests and nurseries. Corals are a prime example of a coevolutionary species of life. They live in colonies and continuously secrete a hard calcium-carbonate skeleton that protects them and provides the infrastructure for the colony. Colonies grow outward in multihorizontal levels resembling densely populated human cities. Reefs exist throughout the shallow waters of tropical and subtropical regions. Coral can manufacture their structures only in seawater with a certain temperature and acidity. While they are resilient to natural events, such as hurricanes, they are being killed off by the assault on them from multiple anthropogenic sources. The human causes of coral-reef collapse include agricultural waste, fertilizer runoff, sewage, overfishing, coastal development, and ocean acidification. Experts estimate that 33 to 50 percent of the world's coral reefs are dead or dying (i.e., functionally extinct). Along with amphibians, corals are one of the world's most critically endangered animals.[20]

Due to global warming, the world's oceans are absorbing too much excess carbon dioxide, which is causing increased acidity. Acidic ocean water melts calcium carbonate, which is the principal composite material of shellfish and coral. The world's oceans, rivers, and lakes maintain a pH (acid/base ratio) level that allows for life to flourish in part due to the absorption and transformation of $CO_2$ into bicarbonate and hydronium ions. If there is an overload of $CO_2$, fresh- and saltwater increase their acidity (H+ ion concentration) and thus decrease their pH levels. For the past several hundred years, oceanic pH levels have been at 8.2 on a scale from 0 to 14; they are now at 8.1 and are expected to be at 8.0 by 2050 and at 7.8 by 2100. These figures translate to an oceanic-acidity increase of 50 percent by 2050 and 100 percent by 2100. A pH level of 7.8 completely shuts down calcification.[21] Twenty-second-century ocean acidity could reach levels not evidenced since the Paleocene-Eocene transition fifty-five million years ago.

Oceanographers also report the existence of more than 500 "dead zones" where most of the oxygen has been depleted, largely because of human agricultural runoff exacerbated by global warming.[22] Nutrient-laden waste leads to an explosion of algae that eliminate the oxygen needed to support marine life. Cyanobacteria spread and wipe out zooplankton and fish, accumulate and decompose, and are eaten by microbes that produce toxic hydrogen-sulfide gas. The current largest dead zone is the Baltic Sea, followed by the Gulf of Mexico off the coast of Texas and Louisiana. The Mississippi River drains into it, dumping much of the Midwest's agribusiness waste. Other major dead zones exist in the Great Lakes, the North Sea, the Lower Saint Lawrence River estuary, and the Chesapeake Bay, and off the coasts of Oregon, Japan, and Great Britain. At its height, a dead zone becomes a huge, toxic, green-slime soup similar to what our planet was like 2 to 2.5 billion years ago.

Overfishing has resulted in the collapse of many big fish populations as well as reducing their individual sizes by 50 percent or more. The 2014 Food and Agriculture Organization (FAO) of the United Nations State of World Fisheries and Aquaculture Report indicates that 80 percent of global fish stocks are fully or overexploited.[23] Commercial fishing is now harvesting once-virgin fishing grounds and fishing down the food chain to catch juvenile fish and smaller species. Huge armadas with GPS technology, spotter planes, and processing ships scour the oceans. Sea life does not have a chance. Unwanted catch ("bycatch") accounts for millions of tons of sea animals that are thrown back dead or dying. Regulatory regimes, such as the International Commission for the Conservation of Atlantic Tunas (ICCAT), are largely controlled by the commercial fishing industry.

The volume of human debris in the world's oceans, our "plastic footprint," rivals our carbon footprint. Although the media focuses on large debris (such as shipping containers, airplane and tsunami wreckage, and tanker and oil-platform spills), most marine garbage originates from land (storm-drain runoff, industrial waste, sewage, garbage, plastic bags, bottles, Styrofoam food containers); consists of microplastics (bits smaller than a penny); circulates in large, dispersed areas or patches; and has sunk to the depths or bottom of the ocean (only 20 to 30 percent of man-made waste is on the surface or in the upper water column). While plastic breaks down into smaller and smaller pieces, it does not disappear. It takes anywhere from twenty (plastic bags) to six hundred years (fishing gear) for plastic to decompose into microplastic. It has been estimated that on average, more than twenty thousand pieces of plastic can be found in a square kilometer of ocean surface water. Many areas of the world's oceans contain more microplastic than plankton.[24]

Ocean garbage circulates in five massive gyres, with the largest being the Great Pacific trash vortex that covers an expanse of more than seven million square miles and consists of three major convergence zones off the coast of California, northeast of Hawaii, and off the coast of Japan. The rotational pattern of ocean currents creates gyres of microplastic soup as well as a highway that circulates human trash within and between major convergence zones. These trash islands are home for "skates" (*Halobates*), small insects that skip over the ocean surface, eating plankton. Plastic garbage provides platforms for laying their eggs. Ocean insect swarms are on the rise. Microplastics also absorb seawater pollutants, end up in the digestive systems of animals, and increase toxin levels, which are passed up the food chain. Countless fish and marine animals die from ingesting plastics as well as getting tangled up in floating fishing line and gear.

Aquaculture has been touted as a solution to the problem of feeding eleven billion people by 2100 in the face of declining wild fish stocks. The industry is fourteen times bigger today than it was in the early 1980s: 47 percent of all the seafood consumed by humans is now farmed. Asia, particularly China, accounts for nearly 90 percent of all fish farming. Fish are more adaptable to selective breeding than are land animals, with more than four hundred marine species capable of being farmed. They grow to maturity faster and have a very low feed-conversion ratio, meaning that it takes a little more than one pound of feed (pellets, fish meal, and krill) for many fish to gain one pound of body mass. Pigs require close to three pounds and cattle up to seven. Most fish farmers raise their stock in intensive, industrial-scale, densely packed pens and make heavy use of antibiotics and pesticides. The most commonly farmed species include carp, catfish, clams, mussels, oysters, salmon, shrimp, trout, sturgeon, and tilapia. There is also a growing trend toward shellfish farming mixed with kelp and other aquatic plants, which is better for the environment since oysters, mussels, and scallops as well as plants filter the ocean water.[25]

Tilapia, native to Africa, has become the world's most popular and, by industry standards, ideal factory fish. Raised primarily in China, the Philippines, and Central America, it will eat almost anything, absorbs food faster, is disease-resistant, can survive crowded conditions, reproduces easily, is very amenable to artificial selection, and has a "nonfishy" taste that makes it appealing to broader consumer markets. It is the broiler chicken of the sea. These advantages are, of course, from the perspective of the fish industry. Tilapia is typically farmed in unregulated, subpar, polluted conditions that give rise to algae explosions. They are an aggressive and invasive species, and when they escape their enclosures, they are hard to get rid of, dominate ecosystems, and interbreed with native fish populations. They are heavily treated with antibiotics and are the least-nutritious fish, with low levels of omega-3 fatty acids since they are raised on corn and soy.

We know from scientific studies that the brains of fish are more complex than previously understood. They have an amygdala that processes basic emotions and long-term and spatial memory used to navigate and migrate. Many fish build nests and hunt jointly for food, and some use tools. Fish have complex and distinct vocalizations, communicating within and across species. The oceans are rich in fish talk. They also have pain receptors. Under overcrowded conditions in tanks, ponds, or cages, they experience stress and often attack other fish and bite off their fins. As biologist Victoria Braithwaite discusses in *Do Fish Feel Pain?* (2010), it has been common practice to slaughter fish by pumping them into carbon dioxide–saturated tanks to suffocate them. Once they stop moving, their gills are cut, and they are left to bleed out on tables packed with ice. Research, however, indicates that $CO_2$ saturation is painful, that fish excrete ammonia as they struggle, and that immobile does not always mean unconscious. Their metabolism slows down and the ice prolongs their misery, since they are cold-blooded animals.[26]

Extinction rates among aquatic species are highest among corals, mollusks, crustaceans, sharks and rays, sea turtles, manatees, seals, sea lions, and tuna. Five of eight tuna species are critically endangered, none worse than the majestic, giant bluefin tuna. These "tigers of the sea" are built like torpedoes for speed and power. Metallic blue on top and silver and white on the bottom, the Atlantic bluefin can grow up to fifteen feet, weigh fifteen hundred pounds, dive to depths of four thousand feet, swim fifty miles per hour, and live for forty to fifty years. Prior to the 1970s, tuna was regarded as a garbage fish ground up for cat food and military rations. But with the development of Asian and American sushi and sashimi markets and aggressive Japanese fishing, all bluefin populations, Atlantic, Pacific, and southern, are now near collapse levels. The majority of tuna industrially harvested today are juveniles that have not reproduced.[27]

One of the most severely threatened classes of marine vertebrates are *chondrichthyes*, fish with skeletons made of cartilage rather than bone, such as sharks, rays, and skates; 20 percent of more than one thousand species are on the path to extinction. The shark is the most maligned and misunderstood of sea animals. Misinformation is packaged by media corporations into phony documentaries; pseudoscientific educational series; and sensationalist, silly, and stupid "shark" and "monster" week programs. On average, sharks kill ten human beings per year, but the estimated number of sharks killed by humans annually is one hundred million.[28] "Finning" involves cutting off the fins of sharks and selling them to Asian markets so the collagen fibers can be processed into "shark fin soup," a tasteless, gelatinous "delicacy" and traditional symbol of prestige, wealth, and good fortune that is often served at weddings. Finless, bleeding sharks are thrown back into the sea, most often alive, where they drown (without fins, they cannot swim and process water through their gills into oxygen), are eaten by other fish, or starve to death.

Sharks are a high-volume unwanted catch because they share similar habitats with highly prized, target species, such as tuna, crab, and shrimp. Half of all the sharks killed by humans each year are bycatch. A recent analysis of Australian and American newspaper articles on sharks revealed an overwhelming focus on attacks and sharks in movies and on television, with only 11 percent of the content related to shark conservation and science.[29] One of the oldest living species on the planet, sharks evolved during the

Devonian Period 420 million to 358 million years ago. Sharks police habitats and protect them from invasive predators, thus keeping predator-prey relations in balance. One key disadvantage that they have, besides being brutally preyed on by humans, is their slow reproductive rate. Sharks do not lay hundreds or thousands of eggs like most other fish. They take up to 15 years to sexually mature and give birth to only one pup per year.

Sea turtles are also in trouble: 5 out of 7 species are endangered (Green, Hawksbill, Loggerhead, Leatherneck, and Kemp's Ridley), and 3 critically (Kemp's Ridley, Leatherneck, and Hawksbill). Sea turtles are air-breathing, marine reptiles, and their severe decline is due mainly to humans—overkilling for their eggs, meat, leather, and shells; pollution and plastics; coral-reef decline; loss of their nesting beaches due to coastal development; frequent entanglement in fishing lines, trawls, and gear; being hit by boats; and mistaking floating plastic for one of their favorite foods, jellyfish. The rarest is the small Kemp's Ridley turtle of the Gulf of Mexico, with only 500 remaining. The Leatherneck can grow to 7 feet and more than 2,000 pounds, dive to more than 4,000 feet, has a leather rather than a bony shell, and has the widest global distribution of all reptile species. Its Pacific population is in serious collapse; since the mid-1970s, its population of nesting females has declined globally from 115,000 to around 26,000. The Hawksbill faces continued poaching for its beautiful gold and brown shell and the loss of its coral-reef habitat.[30]

All of these major trends are converging into a perfect storm that has resulted in another development—the explosion of jellyfish blooms. Larger and more frequent infestations that cover several thousand square miles are occurring all over the world. These swarms are not simply closing beaches but also clogging the cooling systems of nuclear-powered ships, nuclear reactors, and power plants; invading fish farms; and wiping out entire populations of fish and other marine life. Jellyfish, "jellies," or "medusas" (they are not fish) are among the oldest-known multiorgan animals, having evolved 700 million to 500 million years ago. With translucent, gelatinous bells and long trailing tentacles, jellies live in every ocean and breathe through their skin, and many actively hunt rather than simply drift, stinging and paralyzing their prey. The Lion's Mane jelly has tentacles that can reach up to 120 feet in length, the Nomura grows up to 440 pounds, and the Box jellyfish is highly venomous. Jellies have a low metabolic rate, can survive in poor water quality and low-oxygen environments, are prolific breeders and voracious feeders and eat almost anything, and rather than die in a conventional sense, they decompose, reaggregate, and regenerate.

Marine biologist Lisa-ann Gershwin describes jellyfish as a "weedy species" analogous to cockroaches. They are highly adaptable and thrive in destabilized habitats, rapidly multiplying and dominating environments. Jellies survived all of the "big five" mass extinctions.[31] Complex ecosystems that check and balance their growth have kept jelly blooms from taking over, and biodiversity keeps jellies from aggregating to form biomass killing zones. Yet today complex ecosystems are disintegrating. Gershwin describes the Anthropocene as a macroevolutionary event resulting in the "radical simplification" of most marine ecosystems. She endorses Jeremy Jackson's "rise of slime" thesis that global industrialization is transforming marine ecosystems and food webs into simple, microbiotic-dominated habitats.[32] Overfishing has significantly reduced the number of jellyfish predator species. Jellies thrive in warmer, more acidic, low-oxygen dead zones. Human garbage patches provide nesting areas and home bases for jellyfish, allowing them to expand beyond their tropical and subtropical habitats.

Gershwin concludes that humans "are creating a world more like the late Precambrian than the late 1800s—a world where jellyfish ruled the seas and organisms with shells didn't exist."[33] In the late Edicaran Period, 550 million to 540 million years ago, the oceans were filled with simple, soft-bodied organisms—green algae, lichens, fungi, protists, cnidarian, and annelids. Fossil rocks reveal disc, worm, and tube-shaped creatures, centipede-like organisms, and proto-jellyfish. During the Cambrian Period, 542 to 485 million years ago, arthropods emerged, organisms with exoskeletons, modular and segmented bodies, and multiple appendages. The trilobite is the ancestor of today's crabs, lobsters, shrimp, and crayfish.

Our blue planet is increasingly becoming a "green-slime" world, overly exploited and trashed, a murky soup whose evolutionary and ecological stewardship of the planet is in jeopardy. With each passing decade, Earth's oceans more strongly resemble a stew, agitated and simmering in the juices of global warming and human exploitation. What is required is nothing less than the creation of global and regional networks of protected sanctuaries and marine reserves connected by rewilding corridors. These preservation zones will in turn require regional and transnational cooperation among the nations of the world, coupled with much greater regulation of the global fishing industry. The prospects for this shift happening, however, are remote. Thus expect more acidification, dead zones, overfishing, coral-reef disintegration, garbage patches, species extinctions, fewer fish, more slime, and more jellyfish.

## Animals and the Agribusiness-Industrial Complex

The agribusiness-industrial complex is one of the most powerful systems operating today. This "food-to-fork" leviathan consists of a monopolistic corporate power structure; monoculture agriculture; factory farms; cartels that control fertilizer, pesticide, seed, livestock breeding, and biotechnology; university agricultural schools and departments of animal science; a meat-based, processed, fast-food diet regime; supermarket distribution networks; an advertising phalanx; and powerful lobbying organizations that have effectively captured politicians and state and federal bureaucratic agencies, resulting in weak government regulation. Big Ag's great powers include Monsanto, DuPont, Cargill, ConAgra, Archer Daniels Midland, Syngenta, BASF, Bayer, Dow, Koch Industries, Philip Morris, Procter and Gamble, Hormel, Heinz, Mars, Tyson Foods, Foster Farms, Walmart, Kroger, Albertsons, Safeway, and McDonald's. Together, they produce high-yield, low-cost, high-profit, low-quality products. "You are what you eat" is the old adage. Being modern means living in a world of industrialized food.

The great protector of Big Ag is the U.S. Department of Agriculture (USDA), which represents a textbook case of what political scientists define as a bureaucratic agency effectively "captured" by the very industry it is supposed to regulate. The USDA is known by its critics as the U.S. Department of Agribusiness and USDA, Inc. Most of its leadership fits the model of revolving-door, iron-triangle politics. Careers shift back and forth from big agribusiness to trade associations to lobbying firms to Congress to food industry–funded ag schools to the USDA. Very few top-level administrators are from labor, consumer, environmental, or animal welfare groups or family farms. The USDA promotes the Big Ag agenda of the chemical-intensive production of a few monoculture commodity crops and ethanol, concentrated animal feeding operations (CAFOs), biotech foods, the streamlining and privatization of meat inspection, and a faster production line.[34]

The majority of land animals produced for human consumption are processed in large industrial farms or CAFOs. The products of recently invented techniques, the first factory animals were chickens in the 1950s and 1960s, followed by cattle and pigs in the 1970s and 1980s. CAFOs have transformed animal agriculture, replacing the family farm with assembly-line production that confines hundreds to thousands of animals in high-density cages and holding pens and employs intensive industrial technologies in place of traditional land, vegetation, and labor. The ability to raise animals in these crowded conditions was achieved due to advances in animal feed, antibiotics, growth hormones, and livestock genetics.[35]

It is estimated that in the United States, the number of animals killed annually is 10.2 billion land animals, 13 billion finfish, and 40.5 billion shellfish. The number of aquatic animals killed is difficult to calculate, as the fishing industry records its catches in metric tons. Of the 10.2 billion land animals killed in American agriculture, more than 95 percent are chickens. The second-highest number killed are turkeys, followed by pigs, cattle, ducks and geese, sheep and goats, and rabbits. The estimated number of land animals killed worldwide annually is around seventy billion, and the global fish kill is 90 billion.[36]

Since farmed animals are private-propertied commodities, factory farming raises no serious animal ethical concerns from either a business or government standpoint. Problems principally involve human health and environmental issues. But from the standpoint of animal ethics, big agribusiness is a tragic story. Chickens, cows, pigs, turkeys, ducks, geese, sheep, and goats are smart animals that are aware of what is being inflicted on them. They can see, smell, hear, taste, feel, and give voice to their suffering. And we humans intuitively know that most factory farming is cruel and violates reasonable standards of decency. The systematic exploitation and suffering inflicted on factory-farmed animals as well as on the daily lives of animals in slaughterhouses and fish farms have been well documented by Erik Marcus in *Meat Market: Animals, Ethics, and Money* (2005), Mark Hawthorne in *Bleating Hearts: The Hidden World of Animal Suffering* (2013), and Timothy Pachirat in *Every Twelve Seconds: Industrialized Slaughter and the Politics of Sight* (2011).

Thanks to their physiology, the ranching tradition, and federal grazing subsidies, beef cattle (comparatively speaking) have it better than dairy cows, pigs, and chickens.[37] Once they are separated from their mothers after birth, calves are raised on range or pasture land. Before their transportation to "finishing" feedlots, they are castrated, dehorned, and branded. Factory-farmed beef cattle spend the rest of their short lives in feedlots being radically fattened on rations of corn, hormones, and antibiotics. CAFO feedlots contain thousands of cattle in crowded, muddy, manure-layered pens. The final stage, upon reaching market weight, is transportation to slaughter. The normal life of a cow is twenty to twenty-five years, yet factory beef cattle live a mere fifteen to twenty *months*. CAFO dairy cows are confined in metal sheds in stalls or in outdoor feedlots, are artificially inseminated in "rape racks," undergo constant pregnancies, have their calves taken from them twenty-four to forty-eight hours after birth, are injected with bovine growth hormones, are connected to milking machines two or more times a day, and live three to four years.[38]

The modern industrial meat chicken or "broiler" is the most technologically manipulated, abused, and tortured of all factory-farm animals. Industrial broilers are genetically selected for rapid growth, a high percentage of breast meat, and six to seven weeks of life, if one can call it living. Broilers are confined to large windowless sheds with artificial lighting that can hold from twenty thousand to sixty thousand birds. Broiler houses have concrete flooring topped with sawdust, straw, wood shavings, or shredded paper. The sheds are humid and filled with ammonia gas, dust, and bacteria. Chickens are motherless and fend for themselves. Many starve to death. Broilers grow so big so fast that their legs cannot support them, so they spend most of their time lying down on filthy floors. Their feet and legs are full of ulcers and hock burns. They have chronic respiratory ailments. High ammonia levels also cause blindness. The transport of broilers is also brutal. Crews of "chicken catchers" grab them by their crippled, infected feet and legs and stuff them into wire crates. Up to 25 percent are injured, and many suffer heart attacks from the trauma.[39]

CAFO pig farms, also known as "indoor pig systems" and "intensive piggeries," have dramatically expanded over the past few decades. Pigs do not have sweat glands and therefore are sensitive to warm temperatures, sunburn, and heat stress. They wallow in mud to cool themselves. Indoor warehouses allow pig farming to thrive in climates unsuitable for outdoor farming. The life of a breeder sow is one of continual pregnancy for its three- to five-year existence. While wild pigs give birth once a year, CAFO breeders have two litters a year. Breeding sows are first impregnated at seven months. Each pregnancy lasts four months, and newborn piglets are restricted to nursing for two to four weeks; wild piglets are nursed for twelve weeks. Most sow-breeding systems rely on "gestation" crates. During their pregnancies, sows are kept in two-foot-wide pens that allow them only to stand or lie down, not move or turn around. Slat floors allow waste to pass through, but it stills damages their feet. High levels of ammonia cause chronic respiratory ailments. Before birth, sows are moved to "farrowing" crates, where they are forced to lie down and nurse their piglets; the sow is housed in one section and piglets in another to avoid the mother crushing its piglets. After their premature weaning, piglets are placed in "batch pens," which typically hold twenty pigs in a bedroom-size stall with a concrete or metal slatted floor. They are castrated, their tails are cut off, and their ears are notched, usually without painkillers. After five to seven weeks in these "nurseries," they are transferred to finishing pens, fattened to market weight, and trucked to slaughter.[40]

The Humane Methods of Livestock Slaughter Act (HMLSA) became federal law in 1958, was amended in 1978 by the Federal Meat Inspection Act, and was altered again in 2002 with the passage of the Farm Bill. It requires that animals defined as "livestock" be "rendered insensible to pain" before they are slaughtered,[41] meaning they must be fully unconscious and incapable of regaining consciousness. The act requires that methods be "rapid and effective," specifying that livestock can be gassed, electrocuted, or shot with a firearm or captive bolt gun.[42] A religious exemption allows for "the simultaneous and instantaneous severance of the carotid arteries with a sharp instrument."[43] Livestock is categorized as "cattle, calves, horses, mules, sheep, and other livestock."[44] "Other livestock" has been defined as goats and "other equines." Birds (chickens, turkeys, ducks, and geese), rabbits, and fish are exempt.[45] Under Section 4, the secretary of Agriculture has the authority to include other animals as livestock, but to date all secretaries have refused to do so.[46] The HMLSA also contains provisions for handling, which include minimal use of electric prods, noninjurious pens and camps, and proper treatment of nonambulatory animals.[47]

The USDA Food Safety and Inspection Service (FSIS) enforces the law, yet gaping holes in the act and its enforcement undermine its legitimacy in several major respects. The exclusion of birds as well as rabbits and fish makes the HMLSA a 2 percent quasi-solution to a 100 percent problem. The overwhelming majority of animals killed and eaten around the world is chicken and fish, so the chicken exemption is clear evidence of the power of agribusiness over Congress and the USDA. The lack of serious enforcement is another major problem. Inspectors can halt the production line for violations but rarely do, making noncompliance routine in slaughterhouses. Furthermore, most states have customary farming exemption laws (CFEs) on their books that require government regulators as well as judges hearing abuse or cruelty cases to defer to "established methods of animal husbandry."[48] Finally, with regard to killing methods, the problem is threefold—the "stunning" methods, the training and supervision of kill-floor employees, and the speed of the kill line.

Chickens, which constitute more than 95 percent of all slaughtered land animals, are killed using "electrical immobilization." They are shackled upside down on a conveyer belt and dunked into an electrified water bath, where they are neither stunned nor rendered unconscious but are paralyzed. The purpose is to immobilize them so they are easier to handle and to make it easier to remove their feathers. The effect of electric paralysis on the chickens' muscle tissue also makes for a better meat product. Once the chickens are immobilized, a machine cuts their necks, and they bleed out. However, because many birds are not paralyzed, the carotid-artery blades often miss their mark. From here, the birds are deposited into a scalding tank.[49]

Due to the speed at which slaughterhouses operate, animals are routinely beaten and meat hooked, and there are regular instances of animals' being skinned and dismembered alive. The kill line has accelerated to increase productivity. For cattle, the industry standard for the "knocker," the worker who shoots the animal in the head with a captive bolt gun, is 250 killed per hour, yet the actual rate at most plants is 300 to 400 per hour. The rate for pigs in some slaughterhouses can be twice as many per hour. Jobs in the slaughtering and meatpacking industries were once unionized, high-skill, high-paying careers, but they are now nonunion, low-skill, minimum-wage jobs. Most employees are immigrant laborers. Turnover is high in the industry. The result is a lack of skilled, experienced workers and sped-up kill and processing lines, creating a dangerous work environment for employees.

Celebrated animal scientist, animal welfare advocate, and cattle-slaughter reformer Temple Grandin believes that her techniques have made a big difference and that industrial slaughter is now truly "humane." Her innovations have been adopted by McDonald's, Wendy's, Burger King, Cargill, Tyson, and the North American Meat Institute (NAMI).[50] Their adoption, which NAMI "has encouraged its members to subscribe to voluntarily," speaks volumes to the failure of the USDA to do its job.[51] Among her innovations are the curved, single-file chute; the round crowd pen; and the animal welfare audit. The curved, serpentine ramp helps facilitate the natural circling behavior of cattle and sheep. It also prevents animals from seeing people and the end of the chute, with solid sides also blocking their view. With less distraction, cattle are less panicked and play follow the leader, walking nose to tail. The round crowd pen forces cattle to circle around so that they are tricked into thinking they are returning to where they came from. Blood samples from cattle in these pens indicate much lower cortisol (stress hormones) levels.[52]

Grandin's animal welfare audit scores slaughter plants on how well they meet "five basic critical control points" and "five acts of abuse." The five critical control points are (1) the percentage of animals stunned correctly on the first try, (2) the percentage that remain insensible, (3) the percentage that do not vocalize during handling and stunning, (4) the percentage that do not fall or slip, and (5) the percentage moved with no prod. The five acts of abuse are (1) dragging sensible, nonambulatory animals; (2) poking an animal in a sensitive area; (3) driving an animal over the top of another animal; (4) slamming gates on animals; and (5) beating animals and breaking tails. To pass a welfare audit, a plant must have a passing score on all five critical control points and no acts of abuse. Passing requires a 95 percent first-stun rating, 100 percent insensibility, no more than 3 percent vocalizations, 1 percent or less slips and falls, and no more than 25 percent of animals touched with a prod.[53] The audit is a win-win for the ag industry,[54] for it demonstrates that agribusiness cares about animal welfare yet also speeds up the production line. There is more efficiency, more productivity, and enhanced public legitimacy.

Yet despite these reforms, industrial slaughter is outdated and inhumane in how animals are treated, how workers are treated, its methods, its institutional design and procedures, and its regulatory regime. Modern industrialized animal slaughter needs to be institutionally *trans*formed, not simply *re*formed. It needs to be phased out as part of a larger shift toward postmodern farming. Modest reforms within the paradigm of industrial slaughter do not solve the problem. What is needed is a more radical reformist approach that calls into question the very institution of industrial slaughter.

Pachirat's undercover ethnographic study *Every Twelve Seconds* characterizes the industrial slaughterhouse as a "zone of confinement" and a "segregated and isolated territory," in the words of sociologist Zygmunt Bauman, which is "invisible" and "on the whole inaccessible to ordinary members of society."[55] It is analogous to "the prison, the hospital, the nursing home, the psychiatric ward, the refugee camp, the detention center, the interrogation room, the execution chamber, the extermination camp."[56] Pachirat's plant, one of the largest facilities in the country outside Omaha, Nebraska, employed eight hundred workers. The line killed three hundred cattle per hour and "between twenty-two and twenty-five hundred" daily, "adding up to well over ten thousand cattle killed per five-day week, or more than half a million cattle slaughtered each year."[57] The plant itself was separated into highly compartmentalized departments—the front office, the kill floor, the fabrication department, and the cooler.[58] Most employees never came in contact with a living or dying animal. Pachirat points out that only four knockers were directly involved in killing cattle, and fewer than twenty workers were within sight of the killing.[59] Most employees dealt with carcasses and body parts.

Pachirat notes, "Four corporations (Tyson Foods-SBP, ConAgra-Montfort, Cargill-Excel, and National Beef) control more than 80 percent of the U.S. market in beef," with Tyson Foods "the single largest processor and marketer of dead animals in the world, with control of 20 percent of the U.S. chicken market, 22 percent of the U.S. beef market, 20 percent of the U.S. pork market, and poultry operations on every continent in the world except Antarctica."[60] This level of corporate monopolization also exists in the slaughterhouse business, where "fourteen slaughterhouses account for 56 percent of all cattle killed; twelve slaughterhouses for 55 percent of all pigs killed; six slaughterhouses for 56 percent of all calves killed; and four slaughterhouses for 67 percent of all sheep and lambs killed."[61]

Marcus has proposed a "dismantlement movement" as one possible solution to the mammoth power of Big Animal Ag. Its mission is "to undercut and ultimately eliminate industrial animal agriculture" and "suggests that animal agriculture can be taken apart in the systematic manner of a mechanic disassembling an engine—thoughtfully, calmly, and one piece at a time."[62] The strategic focus of the movement is outreach, generational change, exposure, and nonviolent "open rescues,"[63] with its central message focusing on animal ag's "inherently cruel nature."[64] Marcus advocates outreach efforts geared toward young people who are more open to the plight of animals and to changing their lifestyles and diets toward vegetarianism and veganism; he also favors more undercover videos documenting the cruel and abusive conditions in factory farms. Additionally, he supports the formation of tactical alliances with animal welfare organizations, such as the Humane Society of the United States (HSUS), in state-level campaigns to end the use of battery cages, gestation crates, de-beaking, tail docking, and other cruel farming practices.

But animal rights vegan abolitionist Gary Francione rejects this strategy as a form of "new animal welfarism" that, in effect, reinforces big animal agriculture.[65] For Francione, animal rights and welfare positions are fundamentally incompatible ethically and politically. One cannot be a universal animal rights vegan philosophically and morally, yet in one's personal life be a liberal incremental welfarist politically. Francione regards welfarist regulatory reforms as equivalent to "putting mattresses in concentration camps."[66] Welfare reform measures tied to eventual dismantlement achieve the opposite, instead aiding Big Ag. Small changes increase efficiency and productivity, put corporations in a better public relations position with consumers, and make people feel better about continuing to eat meat. Furthermore, all the loopholes in the regulatory laws make them practically meaningless. The movement amounts to feel-good liberalism. Most national organizations, even People for the Ethical Treatment of Animals (PETA), are as corporate as Big Ag. While their narrative is anti-cruelty and justice for animals, their end results are in line with corporate agriculture. In the end, animal welfare, old and new, reveals the structural limitations of liberal reformism and the overwhelming systemic power of the agribusiness-industrial complex.

As an empirical as well as a political question, one cannot definitively tell which strategy has had a greater impact—dismantlement or radical abolitionism. I agree with much of Francione's critique of animal welfare liberalism, yet I disagree with his portrayal of welfarism versus vegan abolitionism as a nonnegotiable, either/or choice and zero-sum game. In the grand scheme of things, incremental reforms *and* radical boycotting have had small effects. Animal rights vegans occupy the intellectual and moral high ground and create committed activists. They also alienate large segments of the public and spend as much time and energy attacking welfare reformers and policing animal advocates and "impure" vegans as they do battling Big Ag. A long struggle requiring a major shift in social norms and habits will need to occur before we see significant institutional transformation.

A third front in the biopolitics of animal agriculture dismantlement differs from animal rights and welfare positions as well as how the rights/welfare debate has framed the future of animal ag. It involves building an alternative farm and food paradigm around new farming models and farming communities. For lack of a better term, I call it "postmodern agriculture." Its goal is not simply an extension of efforts already in place in the form of smaller, organic, and humane-treatment farms and food networks, although this is the direction in which we should be heading. Smart pasture operations (SPOs) that reclaim and return land to pasture to feed animals that are truly free-range, engage in crop diversification and rotation, and are linked to locavore farm-to-table and community-supported agriculture (CSA) play an important role in CAFO dismantlement.

The next step we need to take involves developing new human-animal cooperative farming communities that include animals as coresidents and coworkers. The big challenge is to rethink our relation to farm animals as one of co-laborers working with us in more nonexploitative ways. Can we have citizen farmers who work alongside animal coworkers in more integrated farming communities? This shift also requires integrating new high-tech practices into farming. The goal is not to return to traditional farming but rather to invent new postmodern models. What I have in mind acknowledges the current "agrihood" trend and yet more closely resembles the idea of coevolutionary, interspecies communities. In Chapter 4, I elaborate on the idea of decentralized, associational communities pioneered in the work of anarcho-communitarian Petr Kropotkin and more recently by Bill McKibben.

I part company with universal animal rights vegan abolitionists with regard to the view that we need to completely abolish all animal agriculture and domesticated animals. Domestic and farm animals are integral parts of human society and my idea of posthumanist communitarianism. Domestication is as much a natural coevolutionary adaptive strategy evident in many animals as it is a biopolitics of controlled artificial breeding and domination. The challenge of postmodern agriculture is to distinguish coevolutionary communitarian domestication and nonexploitative animal labor from the modern biopolitics of sequestered industrial animal production. The goal of working toward more nonalienated forms of social labor that is so integral to Karl Marx's vision of human emancipation also needs to become part of the agenda of a posthumanist communitarian ethic and politics in the form of new models and practices of human-animal socially cooperative labor.[67]

## Animals as Neighbors: Life in the Contact Zone

As the Anthropocene unfolds, wild animals have three options: (1) remain in their habitats out of necessity or as a result of being cut off from their normal range due to human development, (2) migrate away from humans, or (3) migrate toward centers of human habitation in search of a better life. Today, more and more animals are urbanized and suburbanized. A kind of reverse reinhabitation is in the works. Animals are headed our way in search of food and shelter, a trend that we refer to as "habitat encroachment." But who is encroaching on whom? In many cases, animals are reclaiming their home ranges taken from them by humans since they have little native habitat left by which to survive. Raccoons and coyotes live in every major North American city. The white-tailed deer population has exploded in eastern Canada and the United States. Feral cat colonies are ever increasing. Baboons in South Africa, kangaroos in Australia, alligators and pythons in Florida, and mountain lions making a comeback and expanding their range in the American West and beyond are just a few examples. Life in the contact zone continues to grow and intensify and is forcing us to rethink the traditional distinction between wild and domesticated animals.

In *Welcome to Subirdia: Sharing Our Neighborhoods with Wrens, Robins, Woodpeckers, and Other Wildlife* (2014), ornithologist John Marzluff chronicles an avian renaissance in progress. From his research in and around Seattle and through surveys taken in other urban and suburban settings around the world, he has discovered that birds prefer suburbia to cities, woodlands, and forests. He notes that he has counted more bird species in New York's Central Park than in Yellowstone National Park.[68] Suburbia is an ideal environment for birds, consisting of a variety of well-maintained microhabitats where gardens, shrubbery, trees, and numerous plant species flourish. Suburbia is "plantopia." And where there are healthy plants, there are insects. Plants, insects, and diverse habitats make for ideal nesting areas. Reliable food and water not only attract birds but also lengthen their breeding seasons, broaden their ranges, and enhance their winter survival rates, thus increasing their reproductive abilities. They breed earlier and produce more offspring.

In terms of their response to urbanization, we can speak of three categories of birds—"avoiders," "adapters," and "exploiters." Avoider species tend to leave or decline once humans invade and transform habitats, as has been the fate of most large mammals. Avoiders include woodpeckers, warblers, and nightingales. Adapters stay and evolve. They include cardinals, magpies, blackbirds, and tits. Exploiters move in and thrive. They include birds found in most urban and suburban environments worldwide—pigeons, sparrows, starlings, wrens, finches, Canadian geese, crows, and mockingbirds. In Marzluff's study of new urban and suburban areas in the Seattle area, he and his students counted ten avoider species, seven exploiter species, and twenty-six adapter species.[69] This information helps confirm what most biologists have known for some time—that birds are one of the most adaptable types of species.

But not is all utopian in subirdia. Feral and free-roaming cats kill 1.4 to 2.7 billion birds in the United States annually.[70] It is also not a healthy habitat for reptiles and amphibians, with a significant decline in the number of snake, lizard, salamander, and frog species.[71] Snakes suffer from cultural persecution, feared and hated by many people all over the world. Amphibians unfortunately require special, stable habitats and are particularly sensitive to human pollutants. Roadways are also death traps for many reptiles and amphibians. Urban sprawl for many of their species has been a "silent killer."[72]

As a citizen of subirdia, I actively manage a small half acre and largely abide by Marzluff's "ten commandments." I do not adhere to the suburban religion of "industrial lawn" maintenance. The well-manicured, excessively fertilized, pesticide-treated, mowed, and watered suburban lawn, the source of petty neighbor competition and disputes, is ecologically a "sterile desert." Marzluff recommends a "shaggy lawn" with more trees, shrubs, flower beds, thickets, brush piles, and native plants.[73] Also, cats should be kept indoors. People should "make [their] windows more visible to birds that fly near them," since death by collision with commercial and residential buildings is the second-leading cause of bird deaths.[74] People should try to minimize night light, for lighting up the night sky disorients birds and disrupts their migrations.[75] Marzluff also recommends offering fresh water and nest boxes, not killing native predators, and fostering habitats that favor native plants rather than nursery stock.[76] I have found in my small patch of subirdia that one can effectively manage a space of coexistence between birds, cats, squirrels, and other local animal neighbors.

We may have come a long way from Alfred Hitchcock's *The Birds* to subirdia, yet all is not well for many birds around the world. As Jonathan Franzen documents in the essay "Emptying the Skies" and as Douglas and Roger Kass's 2013 film adaptation reveals, millions of migratory birds are being trapped and shot all across the Mediterranean, to the point of near extinction in some cases.[77] Southern Europe, the Adriatic and Balkans, North Africa, and the Middle East have always been a major nexus of migratory routes for three hundred species traveling north in the summer to breed and south in the winter to warm African climates. The Mediterranean has always had strong bird-hunting traditions, and many birds are considered delicacies.

While bird hunting is restricted and trapping is illegal in the European Union, birds appear on the menu in restaurants throughout the Mediterranean. Trapping techniques range from traditional nets to lime sticks to metal, mouselike traps. Birds are lured to their deaths by calls on cell phones and iPods. Major killing zones include the coast of Gibraltar, Barcelona, Sicily, Malta, Albania, Egypt, and Cyprus. The slaughter is not simply of songbirds, such as golden orioles, robins, warblers, thrushes, buntings, shrikes, and hoopoes, but also of geese, ibis, and larger raptors. The number of birds killed is estimated in the hundreds of millions.

Jim Sterba's *Nature Wars* (2012) paints a very different picture of the contact zone, which is expressed in the book's subtitle—"The Incredible Story of How Wildlife Comebacks Turned Backyards into Battlegrounds." His main focus is on the Great Eastern Forest, which "stretches from the Atlantic Ocean to the Great Plains" and contains most of the U.S. population and animal life.[78] He specifically focuses on "backyard animals," which occupy the seven-hundred-mile eastern corridor of human sprawl from Maine to Virginia. Sterba identifies four trends that have created a perfect storm of human-animal conflict: (1) the regeneration of the Great Eastern Forest; (2) the great comeback of its traditional wildlife, which was once close to extinction; (3) the growth of human-sprawl habitation (urban, suburban, and exurban); and (4) the development of a denatured, sentimental view of animals by most human-sprawl forest dwellers.

Before Europeans arrived in North America at the turn of the sixteenth century, native peoples had managed the forests and wildlife for centuries with limited damage due to their low-impact cultures, technologies, and populations. Sterba narrates European colonization as a three-wave process: (1) the great deforestation and eradication of wildlife from 1600 to 1900, (2) the late nineteenth- and twentieth-century conservation movement, and (3) postwar suburbanization that expanded into full-blown sprawl and the ensuing growth of exurbias and edge cities.[79] He then profiles the impact of six animals that are the vanguard of what Sterba describes as a "re-invasion"— beavers, white-tailed deer, Canadian geese, turkeys, black bears, and feral cats. How we define the biological, ecological, and social impact of different species often determines whether we regard them as neighbors, nuisances, or threats. At the center of much contact zone politics is the question of what constitutes a "socially acceptable population."[80]

Sterba regards white-tail deer and feral cats as the most severe threats. The damage caused by beavers and geese is significant enough to warrant more aggressive wildlife management. Turkeys and bears, however, have been unfairly portrayed, and their negative impact has been exaggerated. From a historic low of around 350,000 in the 1890s, white-tail deer not only have recovered but have exploded to between 25 million and 40 million and growing.[81] Forest and sprawl belts are rich in vegetation; firearm use is more restricted; there are fewer natural predators; and white-tail deer are smart, fast, agile, and highly adaptable. Even though hunters kill around 6 million annually, the deer population is still out of control, according to some wildlife experts. Sterba cites extensive crop and forest destruction as well as deer ticks carrying Lyme disease. American beavers are amazing ecological engineers whose tree cutting, dam building, and lodges are legendary, but as our neighbors, they can quickly mow down our trees and flood fields, yards, and roads. Canadian geese love suburbia's well-maintained parks, ponds, lakes, golf courses, athletic fields, college campuses, and manicured grass; they also are famous for their excrement, which is messy and abundant, posing health and water-quality dangers. They also have collided with aircraft.

Contact zone politics involves local citizens who typically either love or hate animals, private property libertarians, community activists, ardent defenders of a particular species ("species partisans"), state fish and game officials, local animal shelter personnel, hunters, animal welfare and rights groups, state and local government officials, and the media. All have their particular agendas, which results in high levels of conflict. Sterba concludes, "Because these fights are local, there is virtually no learning curve from one place to another, from one community to the next."[82] What typically occurs is that local government officials hire a "professional wildlife consultant," who recommends culling the nuisance species with sharpshooters, a controlled hunt, or lethal trapping.

Sterba's response to the new nature wars is old-school conservationism. Wild animals are a resource to be managed, not individual sentient beings that have rights or are moral subjects of justice. He sides with the traditional approaches of farmers, ranchers, hunters, fish and game personnel, and professional wildlife experts, recommending "humane" trapping and hunting. Conibear traps are recommended for beavers; controlled hunts, sharpshooters, and reinstituted licensed "market hunting" for deer; flock culling for geese; and roundups and euthanasia for feral cats.[83] Sterba recommends not feeding animals, including birds. He is most critical of sentimental, suburban animal lovers and uncompromising animal rights activists who demonize their adversaries. Sterba also faults the pet industry for portraying contact zone animals as benign "outdoor pets."[84] The professional hunters, trappers, and wildlife-nuisance controllers who are most needed are in short supply. Instead, we have a sadly large number of "junk," "slob," and "trash" hunters who love killing animals.[85] Most hunting clubs include "fair-chase rules" as part of their bylaws and on their websites, a short set of guidelines that urge their members to conduct themselves in a "sportsmanlike" manner and obey all laws and regulations. Hunters in such clubs are encouraged to always work toward improving their skills; make quick, clean kills; and not dishonor the hunter or hunted. Most hunters, however, are not members of these clubs, nor do they abide by fair-chase guidelines.

One needs to keep in mind several important qualifiers when debating hunting. Hunters make up a small minority of the population, less than 5 percent of Americans. Most hunters hunt for fun, not food. It is a cultural tradition and hobby, not an economic necessity. Hunters have a highly disproportionate influence in relation to their numbers thanks to fish and game agencies and the National Rifle Association. The vast majority of hunters are low-skilled amateurs who hunt deer and birds. Most states have minimal standards for issuing hunting licenses. Finally, big-game trophy hunting of charismatic megafauna is the relic of a bygone era of Western imperialism rationalized in a facile manner as a form of bourgeois conservation with monies going to local indigenous communities and national parks and reserves. The rigged nature and frequent illegality of many hunts make a mockery of its pseudo-heroic masculine appeal. The killing of the largest and strongest representatives of critically endangered species does serious if not irreparable damage to the species' gene pool and evolutionary viability.

What then is ethical hunting? It depends on whom you ask. From where I sit, most hunting practices are ethically questionable and in many instances unconscionable. They include luring animals to bait stations; chasing animals with all-terrain vehicles (ATVs) and snowmobiles; tracking animals with packs of dogs wearing global positioning system (GPS) collars; spotting, herding, and shooting animals from the air or road; shooting birds on the ground or animals in hiding; deer driving; taking more than they can use; not tracking and recovering wounded animals; hosting canned hunts where hunters pay to kill exotic species on game reserves and ranches; and simply killing for the fun of it. As many animals are illegally poached as killed legally by licensed hunters. Studies indicate that 18 to 50 percent of animals shot and wounded are not recovered by hunters.[86] Yet state wildlife personnel too often defer to guides and hunters, because state and local agencies are often funded in part by hunters, with most fish and game personnel coming from the ranks of hunters and trappers. Animals on public lands are often managed as crops to be harvested. Traditionally, populations for "game species" have been artificially boosted, while competing predator species, such as wolves, coyotes, and cougars, have been exterminated, thereby distorting predator-prey relations.

Beaver dams and ponds create rich wetland habitats that benefit numerous species. They improve water quality and also control flooding by slowing down the movement of water. Yet they also flood human property, clog drainages and pipes, and cause crop and timber loss. Beavers cut down a lot of trees. The main reason that beavers cause problems is that humans continue to expand into rural areas where beavers live. So who is invading whose habitat exactly? Since the harm is mutual—and on the part of beavers, nonlethal—balanced nonlethal solutions should be pursued. But lethal solutions are often pursued due to state laws, which reflect private-property interests and trapping and hunting traditions.

Since beavers are tenacious master builders, destroying their dams and lodges is largely ineffective—they can rebuild them in twenty-four hours or move downstream. Lethal trapping is often praised as the most practical, decisive, and cost-effective method, and the Conibear trap is recommended as the "most humane" because its powerful jaws can break the neck of an animal, resulting in a quick death. Yet this perception assumes the beaver places its neck in the right position. Instead, beavers typically are trapped underwater and drown, which takes a long time since they can hold their breath for long periods, thus making their deaths cruel. Also, since up to a dozen beavers may live in a colony, all must be killed to eliminate the "beaver problem," a difficult and expensive proposition. Killing beavers also creates a lot of collateral damage, since otters, muskrats, raccoons, and birds often end up in the traps. Traps placed next to residential areas also increase the risk of humans, especially children, stumbling onto them. My own view is to pursue individual and community-based mutual habitat alteration. This approach includes a menu of nonlethal methods—placing heavy wire and electric fencing around trees, planting beavers' favorite trees on the front line of their habitat, installing a wire "beaver baffler" around culverts and drains, and laying a PVC "beaver-limiter" or "pond-leveler" pipe to control water flow backed up behind the dam. Communities should also establish easements as buffers between humans and beavers.

Sterba is clearly not a fan of cats or cat lovers. He describes cats as one of the "worst invasive species on the planet" and cat lovers as the most partisan and self-righteous of all animal advocates.[87] The number of feral cats in America, upwards of one hundred million, almost equals the domestic cat population. Critics point out that feral cats kill birds and small mammals, carry disease, and can be territorially aggressive. Furthermore, the much-touted TNR (trap, neuter, return) method of colony management undertaken by citizen volunteers and some veterinarians can have only a very limited impact.[88] It is very difficult to catch all colony cats, prevent new cats from joining the colony, and stop people from feeding feral cats. What we are dealing with are amazing, crafty survivors and hunters that kill for food and fun. They are stealthy, patient, fast, and efficient; have excellent eyesight and hearing; and are skilled ambush hunters. Cats, in sum, are highly adaptable animals; resourceful, prolific breeders; aggressive predators; and skilled hunters and killers. Does this sound like any species you know?

For Sterba, the worst stakeholders in local contact zone politics are zealous animal rights advocates. My own experience here in the West is that they tend to be strident antigovernment, private property, and gun rights libertarians who prefer to shoot, trap, and ask questions later. I witness time and time again conservative libertarians who block what are often modest neighborhood and community-based animal accommodation proposals and solutions, complete with private rights talk, pseudo-constitutional arguments, threats of lawsuits, and a simplified, black-and-white view of the world. The hypocrisy here is that these same people spend much of their time using public lands legally and illegally. They often attempt to bully and deceive regulatory agents and citizens by rationalizing a host of behaviors with a litany of natural and special-access rights and phony historical precedents and claims.

Clare Palmer, Sue Donaldson, and Will Kymlicka acknowledge that contact zone animals tend to be ignored and undertheorized, with most of the focus of animal ethics and politics on domestic and wild animals. Palmer admits that they "are not much discussed in animal-ethics literature, even though they may be the animals we most frequently encounter. And there is no widespread agreement or terminology to describe animals that live in the contact zone."[89] Donaldson and Kymlicka remind us that animals living among us have a paradoxical existence in two ways: (1) they are visible in our everyday world yet "invisible in our everyday worldview," and (2) they "have been amongst the most successful of animal species, finding new ways to survive and thrive in a human-dominated world. But from a legal and moral perspective, they are amongst the least recognized or protected animals."[90]

For Palmer, our obligations to care for and assist animals cannot be based entirely on morally relevant capacities (sentience, cognition, social complexity); we must also weigh the variables of context, relations, and causality.[91] The moral worth of an animal and our obligation toward it is influenced by its backstory. Causality is defined "where human beings have caused, or partially caused, animals to be in the particular situations and contexts in which they are in."[92] Relations include "having an effect, potentially having an effect, or having had an effect on another, or the existence of an interaction between one being and another, such that the effect or interaction makes a difference in states of affairs."[93] Appreciating these factors reminds us that the worlds of domesticated, wild, and contact zone animals are different, and within these worlds exist worlds within worlds within worlds.

Palmer's "contextual-relations approach" is primarily designed to clarify our obligations (and nonobligations) toward wild and contact zone animals. We are obligated to care for and assist domestic animals because we are the cause of their condition of dependency. Wild animals, for the most part, should be left alone ("no-contact, laissez-faire intuition"), unless we are causally implicated in their situation.[94] Contact zone animals occupy the messy middle and are the most difficult to figure out. Palmer classifies them into three main types: (1) "mutualists" (both humans and animals benefit from the relationship), (2) "commensalists" (animals typically benefit, and the impacts on humans are largely neutral), and (3) "contramensalists" (animals benefit at human expense).[95]

Donaldson and Kymlicka develop a different typology to make sense of what they refer to as coresident "liminal" and "denizen" animals: (1) "opportunists" (highly adaptive generalists), (2) "niche specialists" (which occupy established, specific habitats and tend to be vulnerable to human-caused changes), (3) "introduced exotics" (captive zoo animals and exotic pets that escape, are released, or are deliberately introduced as hunting stock or pest control), and (4) "feral animals" (escaped or abandoned pets or livestock).[96] They liken them to refugees, migrant workers, and illegal immigrants. And just as alien residents have basic human rights, so should our denizen neighbors be protected by basic principles of "fair co-residence." We should (1) seek nonlethal solutions, (2) extend to them a basic right of secure residency that increases in significance over time, (3) develop "fair terms of reciprocity" and reasonable accommodation of human-animal mutual interests, and (4) put in place "anti-stigma safeguards" to protect denizens from discrimination.[97]

Historically, there has been a close interrelationship between stigmatizing wild and contact zone animals, denying them some degree of accommodation, and killing them. In many ways, they are too close for comfort in more than their physicality and our perceptions of them as threats. They are highly adaptable, tenacious, competitor species, and we often cannot handle the competition. We assume a strong human supremacist stance, categorically reject coexistence as an option, and adopt a winner-take-all, zero-sum strategy. Eradication prevails over coevolution. Thus, we label them as varmints, vermin, invasive, pests, bugs, filth, and merciless killers. The list of usual suspects is long and in the United States includes wolves, coyotes, mountain lions, bears, raccoons, skunks, weasels, prairie dogs, rattlesnakes, mice, rats, seagulls, pigeons, crows, magpies, bats, carp, catfish, and eel. Kelsi Nagy and Phillip David Johnson II point out that we project onto these "trash animals" our own fears, phobias, and aspects of our behavior and society we find repulsive or are in denial of, including how we characterize marginalized human groups, such as poor, homeless, immigrant, deviant, and surplus populations.[98]

Palmer offers several hypothetical case studies based on real-world situations to test her ethical theory. One scenario involves wild coyotes displaced from their hunting and denning habitat by a new housing development. They are struggling to adapt, and some residents are trying to eliminate them. Palmer guides us through all the relevant variables (context, relations, causality) and potential solutions (reparations, habitat restoration, removal, retrofitting the development, and neighborly accommodations).[99] She concludes that the coyotes have fairly weak claims and that realistic options are limited. Her recommendation is moderate accommodation.[100] The shooting and trapping of coyotes should cease, because they are "sentient, morally considerable creatures" and have a limited victim's claim to their habitat.[101] They should not be fed or actively approached but monitored as an indirect harm. At best, some land could be set aside for multiple use. Palmer rejects the idea of compensatory justice or reparations, because identifying the causal agents (the authorizers, investors, and builders of the development) and assessing responsibility is too difficult. Thus a "causal account" is rejected in favor of a "beneficiary account."[102] The current residents should assume greater responsibility. But the coyotes' case is weak. They have no property rights claims, no sense of justice, and nothing to gain psychologically, nor can they communicate their interests.[103] They must accept "reduced circumstances."[104]

While the coyotes' legal claims may be weak, their territorial, moral, and justice claims are strong. It is wrong to assume that coyotes have no sense of justice and cannot communicate their interests. Further, equal moral, economic, and legal weight should be given to causally responsible parties and to current beneficiaries. Identifying the causal agents and assigning responsibility is not that difficult; the problem lies in bringing an effective legal case into a human-centered judicial system where contact zone animals lack standing. Certainly direct harm in the form of injury, damages, loss, and wrongful death can be verified. A case could be brought by animal advocates to move the policy process over time in the direction of a new set of precedents giving animals more standing. Just as every development requires an environmental impact report, there should be a legal requirement in every real-estate venture to include an indigenous animal habitat impact report. I also think that Palmer simplifies the residents' responses, for they likely would be divided into three groups—coyote advocates demanding some form of reparations or habitat restoration, liberal welfarists seeking Palmer's recommendations for limited accommodations, and "the only good coyote is a dead coyote" advocates. One could envision a response that pursues short-term accommodations and activist coyote protection along with a longer-term strategy of habitat restoration and rewilding.

In Palmer's subirdia scenario, a nest of blue tits located "under the eaves of the roof of a suburban house" is attacked by a magpie. All the chicks but one are killed and eaten. The last chick falls out of the nest and hops into the neighbor's garden, where her cat begins to close in on the chick. The cat's owner is outside, as is the owner of the suburban home where the blue tits live.[105] Should we intervene to chase the magpie off and stop the cat as well, in both cases to save the blue tit chick? The obvious answer on the face of it is yes, of course we should. Yet Palmer frames the scenario as one in which our primary obligation is to assist, not to prevent harm.[106] Furthermore, there are three animal lives and behaviors to consider as well as their interrelationship. And in keeping with Palmer's ethic, our primary criteria of assessment are context, relations, and causality. Palmer concludes the following: there is no obligation to intervene with respect to the blue tit–magpie relationship. Although they are both residents of the contact zone, they have no direct connection to humans with respect to causal responsibility.[107] However, as a domestic pet, the cat "loosely" obligates the owner to exercise control over the animal. Human causal responsibility exists in this relationship.[108] The motivation here should be not sympathy for suffering, emotional contagion, a human-animal kinship connection, contact zone community feeling, or a sense of justice as fair play or balancing interests but rather our human "causal entanglement" and assessment of cause-and-effect relations.[109] The facts that the magpie has already had a sufficient lunch or dinner and that a pet cat is let outdoors in subirdia do not carry much weight. Human property ownership and relations outweigh Marzluff's subirdia ethics.

In her attempt to operationalize and justify her philosophy, Palmer makes her case studies overly complicated. They are written for ethical philosophers and attorneys. In the real world of interspecies encounters, people who care about animals respond to contexts of suffering, violence, harm, and conflicting interests by drawing on the resources of their experiential and sociocultural lifeworld as much as on ethical principles carefully vetted by logical analysis and access to scientific knowledge. We respond as sentient beings first and foremost and then develop a rational actor strategy. Relational affect is as important a variable as relational cause and effect. In the world of practical ethics, we respond by triangulating the voices of reason, lifeworld, and biopolitics.

Palmer's contextual approach and delineation of three different spheres of wild, contact zone, and domestic animal relations call into question the strong universalistic egalitarian ethic that all animals are equal as individuals and as species. While all animal life-forms are equal in their elemental evolutionary sentience, they are also equally different in their specific individual and species population adaptations to their environments. All animals are the same and different constitutively and contextually. The problem here is that while we should ethically relate to them as both same and different, in our everyday lives we tend to relate to animals as different and unequal. The main battlegrounds in animal politics in the twenty-first century will involve the plight of critically endangered species on the threshold of extinction, the fate of the world's ocean inhabitants, the future of industrial animal agriculture, and the challenge of human-animal relations in the contact zone. The battles fought, big and small, will unfold as the clash of competing biopolitics.

# 3

## POSTHUMANIST ETHICS

Man has been educated by his errors. First, he always saw himself
only incompletely; second, he endowed himself with fictitious
attributes; third, he placed himself in a false order of rank in
relation to animals and nature; and fourth, he invented ever new
tables of goods and always accepted them for a time as eternal and
unconditional.

—Friedrich Nietzsche, *The Gay Science*, Book Three, Aphorism 115

## The Idea of Posthumanist Ethics

The human nature question today is at a crossroads. Advances in evolutionary biology, paleo-anthropology, neuroscience, genetic engineering, synthetic biology, and artificial intelligence are redefining the human animal. The Western ideal of modern humanism has come under greater scrutiny as the world, pushed to its limits by turn-of-the-twenty-first-century globalization, is remaking itself and forcing all life-forms to come to terms with the consequences of a changing biosphere and new era of evolution. The modern human narrative has taken on a more posthumanist story line.

The modern humanism of John Rawls and Jürgen Habermas; the postmodernism of Michel Foucault, Gilles Deleuze, and Jacques Derrida; and the environmental ethics of sustainable development continue to influence contemporary thought. Yet today, animal ethics, posthumanism, transhumanism, and evolutionary ethics are leading the way in innovation and creative disruption. Animal ethics continues to expand its influence as it translates the findings of animal studies into new approaches to human-animal relations. Posthumanism combines the insights of philosophical and literary postmodernism with animal ethics in its critique of modern humanism.[1] The transhumanist goal of a biotech re-engineered human nature conjures up visions of autonomous artificial intelligence, bioexistential overcoming, and the transcendence of conventional moralities.[2] Evolutionary ethics continues to evolve beyond the pioneering work of Charles Darwin, E. O. Wilson, and Richard Dawkins. It is evident in the research and writings of Frans de Waal, Patricia S. Churchland, Robert Boyd, Peter J. Richerson, Kim Sterelny, Michael Ruse, and David N. Stamos.

I contend that a valid posthumanist ethics can be constructed and justified on the basis of work done in coevolutionary neo-Darwinism, biocentric ethics, *umwelt* phenomenology, social constructionism, and postanthropocentric animal ethics. Posthumanism is not only an ethical outlook but also an ethos dedicated to developing social, cultural, and political practices that reconfigure the way we understand, relate to, and treat animals. The poet Gary Snyder captures the spirit of posthumanism nicely:

> We human beings of the developed societies have once more been expelled from a garden—the formal garden of Euro-American humanism and its assumptions of human superiority, priority, uniqueness, and dominance. We have been thrown back into the other garden with all the other animals and fungi and insects, where we can no longer be sure we are so privileged. The walls between "nature" and "culture" begin to crumble as we enter the posthumanist era. Darwinian insights force occidental people, often unwillingly, to acknowledge their literal kinship with critters.[3]

The assertion that posthumanism is an evolutionary ethic rests on five central beliefs. First, the origin and purpose of morality lies in evolution as a biological adaptation designed to increase the fitness of individuals and groups through the regulation of social life. Second, morality exists in other social animals besides humans. Third, human morality has evolved in tandem with our species' enhanced capacity for gene-culture coevolution. Fourth, one can base a normative ethic on evolutionary thinking. Five, one can develop a coevolutionary ethic based on the previous four beliefs.

Posthumanism is also a socially constructed ethic. Most of our daily worldly encounters occur within human-engineered environments mediated by multiple social constructs. Like John Searle, I believe that social artifacts are ontologically connected to natural or "brute" facts even under ultramodern conditions.[4] Yet I remain sympathetic to the postmodern position that this connection is increasingly more remote, segmented, and perspectivist, the product of different cognitive frameworks, language games, and social environments. This attitude, however, is not radically relativist in the sense of the incommensurability of worldviews. Perspectives overlap and therefore are capable of varying degrees of translation.[5]

The road to my idea of a posthumanist animal ethic is paved by work done in evolutionary ethics, coevolution theory, biocentric ethics, phenomenology, and phenomenological biology. Posthumanism as a coevolutionary, biocentric, lifeworld-based ethic constitutes the infrastructure of a more prescriptive animal ethic. As I have stated, it explains the *how* and *why* of animal (which includes human) morality, which I believe is critical if we are to arrive at the *who* and *what* of a credible normative ethic. Posthumanism deepens and broadens the scope of what an animal ethic should be about. It is not just about the treatment of companion, farm, research, contact zone, and critically endangered mammals or whether animals (read largely mammals) should be classified as persons or property; instead, it is about all sentient life that inhabits the biosphere in the twenty-first-century Anthropocene.

Ethical thought tends to undervalue and therefore underestimate and undertheorize the role of evolutionary and ecological dynamics as well as the bodied lifeworld and biopolitics in moral conduct. The voice of reason is not the only determinate of moral life—the voices of biology and the lifeworld are equally powerful and influential, if not more so. Reason is the voice of the universal. The voice of the lifeworld is one of greater particularity within fields of experience. The tug-of-war between reason and lifeworld shapes moral life. This struggle is especially the case with animal ethics, as aptly demonstrated in Hal Herzog's book *Some We Love, Some We Hate, Some We Eat: Why It's So Hard to Think Straight about Animals* (2010). He admits that he occupies "the troubled middle."[6] Animal ethics consists of shades of gray, not black and white, due to the complexity of the issues, the infancy of animal studies, and the diversity of life-forms and environmental factors that must be taken into consideration.

Against the background of the case I make for a posthumanist ethic that is coevolutionary, biocentric, lifeworld-based, and postanthropocentric, in the final section of this chapter, I develop a more determinate and prescriptive animal ethic. I do this by working through what I regard as the most influential perspectives in contemporary animal ethics: (1) the universal rights, vegan abolitionism of Gary Francione and Gary Steiner; (2) the utilitarian new animal welfarism of Peter Singer; (3) Kathy Rudy's affective connection ethic and narrative of "loving animals"; and (4) the postmodern posthumanism of Cary Wolfe and Matthew Calarco. The critical triangulation of these positions offers us the resources with which to develop a strong animal ethic with respect to theoretical and practical wisdom. I propose an alternative that I refer to as "posthumanist communitarianism" and "*humanimal* coevolutionary communitarianism." My yardsticks of evaluation are Aristotelian *phronesis* and my idea of a three-legged "ethical stool" whereby ethics is conceived of in terms of three essential inputs—objectivity, subjectivity, and intersubjectivity—that inform, check, and balance each other.

## Posthumanism Is an Evolutionary Ethic

A significant rupture in Western anthropocentric thought occurred with the appearance of three books by Darwin—*The Origin of Species* (1859); *The Descent of Man, and Selection in Relation to Sex* (1871); and *The Expression of Emotions in Man and Animals* (1872). Before Darwin, the majority of Westerners, including philosophers and scientists, believed that life consisted of immutable species created separately, that they were the products of a metaphysically designed process, and that humans occupied an exceptional and superior place in the order of things. Neither Darwin, nor Alfred Russel Wallace, nor Gregor Mendel discovered biological evolution, but they verified its principal causal mechanisms—natural selection, variation, heredity, differential reproduction, genetic replication, and speciation. While evolutionary naturalism eventually became the accepted scientific life paradigm, it was not until major discoveries had been made in population genetics, paleontology, and planetary geology that the modern neo-Darwinian synthesis was fully established in the 1940s. The theory and facts of evolution are now paradigmatic science, yet as a cultural worldview, it still remains highly contested in the popular mind.

With respect to morality, two questions have concerned modern evolution theory since Darwin. First, how do we account for moral behaviors, such as altruism and social cooperation, when natural selection compels individual organisms to maximize their own survival and reproductive fitness? Second, is morality unique to humans, or does it exist in other social animals? Darwin's answers to these questions in *The Descent of Man* are largely on the mark, for he hypothesizes that morality evolved from "social instincts" in animals that had in turn evolved from "parental and filial affections."[7] In chapter 3, he writes, "The difference in mind between man and higher animals, great as it is, is certainly one of degree and not of kind."[8] Darwin identifies several higher emotional and intellectual faculties (curiosity, imitation, attention, memory, imagination, reason, abstract conceptualization, self-consciousness, mental individuality, language, sense of beauty, and belief in God) and concludes that all but two of these (abstract conceptualization and belief in God) are evident in animals.[9] He also identifies several social instincts common in most animals—group affiliation, sympathy, altruism, deference to authority, separation anxiety, seeking approval from group members, and self-control.[10]

In humans, "the moral sense" evolved beyond basic social instincts with the development of a conscience that enables us to reflect on our actions and their effects on others, language that allows us to communicate "the wishes of the community" and create moral rules, and cultural learning.[11] Like other animals, humans are inclined to gratify their own desires at the expense of others. The selfish instincts are stronger than the social instincts, but only in the short term. Once satisfied, they disappear rather quickly, while the social instincts have a more lasting effect.[12] Darwin believes that aided by conscience, good habits, and cultural evolution, our moral sense could become "more tender and widely diffused."[13] He concludes that any animal with social instincts can acquire a moral sense if its brain grows to the degree that higher mental powers appear.[14]

Darwin also hypothesizes that what drives evolution in higher animals may not be entirely natural selection but also intergroup competition or "group selection." Groups that contain members with mutualistic and altruistic dispositions have a survival advantage over groups composed mainly of selfish individuals. The struggle within a social group between selfish and altruistic traits is the driving force behind the formulation of morality, whose main function is the regulation of social cooperation.[15] Most evolutionary biologists do not subscribe to group-level genetic selection. While it is a theoretical possibility, in reality it is largely the effect of selection occurring at the cellular and organism levels.[16] However, as an explanation of human social and cultural evolution, group selection has much stronger support.[17]

The breakthrough in explaining biological altruism came in the 1960s in the pioneering work of William D. Hamilton on "kin selection" or "inclusive fitness."[18] The evolution of a genetic disposition for other-directed behavior that benefits genetically related kin to maximize the reproductive fitness of the kinship group is consistent with natural selection. Hamilton proposes that altruistic acts occur mostly between individuals who share the same genes, and the cost to the individual donor, while reducing personal fitness, increases the overall fitness of its relatives. The theory of reciprocal altruism was developed in the 1970s by evolutionary biologist Robert L. Trivers to explain altruistic behavior among unrelated individuals of the same group, in the same species, and between individuals of different species.[19] It occurs when one organism (the donor) provides a benefit to the other (the recipient) without expecting immediate reciprocity—although there is an expectation of reciprocity in the future. If I scratch your back, you are expected to scratch mine. Social animals exhibit kin selection and reciprocal altruism. While kin selection has a direct genetic explanation, reciprocal altruism involves a much more developed capacity for social cooperation. These two strategies have evolved much further into forms of greater generalized reciprocity, whereby unrelated individuals cooperate with each other. While prevalent in humans, general reciprocity has also been documented in chimpanzees, vampire bats, and rats.[20]

Churchland traces the source of morality in mammals to brain chemistry and the role of neurochemicals in the development of attachment and bonding.[21] The social emotions and sentiments that bond social animals are the product of neurochemicals that facilitate maternal care, parent-offspring bonding, and pair bonding.[22] In mammals, the hypothalamus and amygdala provide the neurobiological platform for the expression of social emotions and attachment morality. The hypothalamus is the body's thermostat, regulating body temperature, eating, growth, sex, sleep, pain, and stress.[23] It also produces oxytocin and vasopressin, which figure prominently in pregnancy, mate attachment, parenting, and social bonding. The amygdala, part of the limbic system, plays a key role in the formation and storage of memories and how we react emotionally to experiences.

Oxytocin plays a key role in mammalian pregnancy, childbirth, lactation, maternal bonding, and early child-rearing. During pregnancy, the brain and body become biochemically maternalized.[24] Offspring survival becomes paramount. Oxytocin levels and receptor densities are naturally higher in females than in males and increase considerably during pregnancy, childbirth, and early motherhood. Arginine vasopressin, which has higher levels in males, is associated with mate bonding and defensive aggression in the protection of kin, among other things.[25] Long-term mate attachment is rare in mammals, although it is common in birds. Long-term monogamy in humans and prairie voles is correlated with very high oxytocin and vasopressin receptor densities.[26] Oxytocin is currently enjoying celebrity as the "love and trust hormone" that plays a key role in the sexual arousal, maternal bonding, breaking down of social inhibitions and anxiety, pain and stress relief, and social cooperation of many animals and humans.[27] It can help switch on positive in-group social emotions as well as aggressive social emotions in defending group members against threats from outside groups. This pattern is consistent with the idea of group selection.

Primatologist and ethologist de Waal defines morality as an evolutionary adaptation common in social animals and expressed through social emotions. He also identifies a sense of justice in some mammals. De Waal's case in support of animal morality and justice is grounded in firsthand experience with chimpanzees, bonobos, and capuchin monkeys. Morality for de Waal is best understood as a "bottom-up" phenomenon, the product of millions of years of biological and social evolution and not just a thin veneer or cultural overlay.[28] Justice is a type of moral behavior that developed as a solution to resource acquisition and competition. Many mammals and some birds have a sense of fairness, reciprocity, and equity, and they express these motivations and behaviors in species-specific ways.[29] Animal morality and justice are both similar to and different from human morality and justice.

Morality is expressed at its most basic level in the experience of "emotional contagion," which involves an involuntary, physiologically observable emphatic reaction to the pain, suffering, or distress of a fellow species and/or group member.[30] This trait has also been observed across species and is the basis for more complex forms of animal moral behavior. Morality manifests itself at different levels in conjunction with various levels of social and cognitive complexity and behavioral flexibility. For de Waal, not only complex animal societies but also complex animal cultures exist.[31] Culture is defined as the creation of new or modified nongenetic behavioral patterns through learning and their transmission through established social structures. The key characteristics of animal societies include individualization ("members recognize each other individually and form variable relationships built on histories of interaction"), longitudinal stability ("species with long life spans have long-term or multigenerational relationships"), and cultural learning ("social behavior and survival strategies are subject to strong learning effects").[32]

De Waal identifies three levels of morality in mammals—moral sentiments, mores, and moral reasoning.[33] Moral sentiments are the product of a mammalian neurochemical and emotional infrastructure. Mores, or "community concern," involve the recognition and enforcement of in-group norms via social pressure and rules to maintain and strengthen in-group solidarity. Moral reasoning, most evident and evolved in humans, involves reflective judgment based on the ability to abstract from the concrete behavioral level and modify social habits and emotional responses. Nonhuman animal morality operates at the first two levels, while human morality encompasses all three levels. With respect to reciprocity or "justice," de Waal also identifies three levels of expression—first-order fairness, second-order fairness, and universal community concern.[34] Many animals have a sense of first-order fairness, which involves specific and immediate behavioral reactions to perceived inequity or unfairness in the distribution of food or resources. Second-order fairness, discovered to exist among great apes, involves the ability to have a preference for fair outcomes in general. Third-order fairness, found in humans, involves the ability to adopt a more universal and impartial moral perspective.

Dale Peterson agrees with Churchland and de Waal in two key respects: (1) morality predates hominids and functions as two interrelated systems of social and emotional attachments as well as informal and formal rules, and (2) attachments are more general, primary, pervasive, and undervalued than moral rules.[35] While the limbic system generates emotional responses and affective attachments, the neocortex houses cognitive and linguistic faculties. Most modern theories of morality define ethics in terms of personhood, rational agency, formal reasoning, and written rules. Animal morality is displayed in behavioral and emotional terms and is most evident in social play, where moral norms are learned, rehearsed, and reinforced. Moreover, moral systems differ with respect to species and populations. Different moralities between and across species and across species populations "are differentially characterized by fine-tuned evolutionary adaptations to the demands of their species' particular social and ecological niches."[36]

The biological cutoff for animal morality typically is mammals and birds, yet drawing the line with regard to animal morality is difficult, if not impossible, without a degree of arbitrariness. Since extended parental care is a form of moral behavior, we would need to include reptiles, which exhibit mother caring behaviors. Crocodiles and alligators are good examples. Females closely guard their egg nests, and when the babies are ready to hatch, they make a chirping call. The mother digs up the eggs, gently helps her offspring break open the eggs, and carries the hatchlings to the river in her mouth. Crocodile and alligator mothers continue to guard, help feed, and parent their offspring for six months to two years. Newborns follow their mothers everywhere. In some cases, male and female parents share these duties. And the octopus is as intelligent, emotionally complex, curious, playful, and clever as any vertebrate or "higher" mammal, as are many other invertebrates.

Peterson characterizes our thinking about animals as one that "oscillate[s] between false anthropomorphism (an exaggerated assertion of continuity) and false anthropo-exceptionalism (an exaggerated insistence on discontinuity)."[37] Most humans defend the view that only humans have morality. While animals display moral behavior in the instinctual sense of caring for offspring and fellow pack or herd members, they lack the attributes of moral personhood. They are "moral patients" worthy of moral consideration, but they lack the capacity for moral agency. They cannot reflectively evaluate their motivations and actions, give reasons for their actions, articulate their moral choices, or take responsibility for their actions, since they lack the capacity for autonomy.

In answering the question of whether animals can be moral, philosopher Mark Rowlands argues that animals are neither moral patients nor moral agents but rather "moral subjects."[38] Designating animals as moral patients underestimates and undervalues them, but designating them (largely mammals and birds) as moral subjects hits the mark. Moral subjects are those animals that act for moral reasons, which can be emotions with identifiable moral content or moral feelings directed at a particular object or subject. To be a moral subject is to be motivated to act by moral reasons; in the case of animals, this motivation takes the form of moral emotions. Reflection on motives or reasons is not required to act morally, nor is formulating or acting on principles, adopting an impartial stance, or making propositional moral claims. Humans have these capabilities, which animals lack; therefore, humans have more ways of acting morally. But none of these human attributes is absolutely necessary for acting morally.

Animals are not moral agents, largely because they do not need to be. Recognizing them as moral subjects is necessary and sufficient for their moral status. Second, the traditional definition of moral action involving intentionality, propositional states of consciousness, and normative self-governance is incongruent with the actual practice of morality.[39] Rowlands concludes that the real drivers of moral behavior are more external than internal, the requirements of being a social animal and living a group-oriented life.[40] This motive is clearly present in numerous animal species.

Many scientists and philosophers working in animal ethology, cognition, language, and agency studies are finding ample evidence that many mammals and birds demonstrate most of, if not all, the core human capacities of personhood. They have a subjective identity and social consciousness, know when they have done wrong, take responsibility for their behavior by submitting themselves to the group for judgment, and therefore have agency and a sense of justice.[41] Animals reason in a Humean-like fashion as associational, inductive, and cause-and-effect thinkers and learners. As evidence builds in favor of animals' having a broad array of human attributes—albeit at lesser levels of development—the more the idea of personhood is recalibrated to shore up the defenses of human uniqueness. When a new mental or social skill in an animal is discovered, many scientists and philosophers change the definition of cognition, self-awareness, agency, and culture. Animal research typically reaches one of two conclusions, both of which are anthropocentric: (1) on the one hand, analysts redouble their efforts to defend human exceptionalism, but (2) on the other hand, in revealing greater similarities and continuities between humans and animals, animals become more worthy of our recognition because they act more like us.

Yet from a posthumanist ethical standpoint, these findings provide us with supplemental and corroborating evidence. The moral status of animals emanates from their evolutionary sentience and our existential, bodied, experiential connection with them as living beings. Our natural moral sentiments and lifeworld experiences constitute the infrastructure of animal ethics, core components of our biological nature, evolutionary heritage, and the habitats we share with other animals. Our moral connection to animals is rooted in our evolutionary biology, which has programmed us to be highly social and cultural creatures. Rationalist, linguistic, and individual-agentic criteria of a fundamental human-animal moral distinction are key features of the anthropocentric cultural superstructure we have constructed to maintain our civilization.

The standard charge against evolutionary ethics is that it violates David Hume's famous distinction between facts and values—one cannot derive an "ought" from an "is." Yet what he meant is that one cannot derive values from natural facts directly and as a matter of logic. Our passions, social sentiments, and reasoning brain translate our encounters with the world through psychological "laws of association." Reason cannot represent the empirical world to us in a mirrorlike objectivist manner, because it is always filtered through our senses and emotions. Human nature consists of selfish as well as altruistic dispositions that create moral sensibilities that are further refined by our reasoning faculties. So in this sense, we derive values from facts, but indirectly and not fully. Hume concludes that moral valuations of right and wrong are more like aesthetic judgments of taste than logical axioms. Reason plays multiple roles in shaping our moral conduct: it helps refine our passions, determines the best means to achieve the objects of our passions, and provides justifications of our actions, more often *a posteriori* than *a priori*.[42]

Hume is frequently cited in animal studies scholarship for several reasons: (1) his associational theory of human perception and cognition offers a compelling account of the mental lives of animals, (2) his moral theory of natural sympathy and sentiments aligns well with the emotional lives and behavior of social animals, (3) his account of the similarities and differences between humans and animals is not as stark as we have been led to believe, (4) he identifies a distinction but not a dichotomy between facts and values mediated by the role of the passions in connecting valuation to worldliness, and (5) along with Darwin, he has helped in the development of ethical naturalism and evolutionary ethics.[43]

In *A Treatise of Human Nature* (1738), Hume locates the source of mental activity in the inferences generated by sense impressions and sustained by three "laws of association"—resemblance, contiguity, and cause and effect.[44] Most reasoning in humans as well as animals consists of chains of causal inferences built up from past experiences. For Hume, cause-effect associational reasoning is the predominant form of rationality operating in animals and in humans. For "animals as well as men learn many things from experience, and infer that the same events will always follow from the same causes."[45] Animals are not guided by logical or argumentative reasoning, yet "neither are the generality of mankind, in their ordinary actions and conclusions."[46] Where humans have an advantage over animals is in our ability "to carry on a chain of consequences to a greater length."[47] We have more reasoning capacity—for abstract ideas, language, uniquely human values, and moral agency. The crux of the debate, of course, is whether this is a difference in degree or kind. Hume believes that animals (largely mammals) and humans have a full set of natural virtues. Yet while animals exhibit moral behavior, only humans are capable of morality in the full sense that he defines as "artificial virtues," or what can be called "second-order sympathies," such as justice and a general, impartial point of view.[48]

Stamos and Ruse follow in the spirit of Hume and Darwin. Stamos describes his view of ethics as a "Darwinized Hume," while Ruse's is "essentially that of David Hume brought up to date by Charles Darwin."[49] Evolution can explain the nature of morality, its origin, purpose, and functioning. But can we derive a prescriptive ethic, a set of moral rules and substantive norms of right and wrong, from the fact and theory of evolution? The answer is yes and no. Evolutionary biology can inform and contribute to a normative ethic. What we cannot do is derive an objective, rationalist, universal ethic from the fact and theory of evolution. We logically and psychologically believe our morality to be rational and objective, because we are biologically and culturally wired to believe that norms are justified in this manner and are binding on all moral and rational beings. Our biology, Ruse argues, makes "moral claims seem as if they are objective!"[50] Stamos argues that the human species does possess a natural biosocial ethic that can be explained by evolution theory. However, there is a wide variance in the actual mores of particular societies and cultures.[51]

Posthumanism is an evolutionary ethic. However, the posthumanist condition is not simply biological—it is also sociocultural. Evolutionary naturalism is certainly necessary, but it is not sufficient in understanding posthumanist ethics. Posthumanism is more precisely a coevolutionary ethic.

## Evolution as Coevolution

The term "coevolution" is biological in origin, defining a relationship between two or more species that reciprocally alters their evolution.[52] Coevolution manifests itself in a diversity of relationships—symbiotic, predator-prey, parasite-host, competitor, and mutualistic. It occurs on many levels from the cellular to the development of covariate traits between different organisms, species, and populations. It is essential to the sustainability of ecological communities. Specialized relationships develop across species. Several species mimic the behavior or appearance of other species to enhance their fitness. Coevolutionary relationships abound in nature. Plants, insects, humans, and domesticated animals are the most coevolutionary types of species and the most abundant life-forms on the planet.

Many biologists define coevolution as a change in the genetic makeup of one species in response to genetic change in another species. While many organisms, populations, and species interact with one another and share resources and niches, coevolution can be verified only genetically, not behaviorally. I define "coevolution" in a much broader sense. First, I contend that coevolution has been downplayed in standard evolutionary biology. It is a significant yet undervalued part of evolution, and thus its status within evolution theory needs to be upgraded. Second, I argue that it is the driving force of social and cultural evolution that our species has mastered more than any other. It has given us a major edge over other species and has accelerated our evolution dramatically. Third, I employ coevolution as an ethical concept with respect to how humans ought to rethink our relationships with many animals. Fourth, I use the term to describe an ethos, a set of mores and cultural practices, and a way of being in the world integral to posthumanism that is understood as not only an ethic but a way of life.

With respect to the human evolutionary narrative, it took roughly 6 million years for our species to evolve from its ape ancestors and 2.5 million years for the *Homo* line to evolve. Evolutionary biologists believe that humans and chimpanzees shared a common ancestor and that the *Pan/Homo* split occurred 6.6 to 5.4 million years ago.[53] Fossil remains of *Sahelanthropus tchadensis* and *Orrorin tungenensis* give some evidence in support of this hypothesis. Until the discovery of fossils in the 1990s belonging to the new genus *Ardipithecus*, it was assumed that our original ancestors were australopithecines.[54] The human genus evolved during the Pleistocene epoch with the appearance of *Homo habilis* 2.4 to 1.9 million years ago. Named "handy man" for its hand structure and artifact evidence of tool making and use, its cranial capacity was 20 to 25 percent larger than that of the australopithecines. *Homo erectus* employed a sophisticated Acheulian stone tool technology, was a hunter, and is believed to have used fire not only for warmth and protection but also for cooking meat.[55]

A key adaptive trait of early hominids was social bonding. The development of rudimentary societies provided a key platform for cultural learning and transmission. Sustained cultural evolution took hold much later. There is evidence of a major cultural takeoff, known as "behavioral modernity," that occurred seventy-five thousand to fifty thousand years ago.[56] Archaeological evidence indicates a significant increase in human symbolic and material production—tool making, jewelry and other decorative and ornamental items, weaving and stitched clothing, representational art (cave paintings, sculptures, figurines), shamanistic religion, human burial sites, numerical systems (notched artifacts), long-distance trading networks, huts of wood and stone with fire hearths, and the number of occupied sites.

*Homo sapiens* appeared in Africa 200,000 to 120,000 years ago. Our species migrated to South Africa 115,000 years ago, Southwest Asia 90,000 years ago, Australia 60,000 to 50,000 years ago, Europe 46,000 to 40,000 years ago, northeastern Siberia 30,000 years, and North America 15,000 years ago. We coexisted with *Homo neanderthalensis*, who lived in western Europe and Eurasia until they went extinct 24,000 years ago. Neanderthals lived in small, big-game hunting bands and shared a version of the FOXP2 language gene with modern humans. They were highly adaptable to late Pleistocene Ice Age climates, with heavily muscled arms and legs, a barrel rib cage that housed large lungs, large noses and sinuses to warm incoming cold air, and a larger cranial capacity than and twice the daily caloric intake of humans. The recent sequencing of the Neanderthal genome by the paleogeneticist Svante Pääbo and his team at the Max Planck Institute reveals that the Neanderthal shared 99.5 percent of its DNA with modern humans and interbred. With lower energy needs, a more diverse diet, and more sophisticated tools, *Homo sapiens* assimilated and displaced Neanderthals to the periphery of prehistoric Europe.[57]

By the end of the Pleistocene, all of our *Homo* cousins were extinct. We were able to survive a very turbulent period of climate change associated with late Pleistocene Ice Age cycles. Our particular strength was cultural adaptability, and we came out of the Pleistocene with our brains wired for cultural evolution. It has been our good fortune to have flourished for the past 11,700 years during an interglacial period that has been environmentally stable and hospitable. In the Holocene epoch, accelerated social, cultural, and political evolution took over from biological evolution. What has especially taken off in the past few thousand years of civilized life is institutional evolution. A significant amount of our cultural learning, innovation, accumulation, and transmission occurs through the medium of social institutions and institutional reflexivity. One could argue that modernity represents a period of punctuated cultural and institutional evolution.

Contemporary coevolution theory explains this human evolutionary narrative in terms of two different yet interrelated processes—biological and cultural evolution. The gene-culture coevolution theory of Boyd, Richerson, and Sterelny posits a dual, reciprocal feedback track grounded in the main tenets of neo-Darwinism. Genes and cultural traits are different, yet culture evolves in a Darwinian-like way and therefore can be modeled as an evolutionary process. Culture is part of human biology. The brain's evolved capacity for complex cognition and social learning has enabled us to master cultural evolution. Human populations have accumulated vast reservoirs of adaptive information over many generations and applied these variable pools of learned behaviors and technologies with great flexibility, resulting in constant innovation. Human cultural evolution has also substantially transformed the physical and social environments within which biological evolution and genetic selection operate. Culturally altered environments put pressure on their inhabitants—humans, animals, and plants—which results over time in altered biological evolution. Genes and culture therefore coevolve.[58]

Two key processes at work in cultural production and reproduction are learning and transmission, yet how do these two processes work? Gene-culture coevolution distinguishes itself from innate or massive modularity theories of the brain as well as meme theory. Massive modularity contends that the brain is a collection of specific problem-solving, computational domains or modules that evolved to solve specific evolutionary challenges among Pleistocene hunter-gatherer societies.[59] We have a Pleistocene fixed mind. Meme theory, pioneered by Dawkins, contends that "memes" are discrete units of mental representations or ideas capable of being replicated and passed down from generation to generation.[60]

Sterelny rejects massive modularity, seeing human nature as behaviorally and developmentally more plastic. While every person is genetically programmed, he or she is also shaped by the environment. This influence pertains to the brain as well. Different environments therefore result in different phenotypes. While our brains have some innate, hard-wired features—language being the best example—they also have features whose development is environmentally contingent. This plasticity allows us to generate a diversity of cultures and sustain complex, cultural evolution. Sterelny's view is closer to that of Jerry Fodor, who argues that the human brain is part modular and part general-purpose problem solver, part informationally bounded and part informationally open.[61]

Boyd, Richerson, and Sterelny argue that human learning is part innate and part individualized, but mostly social.[62] Learning is the achievement of specific populations of interacting brains within the context of social niches and institutional structures. Its sustainability and transmission are the result of population dynamics, social cooperation, and cultural group selection. Social learning draws on a diverse menu of local heuristics and can be very messy, biased, and error-prone. Learned behaviors and information are housed in brains, cultural traditions, and physical institutions and expressed in varying ways, from discrete ideas, models, and templates to ideologies, social influence, and discourses.

To be effective and sustainable, sociocultural learning must spread throughout a group or population in an organized fashion. To do this, two coevolutionary mechanisms must be in place—social cooperation and cultural group selection.[63] Cooperation has high costs and takes a lot of work to maintain. Altruism is high maintenance. Thus norms must be in place that make altruism cheap and suppress defection. Systems of rewards and punishments, social integration, group identity, and morality all reduce the costs of altruism and make free riding and defection more costly. When costs and punishments of norm violators are spread out across the group, cooperation becomes more of a positive-sum game.

For Sterelny, the key to our species' ability to rapidly evolve culturally is "downstream, cumulative, epistemic niche construction."[64] Niche construction involves organisms' altering their environment to increase their chances of survival. Niches are protective shields or filters that blunt, deflect, and channel the often brute forces of natural selection. Traditional Darwinian theory stresses environmental pressures on organisms as the driver of adaptation. Niche construction involves organisms' changing their environment, which alters the dynamics of natural selection. All animals are niche constructors; for example, beavers construct elaborate dams that create new ecosystems within already existing ecosystems. Yet human niche construction dwarfs all other species, modifying not only the physical and social environments we inhabit but also our cultural environments. We are ecological and epistemic macroengineers. Constructed niches provide specialized learning scaffolding. Cultural evolution is essentially the multigenerational, epistemic modification of a constructed social environment.

Coevolution theory offers a compelling narrative of human evolution. It is also important to note that cultural evolution, like biological evolution, is not linear. There is as much discontinuity as continuity to cultural change and as many maladaptive as adaptive cultural traits, traditions, and institutions. Cultural evolution can lead to stasis, dead ends, and collapse. Cultures often dismantle or destroy institutions and get locked into group-think strategies that lead them off the cliff. Our species has demonstrated that it has one of the greatest capacities among all species for developing coevolutionary relationships. Unfortunately, human history is littered with equally numerous examples of humans' developing relations with other species and habitats, leading to destruction and extinction.

Coevolution is a core value in posthumanist ethics and a cultural strategy in response to the plight of animals in the Anthropocene. While anthropogenic in origination, it is not anthropocentric in its premises, means, and ends. In principle, it believes that the adaptive fitness of humans and nonhuman animals is enhanced by mutualist relationships. I refer to this approach as a form of "*humanimal* coevolutionary communitarianism." The idea of coevolution as an ethos speaks to a conception of ethics as more lifeworld-based and less moralizing according to a rulebook. "Ethos" in the classical Greek meaning of the word means the social character of a community or the accustomed place or habit of a people. Ethos is the root of *ethikos*, which means to demonstrate moral character. A person's moral character emerges from the social character of his or her community. Martin Heidegger defines ethics in terms of dwelling, finding an abode in which one is at home in the world. In the premodern world, ethos determined one's sense of ethics. In today's more globalized, multicultural, and highly mobile world, one cobbles together an ethic out of the ethos of a plurality of places and cultures. Ethics is more of a spatial-temporal journey, yet Heidegger is onto something when he describes ethical dwelling as a homecoming and form of reinhabitation, of finding one's place in the world not merely psychologically but in terms of physical place and community.[65]

Understanding the relationship between ethics and ethos is important. Ethics is our idea of the good, whereas ethos is the community or space that nurtures this idea and the place where it is actualized. Ethos is the infrastructure, while ethics is the superstructure of moral life. The ethos of coevolution draws on several influences—the fact and theory of evolution, lifeworld experience, biosocial networks and communities, social practices and mores, and institutional knowledge/power regimes. The selection, integration, and expression of these influences are achieved through what Aristotle identifies as *phronesis*, or practical judgment.[66] In this sense, trans-species coevolutionary communitarian ethics has more in common with Aristotelian ethics than with modern deontological and utilitarian ethics.

From the perspective of evolutionary biology and in a strict scientific sense, much of what I have described thus far as coevolution is coexistence. My response is that coevolution and coexistence are two different yet interrelated processes and types of relations. Coexistence refers to the creation of niches whereby different species and populations can live among each other, have their own space, and minimize competitive struggle. This arrangement is referred to in ecology as "niche differentiation."[67] Coevolution refers to two or more species' being relationally involved in each other's existence in a way that alters each other's behavior. I define it as a cultural strategy and way of life constructed to not only further mutual coexistence among species but also create trans-species communities and cultures.

Our relationships with animals take on many different forms. There are people whose principal focus is a particular type of animal—companion animals, farm animals, wild animals, endangered species, charismatic megafauna, research animals, or contact zone animals. Other people's lives revolve around a particular species or breed—dogs, cats, horses, chickens, pigs, rabbits, raptors, parrots, crows, snakes, bees, butterflies. Others are more ecological, connected to desert animals, tropical forest animals, deep sea animals, coastal animals, river animals, arctic animals, or animals of their specific bioregions. People are connected by way of their social and cultural upbringings, emotional dispositions, ethical principles, particular conversion experiences, or life circumstances.

We live in a time of two interrelated trends—accelerated global animal exploitation and extinction as well as increased animal advocacy, preservation, and coevolution. If a coevolutionary ethical and cultural strategy is to gain traction, it must find a home and anchor in viable social networks, cultural niches, and institutions. I elaborate on my idea of a "posthumanist archipelago" as this home in Chapter 4, but briefly, the posthumanist archipelago connects biosocial networks and communities through which *hum-animal* coevolution can take place and be passed on to future generations as evolving traditions. This passage is the ultimate goal of coevolutionary ethics, a trans-species ethic successfully housed in biosocial networks, niches, and institutions so that a new line of human social and cultural evolution can take hold and a new social contract can be negotiated over time.

## Posthumanism Is a Biocentric Ethic

Posthumanism is a biocentric ethic in that it regards all living things as having inherent value by virtue of their existence. While all human values and beliefs should be understood as anthropogenic in that they originate with human beings, anthropogenic values do not need to be anthropocentric. Posthumanism's biocentric ethical outlook differs from many environmental as well as animal ethics, which are constructed on explicit or implicit anthropocentric foundations. Environmental ethics from Aldo Leopold to J. Baird Callicott to deep ecology are ecocentric in that their conceptions of the intrinsic value of nature are expressed holistically. The ecosystem, biotic community, or greater ecological good is the primary unit of moral valuation. This holism is grounded in evolution theory, ecology, and conservation biology. The preservation and integrity of the ecological community takes precedence over individual species or organisms. Ecological wholes are biologically, scientifically, and morally prior to their component parts. Callicott argues that any attempt to confer equal moral consideration on individual animals and plants within an ecosystem amounts to anthropocentric extensionism.

Most animal ethics affirm the value of individual animals. This moral determination, however, varies, depending on which criteria of valuation one adheres to. The basis of moral worth ranges from cognitive capacities to sentience to context and relational status to the intrinsic value of life itself. Animal advocates question environmental ethics with respect to its functionalist approach. The value of an animal is relative to its ecological value, defined by its role in the ecosystem. Feral animals, nuisance animals, nonnative and invasive species, and surplus populations are of lesser or no value. Mountains and rivers are often afforded greater value than their inhabitants. Environmentalists mainly address the condition and status of wild animals and make a distinction between our duties to wild animals and domesticated animals. The main focus of most animal ethics is the status of domesticated and captive animals.[68]

The biocentric ethic developed by Paul Taylor in *Respect for Nature* (1986) occupies a unique position in nonhuman ethics, sharing common perspectives with environmental and animal ethics while at the same time distinguishing itself in some fundamental ways from both. I believe that Taylor's biocentric outlook on nature provides another critical resource one can use to aid one's thinking in working toward an animal ethic constructed on strong postanthropocentric foundations. Taylor's ethic rests on four core principles and beliefs. Our common evolutionary origins and environmental circumstances with other species make us "members of the Earth's Community of Life."[69] This belief correlates with understanding "the natural world as a system of interdependence."[70] No species or organism is independent of the biosphere, including humans. While humans distinguish themselves from all other species by their ability to radically transform and control natural environments, they are ultimately dependent on biotic communities. However, Taylor makes clear that these principles do not necessarily result in "a holistic or organicist view of environmental ethics."[71] The ecocentric "position is open to the objection that it gives no place to the good of individual organisms, other than how their pursuit of their good contributes to the well-being of the system as a whole."[72]

While Taylor's first two principles are holistic and environmental, his third principle focuses on "the lives of individual organisms" and the importance of understanding that each living thing "has a life of its own." The idea of intrinsic worth pertains to "individual organisms as teleological centers of life."[73] Taylor justifies this assertion with respect to two lines of evidence. The first comes from advances in the practice of science itself, and the second comes from our experiential lifeworld. Both increasingly confirm "the uniqueness of each organism as an individual."[74] Furthermore, the "internal functioning and external activities" of all life-forms, "whether conscious or not," reveal purposive behavior in the very basic sense of "a unified, coherently ordered system of goal-oriented activities that has a constant tendency to protect and maintain the organism's existence."[75] More than this, as one becomes more familiar and involved with a particular organism, it "comes to mean something to one as a unique, irreplaceable individual."[76] It has a good of its own distinct from a greater holistic or statistically valid good.

Biocentric consciousness accords greater value to "what it means to be an individual living thing" that spends its life "striving to preserve itself and realize its good in its own unique way."[77] It seeks to "sharpen and deepen our awareness of what it means to be a particular living thing."[78] At the same time, understanding living things as individualized centers of life "does not involve 'reading into' them human characteristics."[79] Trees and protozoa are not conscious but are goal-oriented and have "a good of their own."[80] Each organism has "its own idiosyncratic manner of carrying on its existence in the (not necessarily conscious) pursuit of its good."[81] This is tied to its sentience and sentient interaction with its environment. An inanimate object or machine has value but not yet a "good of its own."[82] However, once more autonomous intelligent machines are perfected, this issue will need to be revisited.

Taylor's final principle, again in keeping with his ethical principle of the intrinsic worth of all life, is "the denial of human superiority."[83] He calls into question three main historical sources of Western cultural anthropocentrism: (1) classical Greek humanism, (2) the medieval theocratic Great Chain of Being, and (3) modern Cartesian dualism.[84] The argument for the unique human capacity of moral agency, whether valid or not, does not translate into moral superiority. Is the "power of photosynthesis in the leaves of plants" inferior to the power of human language?[85] Is the monkey's tree-climbing ability inferior to a human's ability to understand mathematics, or it is that we value mathematics more "because our conception of civilized life makes the development of mathematical ability more desirable than the ability to climb trees"?[86] In the place of human superiority, Taylor places the "principle of species impartiality"—"every entity has a good of its own as possessing inherent worth—the *same* inherent worth."[87]

The central underlying value of the inherent worth of life is conceptualized as a Kantian-like principle and explained by invoking the Aristotelian claim that all living things have a teleological good. Contemporary science has replaced the language of teleology with more functionalist cause-and-effect methodologies. For Taylor, "an organism's striving to preserve itself and realize its good is not identical with the more restricted concept of biological fitness, where fitness means the ability of an organism to ensure the continued existence of its genes in future individuals."[88] He conceptualizes a living thing "not only as a center of life, but as the particular center of life that it is."[89] Thus Taylor assigns primary value to the biocentric singularity of life. All living things have inherent worth in their particularity. This concept runs counter to the holistic approach of the evolutionary and ecological sciences.

The age-old question of whether value exists as an objective, ontological property or is the creation of a subjective valuer perpetuates a false dichotomy. Determining the value of something or someone is a relational process involving a valuer and a worldly being or entity. Value resides in the relationship. Life has intrinsic value, because we experience the distinct phenomenal properties of sentient life-forms. The experience of sentience generates perceptual valuation. We physically register this value and in so doing establish the intrinsic worth of sentient life.[90] Furthermore, human beings are not the only valuers; other beings are capable of perceptual as well as cognitive valuation. All of life—indeed, all of reality—can be regarded as having intrinsic value. At the same time, saying that all life has intrinsic value is not the same as saying that all life has the same equivalent inherent value. Assigning inherent moral worth to intrinsically valued life-forms is as much a subjective and intersubjective process as one of objective determination. Taylor believes that the determination of intrinsic value can be made objectively. I contend that ethics involves the triangulation of objective, subjective, and intersubjective criteria of valuation.

There is also another question to consider: While organisms have a life consciousness designed to live and reproduce, do most conscious animals regard themselves as individuated centers of life? Or do they relate to the world as nodes in biosocial networks and/or members of distinct communities? That is, while we humans may regard them as teleological centers of life, do they perceive themselves this way? My sense is that animals are fundamentally biosocial beings. While they certainly fight for their individual lives, they do not regard themselves in the individuated way we do. But this perception does not invalidate the belief in the intrinsic value of life—it strengthens it. Life has singular *and* collective worth.

Taylor's criteria for a "valid normative ethical system" are modern and neo-Kantian. Valid moral principles and rules must be general in form, "universally applicable to all moral agents as such," applied disinterestedly, and "advocated as normative principles for all to adopt."[91] We should not rely on subjective experience and moral intuition as the basis of moral judgments. Legitimate ethical theory must satisfy "certain well-established criteria," such as comprehensiveness; systematic coherence; "freedom from obscurity, conceptual confusion, semantic vacuity"; and "consistency with all known empirical truths." Taylor appeals to "the concept of an ideally competent evaluator" who relies on "well-established empirical knowledge of all relevant matters of fact" and has a "heightened awareness of the reality of individual organism's lives."[92] A valid ethic must also be capable of being exercised by rational moral agents. Thus, in the end, Taylor relies on modern rationalism and empiricism.

As mentioned, I conceive of ethics as a three-legged stool, with the three legs being subjectivity, intersubjectivity, and objectivity. All are necessary for the stool to function, for each leg informs, checks, and balances the other two legs. The absence of one leg renders ethics imbalanced and unstable. Science matters and philosophy matters, yet so does subjective and intersubjective experience, especially trans-species experience. I give weight to the value of lifeworld experience, intersubjective and interspecies communication, and social constructionism, drawing on the resources of phenomenology, *umwelt* studies, hermeneutics, and postmodernism.

In the thoughts of Heidegger, Hans-Georg Gadamer, and Maurice Merleau-Ponty, meaning and understanding are seen as emergent properties of the experiential lifeworld, the contextual background through which the things of the world appear. Ethical life, as Georg Wilhelm Friedrich Hegel and Gadamer point out, is embedded in historical communities and cultures. It is an ethos, not simply a set of abstract moral principles or imperatives. It is also neither primarily subjective (the product of individual reflection and autonomous agency) nor objective (in a scientific sense) but rather intersubjective. For the postmodernists Foucault and Derrida, reason, language, and power, historically and culturally the defining features of the human condition, implicitly involve a gap, an absent trace, a play, a difference, a resistance that can never be reconciled and that changes with each different context. Ethics reveals itself in its most elemental expression as a form of bodily resistance to the multiplicity of violences we endure on a daily basis, big and small, as we adapt to the normalizing metaphysical and political matrices that shape our identities.

Taylor formulates four basic rules of biocentric moral obligation: (1) nonmaleficence, (2) noninterference, (3) fidelity, and (4) restitutive justice.[93] We have a duty to "do no harm" to a being or entity that does no harm to us.[94] We are equally obligated to tread lightly on living things and biotic communities. This obligation calls on us to do our best "to let wild creatures live out their lives in freedom" from internal (poison, pollution, toxic chemicals) and external (cages, traps) constraints.[95] The rule of fidelity obligates us to not deceive or break a trust with an individual animal in a wild state with the intent to harm it. This requirement to not engage in "deception with intent to harm" directly calls into question traditional fishing, hunting, trapping, and wildlife management.[96] Restitutive justice obligates us when a moral subject or object (biotic entity or community) has been wronged by a moral agent. The practical challenges of these rules are acknowledged by Taylor.[97] Extending human obligations to animals, plants, and biotic entities not only increases conflict but also directly challenges many current human practices. This situation is why the majority of people reject biocentrism as impractical—it implies major cultural and institutional change. Yet to a posthumanist, this need for change is precisely its appeal and strength.

Taylor also develops a framework to address the inevitable "clashes between the duties of human ethics and those of environmental ethics" in the form of five principles of conflict resolution.[98] The principle of self-defense allows "moral agents to protect themselves against dangerous or harmful organisms by destroying them."[99] The principle of proportionality is designed to mediate conflicts between "the basic interests of animals or plants and the nonbasic interests of humans."[100] Basic interests translate as security and subsistence ("the right to life").[101] The principle of minimum wrong obligates us to work toward a solution that will inflict the least damage to all affected parties.[102] Distributive justice pertains to the clash of basic interests between human and nonhuman parties that are judged to have roughly equal moral weight.[103] Restitutive justice pertains to the issue of compensation and reparations for damages.[104] All of these principles are open to interpretation, critique, and tests of practicality. How one defines "harm" is a critical issue, as is determining what "basic" and "nonbasic" interests are. Yet what we are essentially looking at is a framework within which the adjudication of values and interests can take place.

Taylor also makes a crucial distinction between environmental ethics and what he refers to as "the ethics of the bioculture."[105] Environmental ethics pertains to relations between humans and natural ecosystems inhabited by wild animals and plants with minimal human contact (i.e., wilderness). Biocultural ethics pertains to the treatment of animals, plants, and biotic entities within human-created environments and under direct human control. Taylor's ethical system therefore does not primarily apply to how animals and plants should be treated in humanly controlled "artificial ecosystems," so it is not directly applicable to domesticated animals, animals used in research, companion species, animals in zoos and sanctuaries, and contact zone animals. Consistent with most environmental ethics, a distinction is made between wild and domestic animals.

This issue raises several questions. Can one easily make a distinction between wild and human-controlled environs? If the answer is no, which I think it is, then can one make a clear distinction between wild and domestic animals? And if this is the case, can one clearly distinguish wild from domestic animal ethics? With the entire planet under human control, is not most of the world under human management? And if this is the case, and I believe it is, then does this not dramatically restrict the practical application of an environmental or biocentric ethic that applies to only wild animals and plants? Finally, given the scope of anthropocentric planetization, are there any truly "wild" animals left anymore? Does not the Anthropocene hypothesis invalidate the ethic of noninterference with respect to wild animals?

The traditional wild-domestic animal distinction has been replaced with a view of animal life existing within a continuum of domesticated, contact zone, and wild animals. This distinction is central to the thinking of Clare Palmer, Sue Donaldson, and Will Kymlicka. Taylor's classic statement of biocentric ethics still retains its pioneering influence in its view of life as individualized and subject to evolutionary and ecological pressures, its alignment with coevolutionary thinking, its critique of anthropocentric humanism, and its principles of obligation and conflict resolution. As general rules in dealing with sentient animals, we should do the least harm possible, allow them to flourish by weighing the costs and benefits of our assistance as well as noninterference, not deceive with the intent to harm, and seek justice for animals. In addition, all life-forms have the right to defend themselves. And in the innumerable conflicts that result from the clash of human, animal, and environmental interests, we should strive for proportionality, the infliction of the minimum wrong and least damage to all affected parties, and realize that justice is not simply symbolic or procedural but involves a price to be paid and a debt owed. Justice is not merely about recognition and reconciliation but also about restitution and rehabilitation.

Taylor's biocentric ethics also has its limitations—namely, its exclusive reliance on modern rational empiricism as its criterion of norm validity, lack of a well-developed lifeworld perspective, and absence of any discussion of biopolitics and how it frames ethical thought. One recent attempt to develop a biocentric ethic that addresses these deficiencies is the biopolitical philosophy of Roberto Esposito. Esposito agrees with Foucault that redefining modernity in terms of biopolitics, the ability of sovereign power to categorize with brutal efficiency and "immunitary logic" which kinds of life are worthy of protection and which kinds of life we need to be immunized from, profoundly alters "the entire frame of political philosophy."[106] Citing Baruch Spinoza as his inspiration, he recommends redefining life itself and developing an "affirmative biopolitics" that affords all living things communitarian immunity protection. The ethics and ethos of the *bios communitas* is the starting point in countering the power of sovereign biopolitics.[107] Rather than humans' imposing order and normativity on life through the power of sovereign natural right, Spinoza believes that life gives itself order and normativity and therefore makes this norm the basis of "the principle of unlimited equivalence for every single form of life."[108] In Esposito's reading of Spinoza, the normative valuation of life and its juridical institutional expression (i.e., biopolitics) should reflect "the singular and plural mode" of nature, and therefore justice should be understood as "the product of this plurality of norms and the provisional result of their mutable equilibrium."[109]

Biocentric ethics accords moral value to all life-forms—human, animal, and plant—because sentience regards all life-forms as capable of sensory experiences that register as life enhancing or negating and of having a good in accordance with their evolutionary makeup. We are therefore obligated as moral beings to treat living entities as worthy of moral consideration. Yet moral significance is determined by situated valuers. In our valuation of life, we realize that while all life-forms, be they animal or plant, are similar in their basic capacity for sentience, they are also equally different. Different life-forms have different capacities, evolutionary drives, and agendas; are members of different environments and communities; and relate to each other differently in accordance with these different variables. Sentient life is similar and different.

The lifeworld reveals the diversity and particularity of life and how we relate to other sentient creatures. We ethically and practically weigh these similarities and differences in dealing with the diversity of life and its environs. Biocentric ethics makes the case for the universal value of sentient life in its individual singularity. The posthumanist lifeworld reveals this singularity and universality as well as the diversity and difference of life. It is also the nexus within which we enter the lives and worlds of animals, communicate with them, and see how they respond to us. A human-centered animal ethic is a one-way street and communication frequency. The posthumanist lifeworld requires us to listen and learn from animals and be more receptive to their needs, signals, and desires. How do we know what they want from us, what they need, how they relate to us? Do they want our assistance? Do they desire to be part of our community? Do they want to be left alone? Do they want to be members of the next social contract?

# The Posthumanist Lifeworld

Posthumanism is a coevolutionary, biocentric ethic. It is also a lifeworld-based ethic informed by our everyday immersion in the phenomenal and sociocultural worlds of contextualized life. Posthumanist ethics translates lifeworld contents into values, principles, practices, habits, and actions. Its normative validity claims are therefore weighed as much on the altar of existential and affective experience and intersubjectivity as they are with respect to the strictures of scientific knowledge and philosophical reasoning. The relational ontology of human-animal experience is the medium through which knowledge of animals and human-animal relations is produced. The epistemological field created is neither strictly human-centered nor modern in the sense of framing reality and knowing in terms of a narrow subject-object dualism. Interspecies knowledge is a function of diverse biosocial networks and lifeworld ecologies. My desire to "know" nonhuman animals is premised on two beliefs: (1) I can never fully, nor should I be able to, "know" animals in a human-centered manner, and (2) "knowing" them is not the principal or exclusive basis on which I relate to them. Understanding the lifeworld, therefore, is central to understanding posthumanist ethics.

As a core concept in existentialism, phenomenology, and hermeneutics, the idea of the lifeworld (*Lebenswelt*) can be traced to the work of Edmund Husserl, Heidegger, and Merleau-Ponty. It refers to the worldly realm of lived experience that constitutes the context of human intersubjective understanding. Heidegger's revolutionary philosophy of "being-in-the-world" (*Dasein*) offers a deeper ontological understanding of the structure and horizon of human existence. Humans fundamentally confront the world in a preconceptual, practical manner and are immersed in the experience of worldliness as an ongoing event or process, not primarily as cognitive knowers seeking to represent the world epistemologically as a collection of subjects and objects. We possess the capacity to grasp the deeper meaning of existence or being (*Sein*). Yet in the modern world, this ability has been obscured by processes of instrumental rationalization and objectification that Heidegger calls "technological enframing" (*Gestell*). Heidegger redefines the phenomenological lifeworld in terms of a fundamental ontology that seeks to reveal and illuminate the space or clearing within which being is disclosed. The experience of being-in-the-world is an event of existential revelation whose interpretation and understanding require for Heidegger nothing less than a new language.[110]

While Heidegger replaces traditional Western metaphysical and modern epistemological ways of understanding with phenomenological ontology, he remains anthropocentric in his belief that only humans have access to being and the capacity to communicate this experience. Conscious of our finitude, we question our existence and, in so doing, transform biological living into existential worldliness. We are, in Heidegger's view, the only beings who truly "exist." By contrast, animals relate to the world biologically. They neither experience finitude nor question their existence. Heidegger dubs them "world poor." Heidegger's deconstruction of Western metaphysics and modernity stops short of calling into question anthropocentric humanism. Worldliness and being are unique human realities. Thus, while Heidegger opens the door to a new ontology of human existence, he also closes the door to a new post-humanist ontology.[111]

Merleau-Ponty's brand of existential humanism identifies embodied inter-subjectivity as the primary site of human being. His early phenomenology of perception places the perceiving body as the nexus of understanding. Our bodies do not simply filter sensory stimuli and information; they organize our experiences of the body/environment field into a bodied subject. This "lived body" grasps its environment and other bodies perceptually. He coins the term "flesh of the world" to describe the intercorporeal matrix through which animate life experiences itself. He redefines intersubjective understanding as the experience of interacting lived bodies within the context of organic lifeworlds. Bodied subjectivities exist in the world "chiasmically," at the intersection or crossing of multiple fields of experience, and in terms of the potential reversibility of states of being and identity. What determines this subjectivity is the bodily field in which we live, the flesh of the world.[112]

The thinking of Jean-Jacques Rousseau, Hume, Friedrich Nietzsche, Heidegger, and Merleau-Ponty in different ways offers intimations, openings, and bridges to what a posthumanist lifeworld might be like. Rousseau and Hume narrow the gulf between human and animal nature maintained for centuries by Western metaphysical thinking and more recently by modern Enlightenment thinking. Rousseau's ideas of the "state of nature" and "noble savage," while maintaining a distinction between humans and animals, emphasize the animal nature in humans and evaluate it positively as a natural good. Hume's model of associational reasoning implies that humans and animals in many ways think alike. Nietzsche's "will-to-power" worldview radically destabilizes long-standing nature-culture and human-animal dualisms.

A more significant breakthrough occurred with Jakob von Uexküll's introduction of the concept of the *umwelt*. Work in the relatively new field of phenomenological biology as well the trans-species ethics of Ralph R. Acampora and Cynthia Willett bring the idea of the posthumanist lifeworld into full focus. The posthumanist lifeworld answers Thomas Nagel's famous question "What Is It Like to Be a Bat?" Nagel maintains that while we can never fully know the subjective state of mind of another species, we may be able to gain some partial understanding of animal subjectivities.[113] We can travel several roads in the pursuit of interspecies intersubjectivity. One is ethology, the scientific study of animal minds and behavior under natural and seminatural conditions. The other, poetic imagination, is described by John Maxwell Coetzee in *The Lives of Animals* (1999) as "being face to face with an animal," bringing "the living body into being with ourselves" through sympathetic identification, and rendering this experience through "poetic invention."[114] A third way is posthumanist *umwelt* phenomenology.

The lifeworld as the experiential field within which physical connections and communications between different sentient life-forms occur was developed by the early twentieth-century biologist Uexküll's pioneering work in the field of biosemiotics. Uexküll sought to understand how sentient organisms act subjectlike in the ways they perceive and function within their physical and social environments and express this behavior via chemical, visual, vocal, and other signals. The functional contacts and interactions of an organism with its particular environment create its identity. While conventional empirical and behavioral science focuses primarily on cause-and-effect relations, *umwelt* biology studies the subjective life of organisms, their awareness of their existence and environment, and how they communicate this awareness to other sentient life.[115]

Uexküll believes all organisms, plants as well as animals, have *umwelten*, or a signifying lifeworld. All life-forms are not necessarily subjects, but they have phenomenal experiences that are subjectlike. They register and communicate with intentionality even if they are nonconscious, such as fungi and plants. Understood from the perspective of *umwelt* theory, sentience is much more than the capacity to experience pleasure and pain. It is the biosemiotic capacity evident in all life-forms to communicate with their environments. This view of sentience bolsters biocentric ethics.[116]

A growing literature in phenomenological biology is evident in the work of Neil Evernden, Adolf Portmann, Kenneth Shapiro, Elizabeth Behnke, and Traci Warkentin, among others.[117] *Umwelt* studies involve finding out what a particular organism's perceptual capacities are, carefully observing its behavior, and trying to discover which phenomena are significant to it. The key to understanding the subjective world of animals is their bodily postures, movements, and gestures in relation to similar bodies, other forms of life, and their environments. Those who practice *umwelt* phenomenology speak of "intercorporeal understanding," "interspecies etiquette," "kinesthetic empathy," and "somatic attentiveness."[118] *Kinesics* focuses on body movement, position, facial expressions, posture, and gestures. *Haptics* focuses on touch and tactile communication. *Proxemics* focuses on social and personal spacing, proximity, boundaries of body and self, and individual-group dynamics.[119] Most communication in animals as well as humans is nonverbal. Gala Argent reminds us that nonverbal communication is "primarily used to convey affective and relational messages" and is ongoing in daily life, relaying a host of social norms and meanings.[120]

Animals have supersenses compared to the relatively weak, underdeveloped senses of humans, which require us to create supersensory technological extensions. Dogs have a sense of smell that is a million more times powerful than that of humans, with evolved noses that split incoming air into two tracks, one of which is dedicated exclusively to smell. Dolphins see and hear through echolocation, sending and receiving sound pulses processed by their complex inner ears and brains. They can identify different species and individual organisms by processing the sound echoes generated by their internal organs. Sharks are sensitive to electromagnetic fields generated by the movement of marine animals and ocean currents. Birds process multiple spatial fields and navigate their aerial environments through a complex process known as "optic flow."[121] Darwin's last book, *The Formation of Vegetable Mould through the Action of Worms* (1882), is not only a scientific study of earthworms but also a portrayal of their *umwelt*, or what Darwin calls their "habits."[122]

The charge of anthropomorphism often leveled against *umwelt* phenomenology misses the mark in a fundamental way, for it fails to grasp the gap between the human-animal (*humanimal*) experience and its linguistic representation. The phenomenology of sentient interaction refutes the notion that humans simply project their capacities onto or register similar attributes in their encounters with animals. The words we use to describe and explain interspecies experiences remain largely anthropocentric and thus anthropomorphic. What we need, and what is currently underway, is a linguistic revolution to effectively give fuller voice to the posthumanist lifeworld.

Acampora takes up the challenge of posthumanist lifeworld ethics in *Corporal Compassion: Animal Ethics and Philosophy of Body* (2006). Drawing on the moral-sense theory of Hume and Rousseau, Nietzsche's cultural ideal of a postmetaphysical vitalism, Merleau-Ponty's phenomenology, and Uexküll's idea of the *umwelt*, he focuses on "the somatic core of cross-species moral experience."[123] The basis of animal ethics should be the experiential lifeworld reconceived as an intercorporeal, interspecies, somatic body field through which we directly experience the flesh of other species and the physicality of their world as inherently intersubjective and moral. This experience yields an instinctive sense of sympathy, or *symphysis*.[124] The human phenomenological lifeworld is expanded and reconceived as the trans-species symphysical lifeworld. What is experienced is similar to Merleau-Ponty's "flesh of the world."

This interbodied field of animate life knows no human-animal distinction or clearly bounded self-other distinction, for that matter. Heidegger is wrong, and Uexküll is right. Not only do all sentient beings have worlds; many animals are also world-forming in their distinctive biosocial ways of adapting to and altering their local environs.[125]

*Symphysis* describes any physical relationship between two sentient organisms that creates interspecies sympathy or empathy. This idea is similar to what Rousseau regards as natural pity expressed by sentient animals that possess subjective awareness. In *Discourse on the Origin of Inequality* (1755), he writes that humans especially have "a natural repugnance at seeing any other sensible being, and particularly any of our own species, suffer pain or death."[126] Our experience of their sensorium, their *umwelt*, even partial, yields a spontaneous moral feeling and relation. Acampora cites Nietzsche's call for us to return to the body as the site for understanding the nature of moral feeling and to reconnect to our animality to rethink the question of human nature.[127] For Nietzsche, this road needed to be traveled to construct a new cultural ethos.

Trans-species encounters can generate bodied sympathy as well as bodied anxiety and terror. Acampora focuses on the former, but the latter experience, especially with wild animals, is just as real. The experience of "wildness" is a double-edged sword, invigorating and transforming but also with the potential to be life-threatening, a world shaped as much by predation as by coevolution. What is learned is a deeper respect for the lifeworlds of wild animals as well as their plight under the stress of human domination. Returning to Rousseau, he writes that while conflict is endemic to life, the basic emotions of most animals are benign, as they seek their own good in a largely nonaggressive manner. For the most part, encounters are brief and serve no vindictive ends. Thus, "it does not appear that any animal naturally makes war on man, except in case of self-defense or excessive hunger."[128]

Willett's ideas of "interspecies ethics" and "trans-species communitarianism" flow from the conviction that animals are highly communicative and rich in moral codes, cultural traditions, and modes of agency and resistance. She argues rather convincingly that animals have long been speaking to us on many different levels. The problem is that we humans have not been listening. We are not very good on picking up "animal social cues," because we are attuned to a very narrow band of frequencies. We assume that animals must tune in to us rather than us to them.[129] We also tend to have a very modern, linear, subject-centered approach to the world that we project onto animals. We miss their cleverness, their social play, sense of humor, trickster ability, and numerous resistances to our dominations.[130] What perhaps is most important is that we can learn from many animals how to build a more community-based and coevolutionary world. Unfortunately, we are very poor trans-species interlocutors.

Willett distinguishes her approach from liberal animal welfarism, animal rights, and postmodern "response ethics." They rely too much on cognitive, linguistic, and/or legal-personhood approaches; underestimate the agency of animals; and too often portray them as vulnerable victims.[131] In keeping with *umwelt* phenomenology, Willett asserts that many animals display a "subject-less sociality" that is a form of purposive agency "worthy of ethical consideration not just with regard to their appetites but also with regard to biosocial drives, such as touching or licking in the case of a number of species, significant for meaningful living."[132] Sentient signals of connectivity from micro-organisms to higher-cognitive-functioning mammals are transmitted via wave and nodal physicality, "biosocial *eros*," and "affect attunement."[133] Biosocial *eros* refers to "a desire larger than the self," often nonsubjective and/or nonverbal, that connects living things to biosocial fields and networks.[134] Affects are not simply feelings or emotions but rather waves or "clouds" of sensory signals "that sweep across a biosocial field" and should not be understood as "properties or states interior to bound subjects or nonporous bodies."[135]

In *The Lives of Animals*, Coetzee articulates his animal philosophy and morality through the main character of Elizabeth Costello. For Coetzee, reason in the form of modern science and philosophical ethics comes up short in making sense of animals. Reason, concludes Costello, "is neither the being of the universe nor the being of God. On the contrary, reason looks to me suspiciously like the being of human thought; worse than that, like the being of one tendency in human thought."[136] She casts her lot with the poets and a form of shamanistic primitivism that only poetry can fully capture. If we want to better understand the embodied consciousness of animals, we need to seek out those "poets who celebrate the primitive and repudiate the Western bias toward abstract thought."[137] Coetzee acknowledges the power of the *umwelt* in his reference to certain poets' ability to effectively communicate interspecies relations. He cites Ted Hughes and his poem "The Jaguar" as evidence of animal being-in-the-world. Hughes is able to "body forth the jaguar," and thus his rendering is posthumanist, while Rainer Maria Rilke's "The Panther" is humanist.[138] The model is "a primitive experience (being face to face with an animal), a primitivist poem, and a primitivist theory of poetry to justify it."[139] He also mentions the poet Gary Snyder, whose life and work in my view exemplify a posthumanist, lifeworld-based ethics.[140]

Today's hypermodern humancentric lifeworld is highly rationalized, technologically framed, institutionally bounded and contained, segmented and hierarchical, encapsulated in artificial physical spaces, digitally connected yet monadic and isolating, quantifiable, and anthropocentric. By contrast, the posthumanist lifeworld is more biocentric, decentralized and spatial, layered with nonhierarchical biosocial networks, chaotically complex, bodied and fleshy, more invisible to the human senses than visible, and alien to most modern humans. It is in many respects a wild microecosystem filled with diverse organisms, events, languages, galleries, levels, and energies not on our radar screen. Mammalian interaction, the focus of most animal studies, is a small band of the posthumanist lifeworld.

To fully access the posthumanist lifeworld, we need what Snyder refers to as "depth ecology." It "is not just diurnal and a property of large interesting vertebrates[;] it is also nocturnal, anaerobic, cannibalistic, microscopic, digestive, fermentative: cooking away in the warm dark."[141] It "is well maintained at a four mile ocean depth, is waiting and sustained on a frozen rock wall, and clinging and nourished in hundred-degree desert temperatures."[142] Animals have their own narratives and literatures. In the deer lifeworld, it "is a track of scents that is passed on from deer to deer, with an art of interpretation which is instinctive. A literature of blood stains, a bit of piss, a whiff of estrus, a hit of rut, a scrape on a sapling, and long gone."[143] Each species as well as individual organisms have their own *umwelt* narratives. The posthumanist lifeworld is a vast labyrinth that we have only begun to explore.

## Posthumanism Is an Animal Ethic

My approach to animal ethics rests on the foundations of coevolutionary, biocentric, phenomenological, and postanthropocentric thought. As a more determinate, prescriptive ethic, I advocate "posthumanist communitarianism" and "*humanimal* coevolutionary communitarianism." It builds on yet differs from what I regard as the most influential positions currently in animal ethics: (1) universal rights, vegan abolitionism best represented in the philosophies of Gary Francione and Gary Steiner; (2) the utilitarian animal welfarism of Peter Singer; (3) Kathy Rudy's ethic of care and affective-connection narrative of "loving animals"; and (4) the postmodern posthumanism of Cary Wolfe and Matthew Calarco. The main split between welfare and rights advocates can be traced to Singer and Francione, with Rudy and Steiner representing the most recent elaborations of these two positions. Singer and Rudy are part of the new wave of animal welfarism, yet their approaches diverge in their respective commitments to utilitarianism and feminist care ethics. Posthumanism combines a lifeworld-based ethics of difference and a postmodern critique of modern liberal humanism. In addition to Wolfe and Calarco, I would include

Coetzee, Donna Haraway, Cora Diamond, Acampora, and Willett within the category of posthumanists.

As a philosophical ethic, the intellectual high ground is currently occupied by the animal philosophies of Steiner and Wolfe. Both articulate postanthropocentric positions. However, Steiner's ethic is neohumanist, while Wolfe's is posthumanist. I am closer to Wolfe in that my postanthropocentric standpoint is posthumanist, not neohumanist. Yet at the same time, my posthumanist postanthropocentrism is not based on a reading of Derrida on the animal question; rather, it is built on coevolutionary, biocentric, and phenomenological thought. Posthumanism's strength is how it addresses the ontological and epistemological terms of the contemporary animal debate. The critique of the Anthropocene and negotiation of a postanthropocentric worldview is as ontological (how we define existence and being for human and nonhuman animals), phenomenological (how we experience our fellow animals), and epistemological (how we know our fellow animals) as it is moral (how we should treat our fellow animals) and political (how we act toward our fellow animals).

As a practical ethic and a viable political strategy, at least in the short term, what Francione and other universal animal rights advocates have critically labeled "the new animal welfarism" is the predominant mode of action in the animal advocacy movement. It goes beyond the old standards of "humane treatment," "unnecessary suffering," and liberal interest-group politics yet stops short of universal rights and universal veganism, does not advocate the complete elimination of the property status of animals, and seeks a compromise between the improved regulation of animal use and its complete and immediate abolition.

My idea of posthumanist communitarianism, while influenced in different ways by all of these different perspectives, does not easily fit the standard welfare versus rights frame that has defined much of animal ethics and politics. I agree with animal rights theorists and advocates that liberal welfarist regulatory reforms are insufficient and do not address the heart of the matter. Yet I am an incremental rather than a radical abolitionist. Furthermore, I do not approach the plight of animals in the Anthropocene from an animal rights framework. And while I endorse veganism, I do not endorse it as a universal categorical moral imperative. One is not a hypocrite or less concerned about animals if one is not a vegan. My approach emphasizes human–nonhuman animal (*humanimal*) community building. I also place the importance of contact zone animals on equal footing with that of wild and domestic animals.

As mentioned, I rely on the yardsticks of Aristotelian *phronesis* and my idea of a three-legged ethical stool. *Phronesis* is a practical value rationality that applies principles and deliberative reasoning to context-dependent action-oriented situations. Practical wisdom concerns itself with particulars as well as universals. However, knowledge of particulars can be attained only through experience, not through theoretical wisdom. The ethical stool conceives of ethics in terms of three essential inputs: (1) objectivity, (2) subjectivity, and (3) intersubjectivity. Objectivity is the voice of modern scientific and philosophical reasoning. Subjectivity is the product of the individual and social lifeworld, the voice of the body, self, personal experience, and emotional connection. Intersubjectivity is the world of the self-among-others and the encounter with Otherness. All three legs of the stool inform, check, and balance each other. The result is the triangulation of (1) determinate ethical principles; (2) lifeworld context, affect, and relations; and (3) *phronesis*, which includes consideration of causality and consequences.

As a philosophical utilitarian, Singer adheres to the general belief that the rightness or wrongness of an action (or inaction) should be judged on its contribution to the overall happiness of all sentient creatures affected by that action. While some question his utilitarian doctrine, others reject the view that the treatment rather than the use of animals is the main problem. Singer is a preference utilitarian, not a strict Benthamite hedonist. Interest-based utility calculations should be founded in reason, not desire. However, ethics should not be a deontological air-tight system of rules and categorical universals, which often result in unintended bad outcomes. At the same time, we should adopt an impartial, objective point of view, which is the defining feature of modern ethics. To be ethical is to transcend not only our personal self-interested viewpoint but also that of our society and species.[144]

Singer believes that "all animals are equal" in that the equal consideration of their interests should guide ethical action.[145] However, this belief does not mean radical equivalence. All animals do not have the same interests due to the fact that they have different capacities. Two key capacities qualify animals for equal consideration—suffering and personhood. Singer makes a moral distinction between sentient creatures and self-conscious sentient beings who possess self-awareness, preferential interests, and future-oriented intentional agency. Different species have different capacities for flourishing. Comparing the capacities of diverse species and individual animals is not an exact science, yet "it would not be speciesist to hold that the life of a self-aware being, capable of abstract thought, of planning for the future, of complex acts of communication and so on, is more valuable than the life of a being without these capacities."[146] Human life in general is more valuable than other animal life.

This does not mean in all cases, regardless of circumstances, that individual humans are, by virtue of their species-nature, inherently more valuable than other animals. Singer "rejects the doctrine that killing a member of our species is always more significant than killing a member of another species."[147] Yet while antispeciesist, Singer remains anthropocentric in his adoption of human capacities as the yardstick of species evaluation.

Singer places animals in three moral-practical categories: (1) "fully a person," (2) "near-person," and (3) "non-person." Most animals are conscious but not persons. Without self-consciousness, an animal is not autonomous and therefore does not automatically have a right to life. It is clear to Singer that great apes are persons, which justifies his coauthorship of "A Declaration on Great Apes" and his cofounding of the Great Ape Project, which calls on us to legally recognize their fundamental rights to life, liberty, and freedom from confinement and torture. Other animals, such as dolphins, whales, elephants, scrub jays, and parrots, qualify as persons, and those who currently qualify as near-persons, such as dogs, cats, cows, pigs, horses, and maybe chickens, might qualify as persons in the future, pending more research. Fish are non-persons. Singer makes clear that he is open to reclassification based on future research findings.[148]

From here, Singer arrives at his famous ethic regarding the killing and eating of animals. If an animal that qualifies as a near- or a non-person is treated to a good and dignified life devoid of suffering, is killed in a "painless unanticipated" manner, and is replaced with an animal of its species that is assured of a similar life, then killing and eating this animal qualify as morally defensible actions. With no expectation or interest in a future, since a non-self-conscious animal lives in the present, no serious harm is done.[149] If an animal does have the capacity for a short-term future orientation, then the harm would be serious but not absolutely wrong. If animal capacities and interests are not similar, then equal consideration does not translate into similar treatment. The practical policy implication of Singer's animal ethic is the abolition of industrial factory farming and nearly all animal experimentation.[150]

Francione has consistently held the position that all animal use and killing by humans is exploitative, is immoral, and should be abolished. Sentience alone, regardless of cognitive capacity, should be the baseline of animal ethics. Sentience is defined as the ability for responsive behavior indicating consciousness, the capacity for experiential well-being, and the desire and therefore interest in continuing to live. All animals in this regard are equally sentient,[151] and they therefore have the right to live rather than to be harmed or used directly or indirectly by humans, to exist on their own terms, and to live without fear of death at the hands of humans. All sentient life has inherent worth;

should be legally regarded as persons, not property; and should live free of human sovereign dominion. This belief entails a threefold ethical and legal-political position—universal veganism, legal and institutional abolition of all animal use and animal-use enterprises, and total liberation from humans. Anything less is animal exploitation and welfarism.[152]

Francione rejects not only the new welfarism of Singer but also the animal rights approaches of Tom Regan and Steven Wise, which, like Singer's approach, include cognitive preference and "practical autonomy" qualifiers beyond sentience in determining the moral status of animals.[153] The central issue is not whether some animals should be treated as persons due to the fact that they have "similar minds" as humans but that all animals as sentient beings should be treated as persons. As long as animals are legally property, any and all attempts to afford them equal or fair consideration and treat them better amount to very little. For while in some rare instances animal interests may achieve parity or even be weighed greater than human rights or interests, the human-propertied interest will always trump these claims. Francione's universal sentience/rights/vegan/abolitionism translates into a negative-rights doctrine that demands that we not only liberate all animals from human use but also eliminate most human relations with animals, since they are inherently domineering and exploitative. This elimination includes the abolition of all domestication processes and the eventual extinction of all domestic-animal biological lines.

Steiner shares Francione's sentience-only baseline of ethical consideration as well as his universal immunity-rights stance and commitment to veganism. Yet a more holistic, nonanthropocentric conception of justice is required to balance and strengthen what is largely a liberal individualist theory of animal rights. The approach should be rights and justice as mutually reinforcing ideas. Thus, he introduces the ideas of "sentient kinship," "non-anthropocentric cosmopolitanism," and "cosmo-politics."[154] Steiner resurrects the ancient Stoic ideal of belonging (*oikeiosis*) and reformulates it into one of cosmopolitan kinship applicable to all sentient life. Our place in this world should be as citizens of a cosmopolis of sentient beings. Hellenic Stoicism envisions a world community of *zoa politika* capable of participating in *logos* (rational thought and discourse). For the Stoics, humans live their lives at three different yet interconnected levels of being—individuals who satisfy their basic biological needs, members of a familial community of close relations, and citizens of a community of rational souls. Steiner replaces *logos* with sentience and the moral interconnectedness and equality of all sentient beings.[155] This cosmopolis further requires taking a moral vow of universal veganism—thou shall not harm, kill, or eat your fellow cosmopolitan sentient citizens.

Like ancient Stoics, Steiner advocates rational self-control, the overcoming of emotion and sentimentalism, and an ascetic regime—absolute voluntary abstinence from the worldly pleasures of animal flesh and use. Classical Stoicism is not simply a set of ethical beliefs but a way of life dedicated to the pursuit of reason, self-discipline, freedom from passion, and *apatheia*—the capacity for objective, nonemotional, clear judgment. One lives one's life according to the laws of the cosmos and as a citizen of the world. The universe is a material substance permeated by reason and, therefore, a rational order and cosmic whole governed by cosmic justice. In keeping with the spirit of Stoic philosophy, Steiner's animal philosophy consists of four levels arranged in concentric circles: (1) sentient organisms as individuals with rights, (2) modern humanism shed of its anthropocentric devaluation of animals, (3) sentient kinship as the basis of a cosmopolitan moral community, and (4) cosmic holism.

Steiner attempts to "square the circle" by synthesizing modern liberalism with the substantive good of sentient cosmopolitanism. His goal is similar to Hegel's concept of ethical community, or *Sittlichkeit*, in which liberalism's limited view of freedom as individual autonomy (negative liberty) is situated within a larger vision of substantive freedom.[156] The only way to credibly pull this effort off is dialectically, by acknowledging the tensional dynamic between oppositional ideas or realities that cannot be fully reconciled but can be negotiated. Justice takes on a Hegelian-like role in balancing animal rights with a larger idea of what constitutes an ethical community. Hegel, like Rousseau, is postliberal in his belief that the substantive good (positive liberty and the general will) takes precedence over individual negative liberties. If the ethical community is all sentient life, then those who morally and politically legislate on its behalf (i.e., humans) face the challenge of balancing rights with the greater good writ large as the rights of all animals coexisting within a sentient cosmopolis.

Yet what exactly is this cosmic order and principle of cosmic justice that provides the ultimate foundation and justification for Steiner's postanthropocentric, vegan cosmopolitanism? And how does the rational order of the cosmos yield a universally valid ethic of the inherent value of sentient life and moral veganism? Steiner draws on the work of German idealist philosophers, including Hegel, Heidegger (the Heidegger of cosmic holism not contingent throwness), Karl Löwith, and Hans Jonas.[157] Cosmic holism is a general worldview that believes the universe is not a cosmic accident but an ordered whole and that the place of humans in the larger scheme of things is one of being "at home." This belief coincides with the Stoic rational faith in cosmic order, holism, and justice as an objective reality and in Albert Einstein's belief that God does not play dice with the universe.

Steiner's sentient cosmopolitanism draws its legitimacy more as an extension of modern humanism than from cosmic holism and justice. The rationality of the cosmos is a neohumanist projection, not a posthumanist cosmology. Humans are obligated to protect sentient life as an extension of modern humanism and liberal rights, not in the name of a cosmos that somehow speaks to humans and reveals its order and justice. While the relevant ethical community may exist in the minds of some as a sentient cosmopolitan ideal, as a social and political reality, Hegel is correct when he defines ethical life as a substantive ethos that evolves from the sociohistorical circumstances of actual, situated communities that occupy a distinct spatial and temporal place. He is wrong in attempting to rationalize and impose a regulative ideal on these diverse communities in the form of Absolute Idealism, a teleological philosophy of history, and the modern sovereign bureaucratic nation-state. I regard evolution and coevolution theory, science, and ethics as much stronger and more defensible grounds for animal ethics than neohumanist rights and neo-Stoic cosmic holism. The question is not what should be the universal regulative principle of cosmopolitan justice for animals but what justice means for animals in the twenty-first-century Anthropocene.

A more fully developed philosophical rationalist account of cosmic holism can be found in Nagel's *Mind and Cosmos* (2012). Here, he questions the ability of scientific materialism ("physico-chemical" and "psychophysical reductionism") and evolutionary naturalism (the "neo-Darwinian conception of nature") to provide a reasonable explanation of "the cosmic order."[158] Physicalism and evolution theory fail his test of "intelligibility," defined in terms of the proposition that the universe must be "rationally governed," which requires the existence of universal qualitative (teleological) and quantitative (physical and mathematical) laws.[159] In addition to known physical laws, other rational laws must be "irreducible principles governing temporally extended development."[160] Furthermore, the existence of mind (consciousness, reason, intentional agency, and ethics) is a fundamental feature of reality, teleologically embedded from the very beginning of the cosmos and not a byproduct or adaptation of physical and biological evolution.

Nagel is an objective idealist in his belief that the cosmos contains an intelligible order that cannot be explained by science and nonintentional, causal explanations alone.[161] He is also anthropocentric and neo-Hegelian in his belief that the cosmos is structured and guided by an inherent teleology of mind and, further, that human reason, which is "an instrument of transcendence that can grasp objective reality and objective value," is evidence of and capable of validating the existence of this rational order.[162] The unique faculty of human objective reason has the capacity to generate demonstrable factual (science), theoretical (logic), and practical (ethics) truths.[163] Nagel is a moral realist who believes that moral facts exist as objectively verifiable truths, just as natural and mathematical truths do. Valid ethical statements represent objective facts and thus express propositions of rightness and wrongness capable of being logically evaluated as true or false. Their validity is arrived at with reference to the objective facts of the world and rules of logic.[164]

The philosophical discourse of cosmic order is rationalist and idealist in the tradition of Plato, Stoicism, and German Idealism. For me, evolution and coevolution theory do a better job of answering many of the big questions. Evolution is not in the business of explaining the cosmos, because it is a theory of how life evolved on this planet. It is a theory of Earth's evolution, not that of the cosmos. It is also an explanation not of how life began on Earth but of how it evolved. For me, this theory is sufficient. I do not need to know the order of the cosmos to fully function as a sentient, self-conscious Earthling. In adopting an evolutionary worldview, one can also answer questions that Nagel finds beyond the reach of materialist thought—the genesis of life; the complexity and diversity of sentient life that exists today; the existence of subjective, reflexive consciousness; and ethics. The RNA world hypothesis, emergentism, and coevolution theory do a good job of explaining these questions. As for our large, complex brain, which we pride ourselves on—it is a mixed blessing. By overdeveloping our mental powers to adapt, we have in the course of our evolution become neurotic overachievers.

Despite their differences, Singer, Francione, and Steiner all pursue a modern, universalistic, and egalitarian ethical approach, one that is identity- and capacity-based and in accordance with their utilitarian, universal sentient rights and nonanthropocentric cosmopolitan doctrines. The case for extending ethics to most or all animals should be based on objective reason, logical propositions, and rational argumentation. The objectivist leg of the ethical stool far outweighs the subjective and intersubjective legs. Reason is the site of not only the formulation of ethical principles but also individual and collective transformation as well as institutional change. Calarco refers to this as "the problem of logocentrism," which downplays the role of the lifeworld, affect, context, and relational modes of being in ethical thinking and conduct. To assume, as many intellectuals do, "that philosophical argumentation plays the only or even a primary role here is a contentious claim."[165]

The predominant way of thinking in the rights and welfarist traditions is neoanthropocentric. One makes the case for how similar humans and animals are in their capacities than previously believed. Human nature and animal natures are integrated into a biological and ethical continuum. Ani-

mal ethics is measured using this yardstick. Humanism is extended to animals with a list of varied qualifications. Ethics conceived in this way revolves
around revising the definition of "personhood" to defend one of two stand-
points. One holds to human exceptionalism but allows for a more progressive
ethical outlook as to what constitutes moral considerability and significance.
Animals largely remain moral patients, but their status is broadened, extended, and tied to stronger legal and political protections. The other position
seeks a more universal extension of neohumanism to most or all animals
conceived as sentient persons and linked to a stronger model of human rights-
based protection. Both standard and radicalized liberal positions pursue the
greater assimilation of animals within the moral and legal framework of
modern personhood.

Calarco, Wolfe, and Rudy pursue a more lifeworld-based, contextual,
relational, and affective animal ethic in accordance with the ideas and values
of the postmodern ethics of difference and otherness (Calarco and Wolfe)
and sentiment, emotion, and narrative connection (Rudy). Calarco and
Wolfe give greater weight to the intersubjective (more precisely, postsubjective
otherness) leg of the ethical stool and resist being placed in the rights and
welfarist streams. Rudy's care ethic is more subjectivist, placing more weight
on the concrete practices and narratives of "loving animals."

Posthumanism, influenced by the ethics of Heidegger, Emmanuel Levinas, and Derrida, questions several presuppositions of the modernist position:
(1) the idea of human nature based on a subject-centered, identity metaphysics;
(2) the curse of "logocentrism," with its logic of dualistic thinking, binary
distinctions, and arbitrary and rigid inclusions, exclusions, and hierarchies; (3)
the extension of this model in conceptualizing animals; (4) the word "animal,"
which homogenizes the diversity and singularity of life into a false, generalized
Other; and (5) ethics defined in terms of objective rationality and universal
moral laws. The key event in the inauguration of posthumanism can be traced
to Derrida's 1997 conference address, which was later published as *The Animal
that Therefore I Am* and followed by several lectures, essays, and interviews,
including "Eating Well," "Force of Law: The 'Mystical Foundations of Authority,'" "Before the Law," *Rogues*, and *The Beast and the Sovereign*. Derrida locates
ethics in the finitude and bodily vulnerability we share with animals; calls on
us to eliminate the word "animal" and replace it with *animot* to signify the
unique singularity of nonhuman life; problematizes the relation between judgment, morality, justice, and law; and questions the value of the animal rights
approach, tied as it is to modern juridical sovereignty.[166]

Wolfe urges us "to rethink our taken-for-granted modes of human experience, including the normal perceptual modes and affective states of *Homo*

*sapiens* itself, by recontextualizing them in terms of the entire sensorium of other living things and their own autopoietic ways of 'bringing forth a world.'"[167] We have created a panoply of cultural prostheses that have sheltered us from the "flesh and finitude" of life and death,[168] yet we have reached a point in human-animal relations where we can no longer work out our responses to reality "from a safe ontological distance."[169] Consistent with the ethics of Levinas, Derrida, and Zygmunt Bauman, posthumanism advocates understanding animals in terms of how they have historically been framed as a generalized alien Other. The antidote to this long-standing cultural and institutional frame is an ethics of Otherness that flows from our experiential encounters with animals in their contextual singularity and resists rigid categoricals.

Calarco calls on us to adopt an "agnostic animal ethics."[170] He questions the logic as well as the historical record of moral inclusion and exclusion with respect to humans and animals. Why not let the particular context determine the proper ethical response rather than a line drawn by arbitrary power? While the machinery of institutional reality requires demarcations, boundaries, and standard operating procedures, ethical experience does not work this way. Why not adopt a "generous agnosticism"? The great truth here is that institutional reality resists otherness, singularity, contingency, and agnosticism since it undermines efficiency. Most bureaucrats exhibit the exact opposite values and dispositions. The antidote to this logic lies in Foucaultian strategies and tactics of resistance politics.[171]

Calarco invokes Levinas's ethical model of the face-to-face encounter developed in response to the Holocaust.[172] The direct, unanticipated event of a stranger in need entering our lifeworld disrupts our ego boundaries and identity. The encounter reveals our mutual vulnerabilities and compels us to make the fate of the Other our priority. Levinas does not extend this ethic to human-animal encounters, believing that animals have no "face" (i.e., subjectivity). Calarco disagrees, and so do I. We certainly have face-to-face intersubjective encounters with animals that alter our lifeworld. Any sentient being, given the context, has the potential to illuminate the finitude of life and call for our ethical response. Trans-species encounters happen all the time. *Umwelt* phenomenology validates this belief. Principles and practices emerge from the lived nature of encounters that force ethical decisions on us.

Steiner rejects posthumanist ethics because, in his reasoning, postmodernism is a failed philosophy. From Nietzsche to Derrida, we are faced with a worldview in which meaning and identity are viewed as social constructs resting on ever-shifting contexts of radical contingency. As for moral principles, they are essentially a form of domineering instrumental rationality that do more harm than good by binding us to unreasonable, unconditional categoricals. For Steiner, posthumanism throws out the baby (the progress made by modern liberal humanism) with the bathwater (Western metaphysics). More than this, we end up with an animal ethic that is weaker than the welfarist position. We are implored to bear witness to the plight of animals and to offer care and assistance, but we are given no clear principles of action, nor do we make any great sacrifices. Derrida is the major target of Steiner's critique. He zeroes in on four words that reveal the inner truth of postmodern ethics—"Later here signifies never."[173] This comment is in reference to Derrida's famous idea of *différance*, which means to differ and defer. For Steiner, this idea translates into an ethics of indecision. In rendering our relationship to reality one of radical contingency, contextual relativism, and absolute singularity, we are left with an essentially reactive, *ad hoc*, situational ethics.

I subscribe to a less stark account of postmodernism. For Steiner, there is no such thing as a moderate form of postmodernism. Yet, as I argue in *Negotiating Postmodernism*, there are two streams of postmodern thought—one very French and radical (the first wave) and one more moderate and reconstructive (the second wave)—that I call "critical postmodernism."[174] I am also more influenced by Foucault than Derrida. Foucault never directly examines animal issues in his historical-philosophical studies, which focus primarily on exposing in great detail the repressive consequences of modern liberal humanism. Yet his analytics of biopower and biopolitics, as Giorgio Agamben, Nicole Shukin, Acampora, Dinesh Joseph Wadiwel, and Wolfe have demonstrated, can be effectively applied to the condition of animals under sovereign human control in a variety of settings, from farms to slaughterhouses to zoos to shelters to laboratories.[175]

For me, the lesson of Derrida as well as of Aristotle, Theodor Adorno, Hannah Arendt, and Jean-François Lyotard is that judgment is the key to ethics and politics. It involves negotiating the universal and particular, identity and difference. To be modern is to give more weight to the universal and identity. To be postmodern is to give more weight to singularity and difference. For modernists, reason imposes order on the messiness and complexity of worldly experience to produce clarity of purpose, enlightenment, and emancipation. For postmodernists, the lifeworld and exposure to Otherness illuminate existential finitude and contingency. Too much rational mastery occludes difference. Too much difference cripples ethical and political agency. How far, then, is one willing to go? How far is too far? This dilemma is where judgment comes in. It is therefore important that we understand what is involved in serious decision making in all of its complexity and indispensability.

In *Before the Law* (2013), Wolfe makes the case that the best approach to advancing a viable animal ethic is neither rights-based nor welfarist but rather by adopting "the register of biopolitics."[176] Two central ideas influence Wolfe's thinking on how and why nonhuman animals are rendered morally and legally objects and subjects of moral consideration, justice, and legal standing—"the biopolitical frame" and "before the law." The first phrase is in direct reference to Heidegger and Foucault, and the second is to Derrida. Together, they provide an analytic-interpretive framework for understanding the process by which any group of living beings, human and animal, is categorized as "human," "human-like," and "animal" ontolinguistically (culturally) and legally and arranged by apparatuses of biopolitical power (what Foucault calls *dispositifs*) into entities deserving and nondeserving of sovereign protection. Biopolitics in the Foucaultian sense is a deployment of power from the top down (from the sovereign state apparatus) and from the bottom up (through disciplinary matrices of bodily control) that establishes population norms and policies that prepare life itself to stand before the law.[177]

The result is an essentially arbitrary (in the sense of a judge or arbiter with sovereign authority) and biopolitical set of categories, identities, entitlements, and protections that govern human and nonhuman animals—person, citizen, client, consumer, refugee, immigrant, pet, wild, livestock, property, meat, test subject, near-person, nonperson, endangered species. The paradox we face is that we must draw lines to function as moral and political beings, yet the lines we draw are arbitrary. The legitimation of these lines, categories, laws, and rights carries with it a cost equal to and often greater than the benefit. Every right generates a wrong every new inclusion requires an exclusion. Wolfe writes:

> We *must* choose, and by definition we *cannot* choose everyone and everything at once. But this is precisely what ensures that, *in the future, we will have been wrong.* Our "determinate" act of justice now will have been shown to be too determinate, revealed to have left someone or something out. Indeed, this is precisely what has unfolded over the past few decades regarding our rapidly changing understanding of nonhuman animals and how we relate to them. *All* of them? How many? Who knows?[178]

Francione's and Steiner's response to Wolfe would be that the decisive ethical universalism of animal rights, sentient cosmopolitanism, and veganism effectively answers these questions. Yet Wolfe would counter that all ethics require translation into a biopolitics of determinate, not universal, justice. Francione's and Steiner's ethics must stand before the institutional logics of late-modern social systems. Incorporating the systems theory of Niklas Luhmann and Esposito's "paradigm of immunization," Wolfe reminds us that contemporary social and political life is contained within functionally differentiated and bounded subsystems that produce different norms, identities, actors, criteria of rationality, and steering imperatives. The legal system's principal goal is to deploy and police the border between what is legal and illegal and therefore "may be seen as serving an 'immunitary' function for society."[179] Right/wrong and legal/illegal inhabit different domains. This is why, concludes Wolfe, Derrida makes an important distinction between "the exercise of justice" as a sovereign mechanism of inclusion/exclusion and "the event of justice" as the expression of singularity.[180] Law is about immunity protection from others via selective categorization. Luhmann and Derrida converge in what is essentially a reformulation of the legal positivist distinction between morality and law as separate spheres with different norms.

Wolfe's Derridean-inspired posthumanism reminds us that the "animal question" is as much about how nonhuman animals call into question human nature and our own subjectivity as it is about the moral status and plight of animals today. Posthumanism questions anthropocentric worldliness, the belief we are the center of the experiential world. It also reminds us that while we must make decisions regarding the lives of sentient beings, and while we must make and apply rules and laws, they will never be fully just. Justice cannot be legitimately fixed, yet that is precisely what the law and its enforcers do. And within every decision and action lies undecidability, the reality that all decisions and actions include unresolved issues and ambiguities. Undecidability is not the same as indecision. The practice of drawing lines should be a central issue of ethical and political reflection and action.

Utilitarian ethics rejects the inherent value of all sentient life; claims of biocentric, *umwelt* phenomenology; universal animal rights; and posthumanist coevolutionary ethics as well as the "unique singularity of the Other" criterion of postmodern difference ethics. Singer measures inherent value as a function of cognitive ability, which is restricted to those species that are humanlike in their capacity for self-consciousness and intentional, future-oriented interests. Yet this line, drawn as justification for killing animals for food in a "painless unanticipated" manner, is as arbitrary as any other benchmark of animal ethics. All ethics cannot escape a biopolitics that comes before and after the ethical principle or judgment. We all draw lines that we cannot fully justify.

Coming to a determination, justifying our actions, and inevitably negating our thoughts and actions are endemic to the human condition, a dialectic we cannot escape or resolve. The presumed fact that most animals live in an "eternal present" and therefore have no self-conscious concern regarding their death is an anthropocentric conceit. And what adds insult to injury is the accompanying social-utility replacement argument to ensure that the ledger is balanced with regard to overall population happiness. A more "reasonable" justification would be that evolutionary biology, cultural evolution, institutional enablement and constraint, lifeworld experience, and communitarian ethos as well as the "higher voice" of universal reason all play their parts in weighing the who, why, how, and when of killing and eating others. The problem is not the drawing and justifying of lines, which is the nature of determinate judgment, but the failure to fully recognize the competing and countervailing push-and-pull of reason, lifeworld, and *phronesis* in making this determination.

There is another equally significant stream of animal studies and ethics distinct from the approaches of animal rights, welfarism, utilitarianism, and posthumanism—feminist animal care ethics. Pioneered by Carol Adams and Josephine Donovan, and more recently by Lori Gruen and Kari Weil, it engages the animal question theoretically and practically from the perspectives of care ethics, feminist-vegetarian critical theory, ecofeminism, and postmodern feminism.[181] Feminist animal care studies and ethics focus their critical lens on the historical connections between women and animals as "abject objects" and "Others"; the androcentric basis of anthropocentrism; the patriarchal history, culture, and institutions of animal agriculture and the modern food industry; and the limitations of modern rational universalistic ethics. Feminist animal care ethics places center stage the importance of the bodied, social, and emotional relationships we have with animals, understands that these relations are lifeworld-based and contextual, and recognizes that this relational social ontology should be the cornerstone of animal ethics and politics. Emotional connection and reasoning are framed within the context of lifeworld experience, relations, and narrative streams. Critical empathy, trust, friendship, love, and community are central values.

Rudy's ethic of "loving animals" is a variant of feminist animal care ethics, relying heavily on the centrality of affective connection and narrative. Rudy relies very little on feminist theory, however; her animal ethic is a function of the thick descriptions embedded in her very personal/political stories of *hum-animal* relations. The approach is of an animal advocate whose ethical baseline is lifeworld experience, emotional connection, the physicality and bodied nature of interspecies love, and narrative. Rudy believes that the stories we tell about our love of animals go "far beyond principles in detailing the nature of our relationships with [them]" and in doing so will "widen the animal advocacy movement" and "help it become more widely accessible and accepted."[182] The basis of animal ethics should be our personal love for specific animals and their love for us, which opens the door to an enlarged sense of empathy. Rudy rejects the prevailing trend that relegates to the periphery or outright exiles the roles of emotion and affective connection in animal ethics. To the contrary, she leads with emotion and personal narratives. Our subjective and intersubjective lifeworld involvement with the animals we love and our stories about them are the basis of her ethical standpoint.

Rudy contends that animal rights, Singer's utilitarianism, liberal animal welfarism, and posthumanism all share a common deficiency—"they take too much of reality for granted."[183] Animal rights vegans frame the debate in terms of stark either/or dualisms, rely on categorical imperatives that have all the virtues as well as vices of Kantian ethics, and have crafted a politically counterproductive rhetoric of absolute animal freedom.[184] Animal welfarists are not sufficiently committed to systemic and structural changes.[185] As for posthumanists, they provide an invaluable service in deconstructing Western anthropocentrism, and their call for a culture shift and new language of human-animal relations is on target. Identities such as humanity, animal, or species are "not something we are, but something we perform." Thus our very relationships with animals and humans can "be performed differently."[186] Yet posthumanists complicate reality so much that it often cripples them from taking any clear stands on animal issues. They tend to be long on deconstruction and short on reconstructive political agency.

Rudy's ethic is contextual and relational, yet not like Palmer's. Affective connection is her standard of valuation, not causality and effect. Affect, not cause and effect, is the key to animal ethics. Yet, like Palmer, she identifies the different worlds of human-animal relations—the world of dogs, cats, and animal shelters; animal agriculture and diet ethics; captive wild animals in zoos, in sanctuaries, and under private ownership; and animals used in research experimentation and testing. Noticeably missing in her personal travel log and journey into the real world of pets, farm animals, diet politics, zoos, and laboratories is the often forgotten and neglected world of contact zone animals.

Rudy admits that she is a dog lover, an advocate of adopting shelter animals and the much-needed organizational and cultural transformation of public animal shelters as well as private rescues. She is equally a strong advocate of humans' relating to animals as companions and guardians and not as pet owners.[187] Around 7.6 million animals enter shelters in America every year, with around 7.3 million of them dogs and cats. Of this number, more than 3 million are euthanized annually, more cats than dogs. I agree with her assessment of the world of dogs and cats; too many pet owners are irresponsible and relate to animals as toys, impulse purchases, and disposable commodities. Animal companions require time, training, and genuine emotional involvement. They are members of our pack, and they know it. Unfortunately, too many humans do not know or care to know this fact. There are few dumb animals, but many dumb owners. As for animal breeders and consumers, too many are in it for status, money, trendiness, vanity, and varied fetishisms, and they often indulge in excessive eugenic manipulation.

Rudy is strongly opposed to the agricultural-industrial complex. She further fully realizes that individual lifestyle change is not enough, because the problem is systemic. It is also complicated, since we are all caught up in big industrial agriculture and cannot live without it at some level—including strict vegans. Rudy is an advocate of local, organic small farms; cooperatives; farmers markets; and genuinely humane, farm-certified, pasture-raised (not phony free-range) animals and animal products. One can be an ethical animal lover and be a plant-strong/low-meat omnivore.[188] Critics point out that local, small, organic, animal-friendly farms cannot produce enough food for the world and that eating ethically is time-consuming and expensive, a liberal upper-middle-class luxury. Yet one can eat healthier and cheaper on a low-meat or vegetarian diet. It does take time, but given the amount of time we spend in front of TV and computer screens and on social media, making time is not that difficult. What we eat does matter for animals, the environment, and our health, and it points directly to the issues of human population control, diet change, less meat consumption, less corporate capitalism in our lives, and a more communitarian way of life.

Humans were originally vegetarians and became omnivores in the course of their evolution. Meat eating among the majority of humans is a recent phenomenon attributable to industrial modernity. There has also been a shift from eating mammals (cows and pigs) to eating birds (chicken and turkey). Beef consumption is down in America but up in newly developing countries and especially in Asia. Eating steak is a symbol of status, affluence, and success. Yet meat is not a healthy food source, the conversion of plants to animals to food is expensive and inefficient, and the claim that we need meat for protein is a myth; we get more protein from plants. Dietary traditions and habits can be changed. However, at the same time, we should not underestimate our omnivorous physiology. We have more flexibility than most animals in developing new tastes and dietary habits. After a short transition period, the body adjusts to its new regimen, and we often wonder why we ate the way we used to.

With regard to the plight of wild animals, many species are in such serious trouble that they would be better off under direct human management. Noninterference is not a realistic option. With regard to many species, we are in an "ark" phase of preservation. Yet which model is most appropriate for wild animals in decline—zoos, private exotic ownership, or sanctuaries? More precisely, what kind of zoos, private ownership, and sanctuaries? While the focus today is on "progressive zoos" that offer more "naturelike" enclosures, Rudy rightly focuses her attention on the corporate takeover and makeover of zoos. Many zoos operate on a bottom-line business model, with a shift toward the greater commercialization of animals and the acquisition of popular charismatic species to attract customers. While zoos promote conservation and education, there is much more breeding for sale; animal trading; separating of families; discarding of sick, old, unneeded, and rebellious animals; and selling of animals for canned hunts than the general public is aware of.[189]

Zoos emphasize that their animals live longer and better than in the wild, yet this claim is certainly not the case with elephants. A highly social, emotional, and matriarchal animal, elephants bond closely to other elephants and live in extended families. Close mother-daughter relationships often last for forty years. Yet in many zoos, they are confined alone or separated from their families. Many suffer from chronic foot disease, arthritis, and pressure sores from standing long hours on concrete or hard dirt surfaces. A tropical animal, they often endure freezing winters in cramped barns or stay indoors, where they are highly susceptible to respiratory infections. Lack of adequate space is a major problem, since elephants are roaming animals and require substantial territory. Many elephants rock and sway neurotically and become aggressive. Being highly social and family-oriented, they are very sensitive to emotional cues and prone to stress, and they can get depressed, stop eating, and die. Their sense of grief is real and profound.[190]

What of private exotic animal ownership? Rudy discovers that some animal owners are for-profit breeders, but most owners are in it due to their attraction toward and love of specific wild species. They are also very resistant to oversight and regulation, quick to cite their private-property rights. While Rudy is sympathetic to their situation, she calls for more oversight and regulation.[191] I agree with her preference for community-based, nonprofit, animal rescue centers and sanctuaries that take discarded, abused, and retired animals from zoos, research facilities, farms, and private owners and offer them a more decent place to live out their days.[192]

I am much more critical of private exotic animal ownership. Many owners claim to be experts on their species but in most cases are amateurs and poor judges of their animals' well-being. This ignorance is why they resist oversight, are quick to defend their private-property rights, and often live in remote areas away from authorities. The exotic animal trade is poorly regulated and a gateway into a bizarre underground of eccentrics, extremists, hoarders, criminals, ignorant hillbillies, animal enslavers, and roadside menageries. The animal trade amounts to slavery at best and an ongoing animal holocaust at its worst. In the United States, only a few states ban the ownership of exotic pets, and an equal number has no regulations at all.[193] I would ban private exotic animal ownership. If one desires to spend one's time with wild animals, then one should undergo professional training and work for a zoo or (preferably) operate, work for, or volunteer at a regulated, nonprofit animal rescue operation or sanctuary.

With regard to animals used in research experimentation, Rudy tries to navigate a "new middle ground" that animal researchers and animal rights advocates can live with. She distinguishes between different kinds of testing: (1) finding cures for life-threatening human diseases, (2) drug and consumer testing, (3) national security testing, and (4) research largely pursued by corporations and universities to advance scientific careers and increase grant revenues. She can endorse only the first type of research and calls for greater scrutiny of the Institutional Animal Care and Use Committees (IACUCs) federally mandated by a 1985 amendment to the Animal Welfare Act. She endorses "the three R's": (1) a reduction in the number of animals used, (2) the refinement of experiments to limit suffering, and (3) the replacement of animals with nonanimal models. She also raises a larger issue of how science is conducted, how scientists objectify their "subjects," and how they rationalize their relationship with lab animals in terms of scientific objectivity. Her recommendation is to turn lab animals into real subjects by giving them names, not numbers, and granting them dignity in exchange for their noble sacrifices to research and medicine. She suggests that scientists and researchers directly care for their animal subjects and establish an emotional connection with them. I doubt that Rudy's solutions will satisfy either researchers or animal advocates.[194]

Most animal testing is neither critically necessary nor well justified. While there have been some medical breakthroughs, the vast majority of research is about big science, the advancement of careers, money, and business as usual. Advocates from major governmental agencies to universities to agribusiness to drug and cosmetic companies are well organized and funded. While several hundred thousand animals from monkeys to dogs, rabbits, rats, guinea pigs, goats, sheep, birds, reptiles, and fish are used annually in research, several million (some estimate one hundred million) mice are used. Their genome is very close to humans, they are compliant test "subjects," and they are easy to "manufacture." They are also exempted from the Animal Welfare Act along with rats and birds. Entire businesses are dedicated to breeding lab mice, so much so that there is a glut in the market—a mouse surplus. Many are gassed, incinerated, or sold to zoos and pet stores as food for other animals.[195]

Steiner regards Rudy's approach as a classic example of "feed-good ethics," "moral schizophrenia," and wavering between two unacceptable polarities of "idealistic sentimentality" and "resigned pragmatism." Steiner sums up her ethic as one in which "husbanding, killing, eating, experimenting on, and perhaps even wearing animals is completely permissible, provided that we 'love' them."[196] Rudy is an anthropocentric animal welfarist who rejects animal rights abolitionism and veganism in favor of the principle of mutual human-animal sacrifice and accommodation—yet animals do most of the sacrificing. In the end, Rudy gives more weight to emotion than to reason. Despite the sincerity of her narratives, their "inner logic" reveals a sentimental liberalism that does not do adequate justice to animals.

Rudy offers us a spiritual interpretation of our connection with animals.[197] The fact that we can love animals and that they have the capacity to reciprocate this love becomes for Rudy a spiritual bond. We make sacrifices for animals by dedicating a significant part of our lives to taking care of and assisting them so they can live a good life. They reciprocate with affection, assistance, and companionship. For Rudy, this bond of mutual love is what exempts animals from harm and, in some cases, our killing them. The community of love is our implicit social contract. However, those outside our community of love are not guaranteed the protections provided to those members of our community, and this inequality is the problem. Rudy's subjectivist ethic yields a pluralistic biopolitics of diverse communities whose internal ethics can range from universal veganism to business as usual. Rudy's critics point out there is no binding transcommunity ethic. Wolfe would agree with Rudy that a universal ethic in the real world of biopolitical reality is impossible to hold to. There is an implicit ethic of least possible harm in all of Rudy's narratives, but what constitutes "harm" varies, depending on the context. This variance is one of the main intellectual impasses in animal ethics that I believe cannot be resolved and, therefore, must be lived with.

As for killing and eating animals—we do this because of biology, culture, and institutional reality. We are physically omnivores and culturally as well as institutionally more carnivorous than we need or ought to be. All three factors, however—biology, culture, power—exert significant influence. Despite the moral baseline of universal veganism advocated by many animal rights advocates, the reality is that vegan and vegetarian recidivism is very high due to issues of health, social acceptance, levels of moral commitment, practicality, and the diets' cost. Yet one often overlooked and undervalued key factor is the fact that we are biologically built to be omnivores. It is part of our evolutionary DNA. Our physiology, brain chemistry, and guts pose a real challenge that should not be underestimated. The very personal, ethical, social, and political negotiation of human biology, culture, and individual will is not a trivial matter.

Rudy's narrative of loving animals is representative of a new animal welfare ethic that occupies a space in between animal rights universal abolitionism and mainstream liberal animal welfarism. This is the world I believe we increasingly find ourselves in today. Steiner makes a very strong principled case that there are very few good reasons for using and killing animals and a host of far better reasons not to. But in terms of approach (affect, lifeworld, narrative) and in how she illuminates the real-world struggles we face in human-animal relations, Rudy's narratives reach and influence more people. Universal veganism is not the holy grail of animal ethics. A plant-strong, low-meat, pasture-raised, locavore, slow-food lifestyle and politics opposed to concentrated animal feeding operations (CAFOs) and the agribusiness-industrial complex represents a credible ethical and political stance in the animal advocacy movement. Rudy pulls us in the direction of an emotionalism that Singer and Steiner warn can too easily justify an arbitrary sentimentality that allows us to love our dogs, cats, and horses yet eat cows, pigs, and chickens. Singer and Steiner pull us in the opposite direction of strong universals that have their own built-in elements of arbitrary distinctions and an undervalued understanding of the posthumanist lifeworld.

As a posthumanist communitarian, I value the insights of animal rights abolitionists, new animal welfarists, and postmodern posthumanists in addressing the plight of animals in the twenty-first-century Anthropocene. My approach is designed not as a replacement for these positions but as another alternative. It is conceived as a postanthropocentric worldview in accordance with the outlook of coevolution theory, biocentric ethics, and lifeworld phenomenology. It aspires to an obligation-based approach that reflects a more communitarian normativity. It is neither rights-based nor cosmopolitan in a modern liberal or neohumanist sense. It is principled not in the sense of categorical moral imperatives but with respect to *phronesis*-based judgment and the belief that lifeworld, context, and relations shape ethical decision making and conduct. Ethical behavior is less about strictly following the moral law or a rule and more about examining how principles guide one on a case-by-case basis.

I question whether the idea of animals as persons and bearers of universal individual rights is biologically, politically, and legally feasible. Advocates of animal rights remind us that what we are really talking about is not a bill of rights but rather a basic fundamental right—to not be treated as property and killed. Yet in practice, animal rights are mammalian rights granted only to certain designated species and types. We project modern individual, human, and citizenship rights onto animals that do not perceive or act as beings that desire humanlike autonomy. I would like to see the animal advocacy movement progress beyond the now-well-established person/property and welfare/ rights abolition dualisms. In addition, we need to realize that the plight of animals in the Anthropocene is not simply solving a philosophical or moral problem and individual lifestyle change. The problem—as well as its solutions—should be framed as one of politics as applied ethics (*phronesis*), communitarian ethos, and an alternative biopolitics. Having said this, what should be the appropriate designation of nonhuman animals if they are neither persons nor property nor subjects of rights or liberal welfare in the conventional sense of these terms? Working within the limits of our language, I would submit that animals be designated as moral sentient subjects of justice and members of the posthumanist social contract with varying degrees of biopolitical community identity, residency, and protection.

Animal rights arguments and welfarism project onto nonhuman animals the modern liberal values of personhood, autonomy, agency, liberty, equality, and rights, which do not embody the capacities, desires, and interests of the vast majority of animals. What most (if not all) animals desire in accordance with their evolutionary makeup and sentient desires is to pursue their biosocial good. The concepts that best represent this purposive behavior are not liberty and equality but rather "the good" and community. Animals are highly communitarian beings and members of their family, hive, pack, herd, flock, niche, reef, pod, colony, nest, and society, pursuing a collective social good. By "community," I mean that animals are biologically, ecologically, and socially highly relational and networked beings.

Steiner admits that a commitment to negative rights and global cosmopolitanism is not enough. Sentient kinship must be felt and relational. It must be affective to be effective. An intellectualist argument for kinship and justice is limited, which is precisely why I believe in the importance of a coevolutionary, biocentric, lifeworld-based ethic. Our kinship and community with animals is calibrated more by our experiential and affective connections to them than by moral equations. Becoming a citizen of the biosphere begins with the concrete lifeworld experiences of the *humanimal* community as well as animal injustices that radiate out to forge larger circles of ethical affiliations and political commitments. Steiner admits, "Whether or not we ultimately retain the language of rights in seeking to protect the interests of animals, it is vital that we retain some conception of justice."[198] I strongly agree.

The "posthumanism" in posthumanist communitarianism has already been elaborated, but the "communitarianism" requires further explanation. I employ the term in several interconnected ways. Communitarianism understands animals as highly relational members of biosocial networks and habitats. Most animals are biosocial networked beings. Their identities are coded not only by their evolutionary and species-being but also by their communitarian negotiation of their particular lifeworlds. I also speak of "communitarianism" to highlight the neglected role of coevolution in providing animals (and humans) with adaptive strategies in building and maintaining biosocial niches and networks. I use the term to emphasize that animal communities, not simply individual animals, are under assault from humans in the Anthropocene. And I employ the idea of communitarianism to refer to the building of new human-animal (*humanimal*) communities that ascribe to posthumanist ethics.

Communitarian networks—blended communities of humans and animals real and imagined—are both the medium and means of posthumanist ethics. It is through communities that an ethical worldview materializes and is instantiated into an ethos. It is through communities that coevolution takes place. It is through communities that biopolitics determines membership, norms, boundaries, and relations. Together, they constitute a multiplicity of social contracts that bind and connect informal networks as well as more formal associations, organizations, and bounded spaces. Different communities will have different biopolitical norms, relations, and policies under the broader umbrella of posthumanist ethics. Their constituents, human and nonhuman, will differ, as will their primary *raison d'être*. Some communities will be built around companion species, others around sanctuaries, postmodern farming, endangered species, reinhabitation, contact zones, and subirdias. Their human residents will also vary from strict vegans to vegetarians to ethical omnivores. Some communities will adhere to a strict "no kill, no eat" biopolitics, while others will allow killing and be morally and politically challenged to define "humane killing" in a posthumanist world. Even though they differ, the practical effects of these communities offer oppositional alternatives to mainstream modernity. As I explain in Chapter 4, the reality of multiple communities and biopolitical contracts is best understood as inhabiting more diffuse, overlapping, and confederal networks and represented spatially as an archipelago. Posthumanist communities do not conform to the modern political-juridical model of sovereignty.

I advocate a middle course that avoids the twin extremes of unconditional universals and radical difference and acknowledges that all ethics, human and nonhuman, cannot be separated from biopolitics and determinate justice. According to Calarco's succinct definition of the ethics of difference, two conditions are paramount—"singularity (the irreducible uniqueness of the Other) and heteronomy (ethical relation and responsibility are initiated by the Other)."[199] Ethical universalism, whether individual categorical (i.e., Kantian) or dialogic (i.e., Habermasian), arrives at rights and wrongs through rational procedural tests largely independent of the lifeworld. Both underestimate the physical, institutional, and normative power of biopolitics with its phalanx of disciplinary apparatuses that operate throughout the social body. They also provide little space for *phronesis*, for the practical negotiation of identity/difference, reason/lifeworld, ethics/biopolitics. Furthermore, in locating the site of ethical-political life in the individual, in the singularity of the event, or in cosmopolitanism, there is little space for or recognition of the reality of situated communities and biosocial networks as the site of animal ethics and politics.

The drawing of distinctions, bounded spaces, rights and wrongs, definitions of legal and illegal, community members, outliers, and intruders is an innate feature of our nature as a particularly evolved social, cultural, moral, and political animal that we share in varying degrees with other animals. It is part of our territorial evolutionary biology, which translates into territorial ontologies, moralities, and biopolitics. Every radical deconstruction and deterritorialization end with a new reconstruction and territorialization. There is an arbitrarily rationalized aspect to all of our lifeworlds and worldviews.

Animal ethics is no different. Lines are drawn between those fully human, less than human, humanlike, animal, and less than animal; between moral agents, subjects, and patients; between self-aware persons and nonpersons; between responsive and reactive life; between "who" and "what"; between animal and plant; between domesticated, contact zone, and wild animals; between family member, community member, and food; and between those we love, those we coevolve with, those we compete with, and those we eat. Traditional animal welfare largely accepts the modern regime of sovereign biopolitics and works within its institutional and disciplinary norms. Universal animal rights advocates tend to downplay or ignore the biopolitical determinants of ethics. Postmodern posthumanists acknowledge biopolitics yet define resistance primarily in terms of radical difference and singularity. Posthumanist communitarianism acknowledges biopolitics yet defines resistance in communitarian terms. It draws on Foucault's idea of biopolitics as well as his ideas of resistance and counter-conduct, Esposito's idea of an affirmative life politics of the *bios communitas*, and the communitarian models of Petr Kropotkin, Snyder, and Bill McKibben.

We must eat others to live. Life requires a mutual sacrifice of life. That is one of the many lessons of evolution. As a moral-practical matter, posthumanist ethics calls on us to shake off our delusional anthropocentric conceit, end our totalitarian confinement of animals and occupation of their habitats, eat much further down the food chain, more fully include animals as protected and entitled members of our communities, and fundamentally renegotiate the Anthropocene social contract. How then does one reconcile the normative ideal of a posthumanist ethics that assigns intrinsic value to living beings, regards animals as part of our moral community, and seeks to more fully incorporate them within a new social contract with the reality of a hypermodern, globalized civilization that has pushed the very processes of evolution into a more competitive life struggle, where environments are becoming more fragmented and destabilized, where species are going extinct at an alarming rate, and where most animals remain largely objects at our disposal? The answer is that we cannot reconcile these values and facts—the best we can do is negotiate this condition. An animal ethic requires an animal politics.

# 4

———

## THE NEXT SOCIAL CONTRACT

———

The philosophers who have examined the foundations of society
have all felt the necessity of returning to the state of nature, but
none of them has reached it.

—Jean-Jacques Rousseau,
*Discourse on the Origins and Foundations
of Inequality among Men*

## Animals and the Social Contract

Animals have always been part of human society and, therefore, members
of our social contract. We have coevolved with them for millennia. The
fates of different animals have risen and fallen in the course of human
social and cultural evolution, the result of ever-shifting logics and boundaries
of inclusion and exclusion as well as status designations from privileged to
product to pariah. They have been and continue to be our close companions,
members of our pack and tribe, bearers of spiritual power, and symbols of our
cultural identity. They also remain our property; a major source of our food
and clothing; useful tools; and a key contributor to our civilized wealth,
status, and power.

Paleolithic humans held an animistic view of life. All things possessed an
elemental life force or *animus*, and there were no boundaries between humans,
animals, plants, and natural entities. Humans had a close relationship with
animals, especially mammals, who lived a social existence as humans do,
whose faces resembled the faces of humans, who expressed emotions as
humans do, who had sex as humans do, whose blood was humanlike, and who
killed and ate each other to live. Cave paintings testify to the close relationship
between humans and animals, with horses, bison, aurochs, deer, bears, mammoth, and big cats most often drawn. The lifeworld of animals was accessed

through shamanistic rituals. The creation myths of totemic cultures regard the first human beings as descendants of animal-people.[1]

The first animal to develop a coevolutionary relationship with humans was the gray wolf (*Canis lupus*). It is believed that wolves became tame in the presence of humans as they scavenged garbage dumps. They gained a reliable food source, and we benefited from their superior sense of smell and hearing in warning of intruders, and their scavenging increased sanitation. As Susan Foster McCarter points out, wolves possess traits that enhance their human compatibility. They are a social, pack animal with "a strongly developed dominance hierarchy system"; are curious and intelligent; and maintain "relationships between individuals that are constantly expressed through facial expressions and body language" similar to humans.[2] The coevolutionary domestication of wolves into dogs goes further back than the old estimate of fifteen thousand years to as long as forty thousand to one hundred thousand years ago.[3]

The advent of pastoral and agricultural life shifted human priorities to the fertility of Earth and the utility of domesticated plants and animals. This change was reflected in creation myths, which focused on the cycle of the seasons and sky, earth, water, and fertility deities. The earliest crops included wheat, barley, lentils, peas, chickpeas, and corn. The first animals bred in captivity were dogs, sheep, goats, pigs, and cows. The domestic cat (*Felis domesticus*), a descendant of the African and European wild cat, domesticated itself around ten thousand years ago, finding itself attracted to agricultural villages whose surplus grain housed mice and rats.[4] The evolution of agricultural society set humans on the path to property-based social hierarchies and war-based expansionism that primarily rewarded the gods' chosen representatives—kings, priests, and warriors. The bull and ram symbolized masculine and patriarchal power, while cattle worship reflected property ownership and wealth.

No other ancient people developed as close a relationship with animals as the Egyptians. Animals were bearers of divine power and shared the afterlife with humans. Animal cults pervaded everyday Egyptian life. The Nile Valley was rich in wildlife—elephants, giraffes, gazelle, ibex, lions, leopards, cheetahs, monkeys, and crocodiles. Egyptians established the first zoos, known as "paradise parks."[5] Deities included Horus the falcon god, Sobek the crocodile god, Sekhmet the lioness-headed goddess, Anubis the jackal-headed god, and Bastet the cat goddess.[6] Cats—*miaw* or *miu* (he or she who mews)—were sacred to Egyptians. They guarded sanctuaries, were associates of gods, were their most favored pet, and were mummified and buried with their human companions. Killing a cat was punishable by death.[7]

Medieval Europeans made sense of their world in terms of a "Great Chain of Being" that held the universe together in a series of natural, human, and supernatural hierarchies.[8] The world was bounded by Heaven and Hell, with ranks of angels, humans, animals, plants, and minerals in between. The status of a being or entity was dependent on its ratio of spirit to matter. The greater the material composition, the lower its ranking in the cosmic order of things. Greater spiritual substance translated into a higher ranking and greater authority over lower levels of being. In *De Coelesti Hierarchia* (The Celestial Hierarchy), Dionysus the Areopagite envisions an angelic hierarchy of three levels, with three choirs in each level.[9] Animals were capable of independent locomotion and possessed physical appetites and perceptual awareness, but they lacked reason, language, and immortal souls. Mammals were at the top of the animal kingdom, followed by birds, fish, reptiles, amphibians, and insects. Birds were ranked above aquatic animals since air was superior to water, as it was lighter and closer to heaven.

The most valued animals were battle and riding horses owned by nobles and knights. These were followed by hawks, falcons, and certain dog breeds trained for royal hunts. Elite game animals included deer, boar, and hare. Cattle remained the most prized food animal. Oxen and draft horses ("heavy horses") were valued for plowing and hauling goods. By the twelfth century, the horse had replaced the ox as the primary draught animal due to the inventions of the padded collar harness and iron horseshoes. Sheep, goats, pigs, and chickens were peasant animals.[10]

In *The Beast Within: Animals in the Middle Ages* (2011), historian Joyce E. Salisbury documents a shift in the medieval worldview in the twelfth century from an absolute human-animal distinction to a blurring of the lines between human and animal. The human-animal border became more permeable. There was greater interest in ambiguous, hybrid, and borderline creatures, evident in bestiary, fable, and penitential literatures; animal trials; and werewolf and monster folklore.[11] *Bestiaries*, or instructional animal dictionaries filled with Christian moral lessons, praised lions, elephants, horses, oxen, and doves while condemning wolves, hyenas, monkeys, foxes, and rats as vermin, associates of the Devil, and prone to demonic possession and shape shifting.[12] Monkeys and apes, named *simia* for their similarity to humans, were generally regarded as stupid, unclean, and humanlike deformities, because they threatened the human-animal distinction.[13] Monsters, such as Grendel in *Beowulf*, were half-animal/half-human hybrids who lived in caves and border woodlands.[14] Animals could be brought to trial for injuring or killing humans, damaging property, demonic possession, or bestiality. Attributing intentional agency and moral responsibility to animals was allowed in judicial proceedings.[15]

Werewolf folklore was common in medieval Europe. Man-becoming-wolf was evidence of devil possession, and werewolf trials involved humans accused of robbing graves, killing and eating children, or dismembering victims. Yet in Celtic, Nordic, and Germanic societies, wolves were regarded as powerful and intelligent human brethren worthy of being honored and emulated. Germans named their sons Wolfgang, Wolfhard, and Wolfram. The belief in man-becoming-wolf was prevalent in warrior traditions. *Hamask* and *hamrammr* referred to changing into an animal. *Ulfhenonar*, Odin's special elite warriors, went into battle wearing wolf skins and headdresses. *Werewolf* meant to wear wolf skins. *Berserkers* (from *berr* meaning bare, without armor) were bear- and wolf-skinned elite shock troops who worked themselves into a trancelike rage before battle.[16]

The advent of modernity brought with it a new era in the human-animal social contract. The "rise of the West" is best understood as a series of overlapping long historical transformations. I identify a distinct Mediterranean modernity from the 1440s through the sixteenth century driven by Italian, Portuguese, and Spanish maritime exploration, the conquest of the Americas, and Renaissance humanism; a Protestant modernity of the sixteenth and seventeenth centuries with its religious-political transformation of Europe, scientific revolution, and birth of the sovereign nation-state system; an eighteenth-century Enlightenment modernity of the American and French revolutions; industrial modernity; a late twentieth- and early twenty-first-century American modernity; and a planetary modernity currently underway driven by a plurality of world influential cultures, political-economic engines, and a shift in economic and geopolitical power to the Pacific Rim.

The transformation of the Western Hemisphere into predominantly slave-based plantation and mining colonies in the sixteenth and seventeenth centuries by conquering Europeans was devastating to its indigenous peoples and its animals. When the Americas were "discovered," an estimated fifty-four million to sixty-one million native peoples lived in numerous and diverse societies and nations. Their impact on the environment and animals was not overly destructive, because their numbers were spread out across the continent, and they had low-impact cultural practices and technologies. Within two hundred years of European contact, their population had been reduced to an astounding six million people due to disease, enslavement, warfare, and genocide.[17] As New World colonialism continued to expand, the need for cheap labor led Europeans to rely heavily on indentured laborers and African slave markets.

By 1600, Europeans had taken over the fur trade from first peoples and aggressively exploited it to the point that by the mid-1800s, beaver, otter, and mink survived in only a few isolated areas. Populations in the millions were reduced to a few hundred thousand. Deer, prized for their meat and skin, met a similar fate. There was a time when sixty million bison and forty million pronghorn sheep roamed the Great Plains grasslands and deserts of North America, but bison extermination became U.S. government policy to defeat the Plains Indians, whose lifestyle was dependent on buffalo. By 1890, fewer than eleven hundred bison were left. Pronghorn extermination was official rancher policy, as they competed with cattle for grass. By the early 1920s, fewer than twenty thousand pronghorn sheep remained. A genocidal war of extermination was carried out against wolves, mountain lions, coyotes, foxes, and other "vermin," using all means necessary—hunting, trapping, and poisoning. Their corpses were displayed with pride.[18]

The modern social contract in its varied historical incarnations has been held together by a set of core beliefs and values. Early modernity evolved out of the collapse of late-medieval civilization and asserted the ontological priority of Man over God and Nature. The rational subject and the power of the human will to master nature and human nature with the tools of modern science came to occupy a sovereign realm once reserved for only God's will.[19] The Newtonian paradigm was deployed through the new tripartite power grid of the nation-state, capitalism, and industrial technology.[20] Max Weber famously analyzes modernity as the triumph of formal-instrumental, means-ends rationality in all spheres of society.[21] The ideology of modern individualism is built on the epistemological power of subject-object rationality. The calculative subject confronts the world as a collection of objects capable of accurate representation, which facilitates their manipulation. This cognitive-object control becomes pervasive in the mastery of not only nature, other species of life, and other humans but also the self.

Ryan Gunderson credits the thinkers of Frankfurt's Institute for Social Research (the legendary "Frankfurt School") with having "more than any other school of critical theory prior to the formation of animal studies" analyzed "society's troubling relationship with animals."[22] They link the long-standing human-animal distinction throughout European history and the modern industrialization of animal exploitation to a cultural tradition that privileged an instrumentalist view of nature and animals as largely means for human ends. More than this, the domination of nature (including animals) has been integrally connected to the domination of humans by humans. In identifying many racial, ethnic, pagan, and "primitive" humans as animals, people justified their exploitation in the name of a paternalistic functionalism. Modern capitalist magnates and fascist leaders embraced particular types of animals to justify their social Darwinian worldviews and policies. Theodor Adorno and Max Horkheimer endorse Arthur Schopenhauer's view of animals as sentient beings deserving of compassion and justice and his rejection of Judeo-Christian and Cartesian-Lockean-Kantian views of animals as soulless machines and property, lacking rationality and moral agency and not worthy of direct moral concern.

In *Dialectic of Enlightenment* (1944), Horkheimer and Adorno chronicle the evolution of Western "enlightened reason" as the emancipation of subject-object instrumental reason from myth, tradition, and metaphysics. Emancipation lies in a kind of knowledge that yields a particular form of power. In the tradition of Weber and Martin Heidegger, and in anticipation of Michel Foucault, they locate this knowledge/power in the means-driven rationality exemplified in industrial technology that results in the "disenchantment of the world."[23] All of reality, inanimate and animate, is fully objectified into a collection of objects and facts amenable to logical, mathematical, and positivist scientific manipulation. Framing the world as a thing unleashed a radical form of modern power. While modern Enlightenment thinkers equate this new form of knowledge/power with human freedom and liberation, Horkheimer and Adorno identify and illuminate its dark side. In "liberating men from fear and establishing their sovereignty," the dialectic ultimately ends up dominating rather than liberating nature and human nature.[24]

The irony of modernity lies in the fact that it does not fully realize that its gospel of rational progress is a secular myth, a reinvention of the mythic worldview. Modern processes of rationalization rely on the great myths of autonomous agency, linear progress, fact objectivity, unlimited knowledge, and technology as salvation. Modernity is "mythical fear turned radical."[25] In premodern cultures, fear of the unknown was mediated by rituals and narratives that produced a collective veneration of the mystery, animism, and power of nature and its creators. Nature, culture, and society were integrated through *mimesis*, the representative re-enchantment of the world through magic, ritual, and narrative. Whereas in traditional society, "animism spiritualized the object," under conditions of modernity, "industrialism objectifies the spirits of men."[26] Modernity deals with this existential fear by cognitively rendering the world completely knowable and capable of human control. For Horkheimer and Adorno, this totalizing control contains totalitarian social and political consequences.

The modern Enlightenment project of rational mastery is today more globalized and postmodern, and it increasingly renders humans as adjuncts to technology. Our ever-tightening control and manipulation of human societies and ecosystems have caused them to become increasingly destabilized. Ulrich Beck calls this condition "reflexive modernization," the emergence of a new "risk society" from the self-destruction of the old industrial society.[27] The idea of advanced late modernity's ushering in a globalized risk society supports the Anthropocene hypothesis. Human sovereign control over the planet is now largely complete, yet the consequences of runaway modernity and biosphere colonization are fully underway in the form of climate change, ecosystem disruption, and species extinction.

## Revisioning the Modern Social Contract

The belief that the authority and legitimacy of human institutions should be based on a mutually binding normative agreement or "social contract" voluntarily consented to by free and equal rational agents is considered to be one of the great achievements of modern political thought. It is most famously elucidated by Thomas Hobbes, John Locke, and Jean-Jacques Rousseau in *Leviathan* (1651), *Second Treatise of Government* (1689), and *The Social Contract* (1762), respectively. Modern social contract theory has a specific function: to legitimize liberal political modernity and establish a regime of rights and obligations organized around the sovereign nation-state, capitalist market economy, and civil society. At its heart is the thought experiment of imagining a prepolitical "state of nature" where relatively free and equal human beings negotiate and decide what type of society and state they would be willing to consent to. The goal of the process is the legitimation of a normative and institutional order.

The theories of Hobbes, Locke, and Rousseau are composites of historical circumstances and normative commitments designed to justify their preferred models of society and state. Hobbes's state of nature as a condition devoid of institutional order and one of "continual fear, and danger of violent death" sets one on the path toward exiting this situation.[28] Our optimal rational choice is to "seek peace" by laying down "a man's right to do anything" and enter into a "pact, or covenant" to create a well-ordered sovereign state.[29] Locke's ideal of industrious individuals pursuing their natural rights rationalizes Protestant liberal capitalism. Rousseau questions Enlightenment rationalism and modern liberalism, in its stead advocating a romantic naturalism and communitarian democracy of the general will. A dissenting David Hume argues, "Almost all governments which exist at present, or of which there remains any record in history, have been founded originally, either on usurpation or conquest, or both, without any pretense of a fair consent of voluntary subjection of the people."[30] Even in the rare instance where consent may have taken place, "it was commonly so irregular, so confined, or so much intermixed with either fraud or violence, that it cannot have any great authority."[31]

Friedrich Nietzsche views social contract theory as a clever but false artifice in legitimizing modernity. In the second essay of *On the Genealogy of Morality* (1887), he poses this question: "To breed an animal which is able to make promises—is that not precisely the paradoxical task which nature has set herself with regard to humankind?"[32] The great achievement of Western modernity—the "sovereign individual," this "master of the free will," who has "the right to make a promise" and who accepts full moral responsibility for his actions—is the achievement of an "immense amount of labor of man on himself during the longest epoch of the human race—before history."[33] Man, "with the help of the morality of custom and the social straightjacket," has been "made truly predictable."[34] The social contract is one of the most cunning of all human inventions. The mass of humanity consents to a life of domestication, with the "herd animal" tended to by the modern paternalistic-maternalistic state.[35]

Liberal social contract theory receded into the background in the nineteenth century with the ascendancy of utilitarian thinking in ethics, politics, and economics. Jeremy Bentham, James Mill, and John Stuart Mill would assert that the foundation of political modernity is neither consent nor natural rights but rather social utility defined as the maximization of aggregate happiness or general welfare. Yet with the appearance of John Rawls's *Theory of Justice* (1971) more than a century later, the pendulum would swing back to social contract theory. His theory of justice is so comprehensive and influential that it revitalized not only liberal social contract theory but also political theory itself. Nearly fifty years later, we still think in the wake of Rawls, even those of us who are decidedly post-Rawlsian.

Martha Nussbaum and Mark Rowlands have modified Rawlsian theory to make it compatible with extending moral rights and legal protections to animals. Traditionally, contract theory has recognized only human rational agents as being the legitimate framers and beneficiaries of the contract. Only moral agents, not moral patients, have full and direct rights and obligations. Yet Nussbaum argues that because the actual framers of the contract are human agents, this does not logically imply that the recipients of contractual protections and benefits need to be rational agents—or human, for that matter.[36] Rowlands goes one step further to argue that human rationality can be conceived of as an arbitrary property of evolutionary biology that qualifies to be put behind the veil of ignorance.[37] The adoption of a modern liberal conception of personhood is therefore not a categorical imperative of social contract thinking. Nussbaum replaces Rawls's Kantian approach with Aristotle and the deeper and broader principle of the diversity, dignity, and flourishing of life.[38] Animals should not be conceived of as objects of sympathy but rather as subjects of justice. Nussbaum's neo-Aristotelian, capabilities approach rejects modern natural rights and utilitarian doctrines in favor of a theory of justice that extends a list of core human capabilities to other species. Other species of life should be afforded the dignity of flourishing just like humans and therefore should be included as members of the social contract.

The standard logic of social contract theory follows a basic three-step process. We begin with an imagined state of nature, original position, or ideal communication community in which rational agents reflect on, deliberate over, and/or bargain about what kind of society and state they would consent to. Following their decision to invest in a social and political order that they deem legitimate, they undertake a second step that involves consenting to a contractual agreement and a set of principles binding on all parties. Persons become citizens. The third step involves the construction of an institutional reality that reflects the contractual agreement and instantiates a social, economic, and political order.

Upon closer scrutiny, it becomes evident that the goal of the social contract—a determinate social, economic, and political order—is baked into the process from the start. Contained within it is a tacit set of assumptions that move us toward the goal of the exercise—a sovereign social reality that has factored in our consent. Our choice is logically and empirically constrained from the outset. This limitation can be demonstrated with respect to all the major thinkers from Hobbes to Rawls. Social contract theory reveals itself to be a political theory, the advocacy of a set of political principles. We would be better off if we fully lifted once and for all the veil that has historically shrouded the social contract.

My idea of the social contract is not based on the traditional premise of a counterfactual thought experiment whose foundation is a hypothetical "state of nature," "veil of ignorance," or "discourse ethics." Nor do I endorse the implicit belief that rational consensus should be the basis of legitimation and the goal of the contract. Further, I do not endorse the idea of a restrictive proceduralism and rules of public reasoning that marginalize, bracket, or require "thin" conceptions of the good as second-order priorities for the sake of a safe, minimalist, procedural ideal of rational consensus. Thus, I do not follow in the footsteps of Rawls and Jürgen Habermas. The heart and soul of the social contract lies in recognizing public space as highly pluralistic and animated by competing conceptions of the good. The goal is not artificial consent but rather the elucidation and testing of alternative models of the good life. Thus, the contractual environment creates a space of existential disclosure and deliberation that more closely approximates Hannah Arendt's idea of a public realm of existential action, Martin Matustik's reformulation of Habermas's discourse ethics that gives greater weight to existential questions in normative deliberation, and Chantal Mouffe's idea of democracy as agonistic pluralism.[39]

Like Rawls, I am concerned with "justice as fairness," but my approach is postliberal, postmodern, posthumanist, biopolitical, and communitarian. I part ways from modern liberalism by including animals as moral subjects of justice and members of the contract. Modern social contract theory does not include animals, because they cannot consent, lacking personhood capabilities (i.e., they are not human). Yet personhood status by itself is not sufficient for consent, even among humans. One must have the attributes of practical autonomy, which the majority of humanity lacks. This is precisely one of the goals of social contract theory: to level the playing field for all humans so that, in theory, they are afforded all the attributes required to engage in a free and equal discourse on the institutional reality they would be willing to support. The status of animals in the social contract has always been at the hands of their human masters. The question is whether we have now reached a point in human social evolution where our relationship to animals and their status should undergo a major cultural and political shift and the social contract be fundamentally revised. I believe we have.

Based on these presuppositions, I propose my idea of a posthumanist social contract. It begins with the real "state of nature" today, the status of the biosphere and the condition of life on planet Earth as informed by the Anthropocene hypothesis. Placed before us is the issue of the impact of our current civilization on the planet's carrying capacity, on the biosphere, and on its inhabitants. What is the current state of the biosphere, our civilization, and the prospects for their mutual sustainability? The focus is not on the human condition but on the condition of planetary life. Implicit in this assessment of the state of nature are two interrelated questions, one empirical and one normative: What is our current state of nature? What ought to be our current state of nature and our place in it? The key word in both of these questions, "our," pertains to all animals, of which humans are one species among many.

The Anthropocene hypothesis frames the contractual reasoning process. It rests on the empirical and normative validity of the impact of several global trends on the mutual sustainability of the biosphere and human civilization— human population growth, distribution, and density; mega-urbanization; advanced capitalist economic growth; the rapid explosion of a global consumer middle class; global energy production and consumption; anthropogenic habitat re-engineering; climate change; and species extinction. The devil is not only in the details but also in how we assign meaning and value to nature, animals, humans, and our current civilization. Regardless of how one analyzes and interprets these megatrends, their interdependence cannot be denied.

As I argue in Chapter 1, one can take three main positions with regard to the Anthropocene hypothesis. One could adopt a conservative or neoliberal stance, reject the hypothesis, and endorse the status quo. Our current civilization should stay the course. The sky is not falling, and we (humans) will prevail. One could adopt a reformist stance, accept the hypothesis with some reservations and disagreements, and yet remain confident that we have not reached a tipping point and that our current civilization possesses the resources to mitigate late-modern anthropocentric planetization. The third position accepts the Anthropocene hypothesis, believes that we have gone beyond the tipping point or should act as though we have, and lacks confidence in the ability and capacity of late modernity to mitigate or reverse current trends. The key here is the "we," which includes humans and animals. I adopt this third position.

Traditionally, the pivotal moment in modern social contract theory has been the legitimation of sovereign consent. I question the paradigm of modern sovereignty. Instead, the pivotal moment becomes one of dissent that directly calls into question the legitimacy of the civilization that has delivered us into the Anthropocene conundrum we find ourselves in. Assessing legitimacy combines abstract normative standards with an evaluation of the particular power structure that exists at present. Legitimacy is a function of "is" and "ought" and of the gap between. Most regimes make claim to a minimalist benchmark of legitimate authority based on express or tacit consent, utility or functionality, or democratic approval. Informed critical citizens lay claim to a higher benchmark of normative legitimacy, not merely utility or functionality. Equating legitimacy with a normative benchmark ups the ante. Equating legitimacy with a posthumanist conception of justice ups it much further. The bar is set high.

The verdict on the sovereign legitimacy of late-modern civilization (what I refer to as "anthropocentric planetization") is intertwined with the question of justice. From the perspective of posthumanist ethics and justice, one cannot endorse the current order of things. I would go further and argue that from a humanist and a posthumanist perspective, the social contract of late modernity is an exhausted artifice. It sustains its hegemony and counteracts normative deficits through sheer technological power over human and animal bodies. Politically, a vote of no confidence in the late-modern social contract translates into personal and political action that reframes the benchmark of legitimacy as one of structural change (a new institutional reality), resistance to the sovereign order, and the pursuit of exit strategies from the neoliberal Anthropocene.

## The Question of Civilizational Legitimacy

How do we define "civilization" today? What descriptors do we employ to bring into focus the dominant institutional power system in the world? I would capture the nature of our present condition using the following words— "Anthropocene," "late modern/postmodern," "neoliberal," "globalized," "high tech," "high consumption," "fossil fuel," "mega-urban," "highly militarized," and "planetization" (i.e., planetary sovereignty). Every human, animal, species of life, and habitat on the planet, from the Amazon interior to inner-city London, from Alaska to Antarctica, from the Great Barrier Reef to Mongolia, from small organic to large corporate factory farms, from the lower atmosphere to the ocean's depths, from megafauna to micro-organisms, from remote desert to Hong Kong, is under the driving influence of this model.

How then do we assess the legitimacy of this juggernaut? This is a difficult task due to the enormity of the artifact under scrutiny. The approach I adopt draws on the model developed by Habermas in *Legitimation Crisis*. To analyze "legitimacy deficits" in advanced capitalist Western societies, Habermas adopts a "system" and "lifeworld" model.[40] He concludes that late-modern societies suffer from serious legitimacy problems that are not simply systemic in how economic and political systems function but reflect deeper sociocultural problems of identity, meaning, motivation, beliefs, and values. While institutions continue to produce adequate levels of economic wealth, jobs, material goods, status, social welfare, and security to keep the system operating for a sufficient majority and to maintain a revolving door of elites in power, doing so comes at a great cost. Systemic support is very shallow, and the reason is to be found in the lifeworld. Self-legitimizing corporate economic and state bureaucratic entities reproduce themselves over the heads of their customer-client-citizens and simultaneously colonize their everyday lifeworlds to keep them sufficiently tethered to and dependent on system steering imperatives. Yet systemic functionality and utilitarian contentment are not enough to make life fulfilling for many people.

Despite the rise of neoliberalism, most advanced capitalist societies still operate within the parameters of a neo-Keynesian, welfare-state model. Advanced capitalism is a tensional hybrid of neoliberalism and neo-Keynesianism. The interventionist regulatory state prevents economic and political collapse. But to maintain their legitimacy, social and political systems manipulate their citizens in a highly paternalistic, passive-aggressive manner. Late modernity has become a banal worker-consumer model of manufactured pseudohappiness. Most people passively "consent" to the system. Their conformity, ritualism, and privatism pass for legitimacy and consent.[41] This passivity obviously will not do for Habermas, who equates legitimacy with a normative ideal of communicative rationality and a robust deliberative democracy of informed active citizens.[42]

Over the course of his career, Habermas's critics have pointed out that while late modernity does indeed have legitimacy problems, his yardstick of legitimacy and proposed diagnosis—democratic communication and deliberative democracy—are untenable in practice. This claim may be true, but one of the great strengths of Habermas's analysis lies in his expansion of the concept of legitimacy beyond its narrow political confines as public confidence in government. It involves the entire scope and depth of society, from macrosystems to microsocial lifeworlds. The legitimacy of late-modern civilization is not simply an institutional problem but a more profound cultural one. It is our way of life and the debate over whether it really is a good life. Here, Habermas is on the right track.

But at the same time, it is much more than this. What has occurred is the systemic colonization of the biosphere and its inhabitants. A globalized, technocratic civilization has colonized not only the human lifeworld but also the lifeworlds of other species. From a posthumanist perspective, civilizational legitimacy is a question of the quality of human *and* nonhuman life, not simply human life.

Posthumanist tests of legitimacy go deeper and are more encompassing. Where then does our civilization fall short? From my nodal point as a posthumanist citizen armed with the Anthropocene hypothesis as my legitimacy test, it comes up short on several major fronts. Deficits are evident in the rate and scope of global warming, the rate and scope of ecosystem disruption, species extinction, our use and treatment of animals, human planetary colonization, the power of the agribusiness-industrial complex over our lives, the quantitative-consumptive rationality models and monopolistic power structures of late-modern capitalist growth economies, our status culture of conspicuous consumption, the declining value of conventional work and quality of jobs generated by late modernity, and the pervasive logic of technology as an end rather than a means.

Even from a more conventional humanist standpoint, the United States is facing multiple legitimacy crises. Its eighteenth-century constitutional system is in a state of functional paralysis. Most of its major political institutions and federal bureaucratic agencies have very low levels of citizen trust and support. Serious issues of social inequality and political corruption are attributable to its oligarchic economic system, which, some have argued, has entered a new Gild-ed Age of dynastic capitalism.[43] American civil society finds itself in a highly polarized and weakened state, with major areas of the country disintegrating, violent, and anomic. The United States is the world's largest prison state. In 2013, its national infrastructure of highways, bridges, railroads, aviation systems, ports, inland waterways, levees, and dams received an overall grade of D+ from the American Society of Civil Engineers.[44] America's imperial national security state is struggling to come to terms with the consequences of two major failed wars. There is evidence of significant reactionary social, cultural, and political responses to major demographic shifts. The United States is also in the early stages of a fully automated/robotics/artificial intelligence (AI) revolution that is destined to eliminate major sectors of its working population, an eventuality for which it is ill prepared culturally and politically. The country is to a significant degree held back by it adherence to the "old modernity" of Protestant individualism, free-market capitalism, and nationalist exceptionalism.

I place *eudaimonia* (happiness as flourishing) center stage in my assessment of late-modern system/lifeworld legitimacy. Legitimacy is a question of justice and the good. Contrary to modern liberalism and the thoughts of Rawls and Habermas, substantive conceptions of the good do not play a subordinate role in moral and political theory; they are on equal footing with questions of right or justice. The distinction between questions of rightness and justice and questions of the good is false. At the heart of the social contract are competing conceptions of the good (sets of values and goods) and the political challenge of how they should be accommodated within a framework of justice.

What does a posthumanist conception of the good look like? In keeping with my idea of posthumanist communitarianism as inhabiting numerous nodal points and niches in a decentralized archipelago, there is a plurality of conceptions of the good. However, one can discern common core values and principles in coevolutionary ethics, biocentrism, animal kinship, environmental sustainability, habitat preservation, species viability, and *humanimal* justice. The elevated status and priority of animals in the social contract directly implies the need to rethink prevailing models of cultural and institutional normalcy.

The legitimacy crisis of the Anthropocene and posthumanism call into question the linchpin of modern social contract theory, which is sovereign consent. Sovereignty and consent are two sides of the same coin, which is power. While the rationale for modern sovereign consent can be traced to Hobbes's *Leviathan*, an equally pivotal event in the discourse of sovereignty can be traced to Foucault's *Discipline and Punish* (1975).[45] Here, he identifies a novel form of power intertwined with modern liberalism. The same regime that constructed the rights-bearing citizen also constructed a form of disciplinary power as a consequence of Enlightenment progress through rational control.[46] Disciplinary power evolved out of a panoply of social administrative practices, agencies, professions, and applied sciences. This web of power relations spread through society, reforming schools, prisons, the police, military, factories, social services, hospitals, and asylums. It transformed individuals into self-policing consensual citizens. Hobbes's sovereign state evolved into a modern administrative-disciplinary state.[47] Disciplinary power circulates throughout society in a capillary fashion, working on bodies (biopower) as well as on individual subjectivities.[48] Power is everywhere in the social body, producing who we are.

Modern Hobbesians see power as vertical, hierarchical, and centralized, with the state as the dominant actor and ultimate sovereign. Postmodern Foucaultians see power as a horizontal, society-immanent, and decentralized phenomenon held together by social networks and matrices. Foucault recommends that we "cut off the King's head" and eliminate the outdated notion of Hobbesian sovereignty,[49] yet both models are alive and well. We have multiple Leviathans coupled with networks of disciplinary power. Sovereign consent is everywhere, at the micro- and macrolevels. It has expanded today into a form of biopolitical population management. We are beholden to many masters, yet believe that we are freer than ever.

I believe that Hobbes and Foucault are particularly relevant, because we live in a time of postliberalism. The age of classical liberalism is over. Its regime of individual autonomy, rights, consent, and constitutional representative democracy is on the wane. The reality of institutional power in the late-modern world dwarfs modern liberalism. The interlocking logics of social complexity, neoliberal corporatism, bureaucratic systems, and the national security-counterterrorism state have rendered much of modern liberalism moot. This situation is precisely why there has been such a resurgence of libertarian rhetoric—the construct of modern individual liberty has largely been deconstructed by late-modern power.

What exists in reality and what has always been the historical norm are a multiplicity of social and institutional networks operating at different levels that are overlapping and intersecting. Day-to-day social life is situated within local environments, which are connected to varied confederations and archipelagos. These networks are, in turn, situated within larger power structures and fields of control. There is no such thing as one sovereign—we answer to several sovereigns and several social contracts, all of which impose on us a set of power relations with their own mechanisms of consent.

From this, we can conclude the social contract does not exist in the singular. There is no unitary, hegemonic, sovereign document, agreement, or tacit social or political construct. There are multiple, overlapping contracts—spatial, horizontal, vertical, elliptical, temporal, generational, micro, macro, and biopolitical. They all compete for hegemony, and they are all provisionally binding and asymmetrical in terms of power, resources, and access. As an artifice of political authority and obligation, the social contract has primarily served the more conservative purpose of institutional legitimation, policy rationalization, elite domination, and biopolitical control. It has rarely served as a force for delegitimation, dissent, and radical reconstruction. The reversal of this logic is long overdue.

Foucault frames the question of consent as one of dissent. We assert our political agency in questioning those institutions and their directorates that speak in the name of sovereign authority. By what authority do they speak, make laws, and give orders? Much of legitimation is a tautology, an exercise in circular reasoning. Consent is to a large extent what Weber characterizes as the rationalization of domination.[50] The sovereign-disciplinary society has already integrated us into its web of power as consenting subjects. Foucault defines social and political reality in terms of disciplinary power networks that shape who we are, what we do, and how we do it. Power flows through the social body vertically and horizontally by way of interconnected circuits and matrices. We cannot escape it and therefore cannot exit from society. Our exit from one power network/social contract lands us in another.

We can, however, resist, for where there is power (and sovereign-disciplinary consent), there is resistance (dissent).[51] Every power network contains within it nodal points and spaces not fully fixed and controlled. Disciplinary matrices and circuits hold power together and stabilize it so that it can be stitched together and built into larger organizational entities. Niches of resistance, countervailing power, techniques, social and cultural practices, and identities can and do thrive in every social network. It is here that new cultural adaptations, specific transformations, and novel practices can be nurtured. Resistance is therefore built into the very nature of power. Every institution, system, and social contract contains within it spaces of rebellion, dissent, resistance, and exit.

The idea of "exit" brings to mind Albert Hirschman's book *Exit, Voice, and Loyalty* (1970). In our relationship with any organization, group, or person, we have three options—leave, complain, or keep quiet and stay.[52] To exit is to terminate one's relationship. Voice is protest and critical feedback coupled with attempts to reform the relationship. Loyalty is conforming and supporting the relationship without spoken reservations. As an economist,

Hirschman focuses on how to correct dysfunctions in organizational performance. Assessing the health of any collective entity involves measuring the interplay of loyalty, voice, and exit among employees and customers. He concludes that the right interplay of voice and exit can help reverse a decline or crisis in an institution. Voice and exit work best together. Too many organizations require conformist loyalty, yet too much loyalty stifles voice. Exit is needed to stimulate voice, but it should be at a slow rate. If there is a high rate of exit, the institution will experience a crisis as its best voices leave for greener pastures. For Hirschman, voice is the key to righting a failing enterprise or relationship. Voice must be cultivated in a constructive way. Exit is also not simply physical but potentially psychological and emotional.

While we can exit a particular institution, power network, or sovereign space physically, politically, or psychologically, we cannot exit society. We can, however, refuse to consent to a particular social contract as part of a process of shifting allegiance to another. Or, as Foucault would have phrased it, we have limited mobility (depending on the resources at our disposal) to exchange one disciplinary network for another. We can rebel, dissent, resist, or exit as part of a process of constructing or inhabiting a different social niche, nodal point, and/or social network. In a world of many sovereigns, we consent to some, dissent to others, and, most importantly, struggle to construct new niches of habitation. We will always be under the authority of multiple sovereigns, most of whom have factored in our consent, whether we like it or not. But we also have the ability as bodied, sentient beings and social and cultural learners to adapt to and to alter the environments in which we live.

The Anthropocene hypothesis, posthumanist ethics, and *humanimal* justice call into question the legitimacy of late modernity. The consequence of this question is the ongoing negotiation of a social and political space in between late modernity and the posthumanist condition, a straddling of voice and exit, one foot in one world and one in another. It is a spatiotemporal location and sense of identity "in" but not fully "of" late-modern civilization. It is an outlook that is postmodern, postliberal, and posthuman yet not antimodern, antiliberal, and antihuman. It rather represents movement in the direction of an alternative social network, cultural niche, and commitment to a different social contract.

## Justice in a Posthumanist World

What political space should animals occupy in a posthumanist world? Currently, they are predominately objects of instrumental value with varying conditions of protection or lack thereof. We have a moral and legal right to own and use animals coupled with an obligation to treat them decently in accordance with their legal categorization and functional status in our civilizational division of labor. In the posthumanist biopolitical contract, animals are nestled within a framework of justice that obligates us to treat them as subjects of justice entitled to living conditions that befit their political status.

Justice is much more than an ethical or political idea or theory—it is a biological, social, and cultural trait evident in human and nonhuman animals, the product of literally millions of years of evolution. Justice is a natural and conventional reality, hardwired in the DNA of social animals and soft-wired in the learned behaviors of cultural animals. Its main function is the regulation of social life through a variety of adaptive behaviors, mores, laws, and institutions. Furthermore, a significant amount of what is commonly regarded as justice is born of a sense of injustice. We know this intuitively, regardless of whether we fully express it in words. This sense is especially the case with animals.

I believe that all animals that live in social groups—and I would add that most animals are social in the sense of inhabiting and conducting their lives within biosocial networks—operate within the boundaries of implicit social contracts or biosocially demarcated, routinized, and regulated spatiotemporal communities. The more complex an animal is, the more its social world takes on a more explicit social structure. In the human animal, the social contract takes on a highly discursive, collectively intentional, and institutional form. Under conditions of modernity and advancing globalization, it takes on an even greater, more explicit specificity and complexity, multiplying into a phalanx of classifications and qualified and quantified norms of identity, power, and behavior. The result is a sovereign biopolitics that has endowed the power elite of the Anthropocene with unprecedented powers, rights, and privileges over all other life and has equally cut them off from the rest of planetary life.[53]

A posthumanist conception of justice challenges this state of affairs. I am not a member of the Anthropocene power elite and therefore do not view the world from the summits of sovereign power. However, I am a member of a sovereign civilizational order and therefore occupy a relatively privileged position in the planetary pecking order. It is from this nodal point that my idea of justice takes shape, one that recognizes animals as subjects of justice that deserve more equitable community membership. I therefore define the next social contract in communitarian rather than modern liberal terms. It is also postmodern in that its location is the system/lifeworld of Western late modernity, yet it does not conform to the paradigm of modern sovereignty. It is also postliberal in the sense of emerging out of the political culture of Western liberalism, yet it is not principally grounded in legalistic and rights traditions.

Furthermore, it does not share a rational-choice utility view of human agency or the progressive optimism of liberalism, modern market economics, and techno-neoliberalism. And when I speak of justice I am not simply talking about human justice—animals also have a sense of justice.

Here, I agree with Frans de Waal's and Marc Bekoff's empirical research findings, which indicate that many animals have a sense of justice as an inherent capability. While de Waal has discovered morality and justice in chimpanzees, bonobos, and capuchin monkeys, Bekoff has chronicled similar behaviors in wolves, dogs, coyotes, and hyenas. For de Waal, justice in animals manifests itself at three levels: (1) first-order fairness, (2) second-order fairness, and (3) universal community concern. Many animals have specific and immediate behavioral reactions to perceptions of inequity or unfairness. Second-order fairness, evident in great apes, involves the ability to have a general preference for fair outcomes. Third-order fairness, found only in humans, involves the ability to adopt a more universal, hypothetical, and impartial perspective guided by reflective, abstract reasoning.[54]

In *Wild Justice: The Moral Lives of Animals* (2009), Bekoff and the philosopher Jessica Pierce identify three "clusters" of moral motivations, dispositions, and behaviors ("a suite of interrelated other-regarding behaviors that cultivate and regulate complex interactions within social groups") that have been empirically evidenced in primates, wolves, coyotes, dogs, hyenas, elephants, dolphins, whales, corvids, mice, and rats.[55] They are the "cooperation cluster" (altruism, reciprocity, trust, punishment, and revenge), "empathy cluster" (sympathy, compassion, caring, helping, grieving, and consoling), and "justice cluster" (sense of fair play, sharing a desire for equity, expectations about what one deserves and how one ought to be treated, indignation, retribution, and spite).[56] The key "threshold requirement[s]" for animal morality are social complexity, neural complexity, and behavioral flexibility.[57] In addition, Bekoff and Pierce advance a "species-relative view of morality" in which norms of behavior vary across and within species.[58]

Bekoff distinguishes between morality and ethics. Animals have morality, while humans have morality and ethics, which is the reflective application of morality.[59] The source of animal morality lies in social emotions. These emotions are the product of biological and social evolution, of mammalian physiology and the expression and enforcement of social cooperation and group cohesion.[60] Bekoff's evidence comes from ethology studies of animals in the wild and captivity, experimental science, and recent breakthroughs in social neuroscience, which include the discovery of mirror neurons and spindle cells in apes, monkeys, whales, and birds that are integral in generating moral emotions and judgment.[61]

Bekoff advances a theory of animal "justice as fairness" that he discovered in his research with canids. Social play is the window into the world of animal justice.[62] Here, animals rehearse, reinforce, and learn species- and group-specific norms and social expectations. While justice is a human normative concept used to evaluate human behavior, it is evident in a host of animal behaviors—inequity aversion, social evaluation, indignation, forgiveness, punishment of noncooperative cheaters, role reversal, and self-handicapping.[63] Justice in animals is "a set of social rules and expectations that neutralize differences among individuals in an effort to maintain group harmony."[64] It varies depending on species type, group size, physical environment, group stability, and relationship longevity.[65] Bekoff also admits that animal justice is built on cooperation and empathy, is the most complex of animal behaviors, and remains the most suspect.[66] Most humans reject the idea of animal justice as anthropomorphic, yet for Bekoff, the real problem lies in the current state of human science and philosophy and their standards of measurement and understanding. The main impediment to animal studies is anthropocentrism.[67]

Nussbaum's attempt to push the "frontiers of justice" beyond the modern liberal social contract to include animals as subjects of justice represents an important chapter in the evolving narrative of justice for animals. Although her approach is neohumanist rather than posthumanist, and she has been criticized for her famous "list" of basic capabilities and idea of a "species norm," it values animals as subjects and agents and regards their desire to live their lives to the fullest of their capabilities as a fundamental question of justice. Despite her criticisms of traditional social contract theory (Hugo Grotius, Hobbes, Locke, Rousseau, Hume, Immanuel Kant) and Rawls (a mix of social contract theory, Kant, and rational choice theory), Nussbaum believes that the social contract tradition remains the strongest approach to justice.[68] Her dual innovation is to replace Rawls's Kant with Aristotle and frame the contract not as a thought experiment to legitimize an idealized sovereign social and political reality but as a biosocial reality in which social animals cooperate to flourish in accordance with their basic capabilities. An expanded neo-Aristotelian conception of "flourishing" (*eudaimonia*) applicable to all forms of life, not neo-Kantian personhood, social utility, or liberal rights, is the framework we should adopt in determining how animals fits into human society.[69]

All social animals are part of "social contracts" by virtue of their evolutionary capacities and adaptive tool kits for creating societies and communities to survive and thrive. Human beings engage in a secondary level of formal contracting to ensure social cooperation. To ensure our continued attachment to society, we must believe it is fair; otherwise, we have legitimate grounds to protest or exit. I am convinced by the available evidence that many animals conduct themselves in accordance with the biosocial contracts that evolution has endowed them with. Humans, as Aristotle surmises, use their capacities for abstract reason and symbolic speech (*logos*) to create political order (*polis*) and therefore are in his mind enhanced social or "political" animals (*zoon politikon*).

In most of the literature on animal philosophy and ethics, Aristotle is singled out as the "founding father" of Western anthropocentrism, biopolitics, and the human-animal distinction. Richard Sorabji argues that in defining morality in terms of the capacity to reason, speak, and deliberate, Aristotle lowers the moral status of animals and our duties toward them.[70] He credits animals with discriminating perception, cause-effect calculation, limited *phronesis*, intentional emotional states, and social cooperation, yet they cannot conceptualize, speak, reason, or believe; lack agency; cannot deliberate; cannot have or be friends; and have no sense of justice. At the same time, they are morally responsible for their behavior, because all acts, voluntary or involuntary, have consequences. And while they lack justice, they can wrong us. Gary Steiner notes that Aristotle's zoological writings (*History of Animals* and *Parts of Animals*) show more continuity between humans and animals, while his writings on human nature (*On the Soul*, *Nicomachean Ethics*, and *Politics*) place greater emphasis on identifying categorical distinctions. The result is an "uneasy tension between his commitment to the natural continuity between animals and human beings on the one hand, and his categorical exclusion of animals from the *polis* on the other."[71]

Catherine Osborne reads Aristotle as less explicit about whether humans are uniquely political. It is the Stoics who maintain a strong distinction between rational humans and irrational animals.[72] While animals lack intellect (abstract thought), intellect is but one faculty of reason. Aristotle regards *phantasia* or "purposive imagination" as a key animal attribute,[73] the ability to produce a mental image not immediate to the senses by drawing on the contents of memory. It is the animal equivalent of conceptual representation in humans. Purposive action does not require concepts, beliefs, or reflective judgment. It requires conscious attraction toward objects of desire, the means to access these entities, and the decision to acquire them. All of these capacities are enabled by *phantasia*. Animals, therefore, demonstrate a form of intentional agency, but they simply do it differently than humans due to evolution. While humans have the capacity to generate abstract representational concepts to manipulate their environments of action, nonhuman animals can generate particulars with greater concreteness and can generalize from repeated memories.

Larry Arnhart also reads Aristotle as more of a gradualist who believes that most animals are social and a few are political. Human beings are not uniquely political animals. What Aristotle means by *zoon politikon* is that humans are the *most* political of all animals.[74] For Aristotle, the "distinguishing characteristic of the political animals is they cooperate for some common work or function (*koinon ergon*)."[75] Insects such as ants, bees, and wasps, as well as cranes, monkeys, apes, and humans, all demonstrate complex social structures that promote "the common advantage of all its members."[76] Furthermore, many mammals and birds are capable of learning and, thus, of developing culture. In this sense, they are political. If one surveys the tradition of Western political thought, Augustine, Thomas Aquinas, Hobbes, Locke, and Immanuel Kant draw much stronger distinctions between humans and animals. In book II, chapter 17, of *Leviathan*, Hobbes details six reasons why humans and animals are fundamentally different: animals (1) lack reason, (2) lack "the art of words," (3) cannot distinguish good from evil, (4) lack the unique and more complex human passions, (5) cannot distinguish private from public life, and (6) cannot enter into covenants. The "agreements of these creatures" are natural, not artificial.[77]

Animals cannot enter into covenants in the manner humans do because they are not human. But this difference is not the critical issue, because they are already part of natural contracts, as are humans. The culture/nature and reason/instinct divides that have traditionally accompanied the human/animal divide in Western history are outdated social constructs. Nussbaum starts from the premise that as a biological fact and basic moral intuition, all sentient life-forms possess deep needs and abilities and the desire to fulfill them by pursuing their particular goods. This approach is expressed in her key concept of "life flourishing." Flourishing is more than Aristotle's idea of *eudaimonia*, or human happiness. It pertains to individual organisms, species, and the plurality of life-forms.[78] In this sense, flourishing is posthumanist. The inherent desire of all life to flourish carries with it the equally fundamental moral intuition that nonhuman animals are capable of and deserve a "dignified existence."[79] Justice in the larger sense, what Nussbaum calls "truly global justice," involves extending the modern social contract to include the "three unsolved problems of justice": (1) people with disabilities, (2) social cooperation beyond nation-state borders, and (3) justice for nonhuman animals.[80]

How then do we operationalize this life philosophy and ethics into a functioning theory of justice? Her starting point is to identify the basic capabilities that different animal species possess in accordance with their nature and environment that animate and structure their particular pursuit of the good. Nussbaum also acknowledges that all life, especially nonhuman life, operates within the biologically enabling and constraining forces and parameters of evolution and ecological processes. Competition and predation should be factored into assessing animal capabilities, flourishing, and coexistence.[81] Another key qualifier is that with humans, we focus on the individual as the bearer of the good and rights, but in the case of animals, the focus should be on species membership and arriving at a "species norm" as our benchmark in determining how different animals are to fit into the next social contract. While moral and political individualism is appropriate for humans, in keeping with the norms of liberal modernity, it is not the principal criterion of animal justice.[82] Different species' capabilities translate into different entitlements and protections. Nussbaum acknowledges that this methodology is anthropocentric and paternalistic, but this is unavoidable. Justice for animals is a form of human justice, and therefore the real challenge is balancing human sovereignty with species' flourishing.[83]

Yet how do we know the basic needs and wants of different animals? Nussbaum proposes that we arrive at a set of practical norms (*phronesis*) for understanding a species' capabilities and its conditions for flourishing that includes science and "sympathetic imagining."[84] Animals flourish and realize their goods by fulfilling their "species being." We need to draw on the best that science has to offer and our emotional resources of empathic identification to arrive at norms of justice. This process of evaluating an animal's species norm must take into account not only those capabilities central to flourishing but also the environment within which an animal lives.

Critics from Cary Wolfe to Steiner to Sue Donaldson to Will Kymlicka to Dinesh Joseph Wadiwel have questioned Nussbaum's species norm principle.[85] Can we really extend basic human capabilities to animals? Is this just another version of anthropocentric extensionism? Furthermore, how does one arrive at ten basic capabilities in the first place?[86] And is Nussbaum not a Rawlsian liberal after all, despite her incorporation of Aristotle into her social contact theory? Is her trans-species ideal of equal flourishing not undermined by the fact that she upholds individual rights and dignity for humans yet not for animals, which are protected at the species and not individual level according to "a high threshold of adequacy" not equality? Thus, in the end, we have a new model of animal welfarism. Also, what is "normal" for a species, and who decides? Norms are socially constructed and biopolitical—they are not simple biological or objective realities. Therefore, the question remains, who decides the species norm? Scientist bureaucrats and bioethicists, judges, animal welfarists, universal rights advocates, postmodernists, posthumanists, communitarians? And is not Nussbaum's goal of benevolent guardianship still a form of propertied ownership? Finally, while this theory may work with respect to wild species, can this norm really work for domestic or contact zone animals who live in highly mixed, interspecies communities?

Animals have a basic set of biosocial needs, capabilities to fulfill them, and a substantive good that animates their lives. We should seek to understand what these are, realize our biosocial connection to animals, and make our mutual coexistence and flourishing a moral and political priority. So, in this respect, Nussbaum's approach makes sense. However, extending a list of human capabilities to animals keeps us in the anthropocentric cage we should be freeing ourselves from. It is reasonable to assume that animals want to live, enjoy bodily health and integrity, have a sensory life and a social life, and have some control or adaptive relation to their environment. But not all animals have the capability to enjoy a rich and complex emotional life, exercise practical reason and imaginative thought, play, or have a life of diverse affiliations. Extending human capabilities to animals is largely an exercise in mammalcentrism. The animals Nussbaum is concerned about, as are most other animal studies thinkers and advocates, are largely our closest relatives.[87] Most animals, the majority of which are insects, have capabilities and conditions for flourishing that are largely alien to our sensibilities and understanding.

I have no problem with employing a species norm as part of a group of criteria. I also support understanding animal needs and wants through science and sympathetic imagination. Assessing the situation of an animal, however, requires more. One must understand its environmental circumstances, the biopolitical context that has shaped its current situation, its value and disposition as an individual organism, and its status as a member of a particular animal or *humanimal* community and participation in its culture. I would also add lifeworld experience to science and sympathetic imagination in ascertaining an animal's capabilities and the conditions it requires to flourish. People who spend a lifetime with certain animals often "know" them better than scientists, veterinarians, and other experts. Those species whose capabilities are more cognitively complex, social, cultural, and individualized, such as mammals and birds, should be treated as such. Yet for those species whose evolutionary makeup predisposes them to be part of a collective entity, a swarm, or a superorganism colony (most but not all invertebrates, which constitute the majority of animals), a more general species norm is appropriate.

What I am most concerned about is ending up with a rigid, hierarchical taxonomy linked to an official state biopolitics administered by panels of "animal experts" whose approach is narrowly scientistic, bureaucratic, and legalistic. This is what I fear that Nussbaum's species norm would become in practice. Her "threshold-based approach," which "focuses on adequacy rather than equality," would likely translate into standards that differ little from current legal standards of "humane" treatment and "unnecessary" suffering.[88] Flourishing would be reduced to adequate species sustenance, which would at best translate into zoolike conditions. Genuine flourishing for the vast majority of animals requires shrinking the human imprint on the planet, putting a moratorium on most development projects, ending the mass killing and slaughter of animals, creating more open spaces, building fewer fences, having fewer people, and respecting the desire to be left alone.

Justice as flourishing in a posthumanist world requires a different cluster of human species norms toward animals that take us beyond Nussbaum's extension of human capabilities, species norm principle, threshold of adequacy, and overlapping human consensus on what appropriate animal entitlements should be. Two key convictions shape my view of justice for animals. The first is that animals are members of our social contract by virtue of our mutual biosocial kinship and that, as fellow community members, they share with us the status of moral subjects and subjects of justice. The second is that by virtue of the historical injustices we have inflicted on animals, they are owed a debt. Justice is biosocial, ethical, and political. It is also historical. It is with this belief in mind that my idea of justice in a posthumanist world relies on six guiding principles that I call the "six Rs": (1) recognition, (2) reconciliation, (3) responsibility to intervene, (4) rehabilitation, (5) restitution, and (6) reinhabitation. These principles constitute a general political orientation toward animals—one, however, that is not mutual and reciprocal. It is asymmetrical, with the scales of justice tipped in favor of animals. We owe them more than they owe us.

Recognition and reconciliation are interrelated and represent a much-needed cultural shift away from long-established and now questioned anthropocentric traditions. This involves re-cognition, a reorientation of our cognitive maps in favor of posthumanist, coevolutionary thinking. Coupled with this shift is a movement toward ending our fundamental estrangement from animals. Reconciliation is a long process of healing our alienation from the realities of evolution and ecological processes as well as our relationships with animals. As a type of conflict resolution, it requires open dialogue and communication as well as honest and open fact gathering. Reconciliation is dependent on the revelation of not only facts but also motivations, intentions, and the consequences of actions. The great difficulty in translating recognition and reconciliation into public policy is the fact that government institutions are anthropocentric and dedicated to defending and serving human interests first. Thus, the level of human support for *humanimal* reconciliation would need to reach a significant level before traditional state agencies would act. A better approach lies with nongovernmental actors and the institutions of civil society taking the initiative in building the necessary communitarian infrastructure for political action.

Justice for animals also requires rehabilitation, which involves a process of restoring many species, populations, and individual animals to a better life and better place in the world. Rehabilitation includes physical, psychological, social, and habitat restoration. Intervention and confrontation in defense of animals is also part of justice in a posthumanist world. Animals can and do speak for themselves. They are capable of agency, yet they lack the power needed to give them a fair chance in a world of overwhelming human domination. The responsibility to intervene is similar in principle to the United Nations Security Council's doctrine of "responsibility to protect" (R2P), which holds that nation-state sovereignty is not absolute and that a state forfeits parts of its sovereignty if it fails to protect populations within its territory from mass atrocities and human rights violations.[89] The same principle holds with animals—nonviolent intervention and protection are preferred but are not categorical moral imperatives. Violence is justified in the defense of one's life, human and animal. With respect to protecting wild animals from genocide, poaching, and extinction, violence is justified as a reasonable course of action. Killing humans who are exterminating elephants, rhinos, apes, and other seriously endangered species is justifiable. Civil disobedience against the abuse of factory-farmed animals, research animals, and other captive animals is justified, depending on the context. At the personal level, if you are beating, torturing, or abusing an animal on your property in plain view, I will intervene and confront you.

Restitution is the most controversial and difficult challenge, for it legally implies a gains-based recovery. The defendant (human) gives up some of its gains to the claimant (animal). Compensatory damages imply a loss-based recovery. Here, we are talking more about reparations. In human rights law, reparations are part of a larger process of "transitional justice" that also includes truth seeking, public acknowledgment of past violations, apologies, possible prosecutions, and institutional reform. For "gross and systematic" violations of human rights and humanitarian law, the United Nations has established a five-stage framework: (1) restitution, (2) damages compensation, (3) rehabilitation, (4) satisfaction (truth seeking, sanctions, public apologies, commemoration), and (5) institutional reforms to protect against a recurrence of human rights violations.[90]

Finally, justice requires reinhabitation. To reinhabit is to seek out a place or habitat that has been altered and/or abandoned by humans and dwell there as an inhabitant. Reinhabitation goes hand in hand with habitat rehabilitation. It is a conscious attempt to restore a place that once flourished as a diverse ecosystem, bioregion, or community of life but was radically altered, damaged, and depopulated by human use, mining, deforestation, fire, drilling, agriculture, pollution, or urban collapse and downsizing. It also equally refers to animals' returning to habitat in recovery. Humans and animals reinhabit and learn to coexist and coevolve as they rehabilitate their mutual home.

Justice for animals also requires new technologies designed to make their lives better and to make human-animal relations low conflict and nonlethal. Animal-appropriate technology (AAT) is a neglected field that needs to be prioritized. We already have a number of AATs in use, ranging from new drugs and medical procedures to meat and dairy substitutes, global positioning system (GPS) tracking systems and smart collars, remote-control photography and video, magnetic fish SMART hooks, contraceptives, drones, and prosthetics for disabled animals. AATs are essential to postmodern farming. We need new and better synthetic meat products. We also need new scientific, medical, and cosmetic testing methods, such as growing human cells into simulated organs and creating more sophisticated computer simulations to eliminate animal use in research. Many animal experiments are poor predictors of how humans will react to a substance. Scientists a century from now will look back on much of modern animal experimentation as neomedieval science. If humans can harness the money, time, resources, ingenuity, and dedication to produce advanced weapons systems, nanorobots, smart phones, superskyscrapers, and missions to Pluto, then surely they can do the same for AATs.

Animal politics in the twenty-first century will likely take place along three fronts that will clash with greater intensity. Within the existing political-legal framework of our current social contract, a select group of human-like and human-loved species will be granted special legal rights, entitlements, and protections as a consequence of neohumanist extensionism. They will mostly be our closest relatives, rare and endangered species, and pets—great apes, pandas, elephants, big cats, dolphins, whales, dogs, and domestic cats. While this new neoanthropocentric regime takes hold to advance the rights of selected mammal species, two other fronts will come to the fore in response and as a result of their own internal dynamics—the agribusiness-industrial complex and posthumanist communitarianism. Animal businesses and consumers will continue to promote property, consumer, and carnivore rights in support of the current regime of animal products. Corporate economic power, government agencies, and cultural and advertising industries will redouble their efforts to portray animals as property and objects of consumption, defending the "free market" of animal goods and services. Liberal welfarists will continue to work toward reforming Big Ag through conventional interest-group politics, referenda, the courts, and organized boycotts.

Posthumanism places communitarian networks at the center of animal politics. This focus differs from identifying the principal locus of change in state bureaucracies, corporations, or interest-group and electoral politics; the legal realm of rights and regulatory law; the policy process; personal lifestyle transformation; or conventional animal advocacy organizations. Posthumanism does not reject these avenues of change, nor does it refuse to engage in these types of animal politics. Stronger legal protections; new conservation policies and practices; veganism; the creation of more rescues and sanctuaries; and the setting aside of more land, sea, and air space as protected habitats all have their place. Of the four spheres of late-modern society—the state sector, the market sector, the public sphere, and civil society, with its formal social institutions and informal networks—it is within the realm of civil society that the next social contract calls home. This is the primary social and political space where the posthumanist archipelago is most visibly anchored. In many respects, posthumanism in practice best lends itself to the world of the contact zone, in mixed communities where animals increasingly find themselves pushed into our homelands as we eliminate theirs. In an expanded sense of the term, the contact zone is ground zero of justice for animals in the twenty-first-century Anthropocene.

## The Next Social Contract: Zoopolis or Archipelago?

The most ambitious and comprehensive animal political theory to date is Donaldson and Kymlicka's neoliberal vision of a zoopolis. They agree with traditional animal rights theorists, such as Gary Francione, that by virtue of their conscious/sentient status as subjective "selves," animals are entitled to universal basic rights. At the same time, they disagree with the political translation of this principle in the form of negative (leave them alone) rights.[91] Their goal is to expand and modify the animal rights approach by instantiating immunity (negative liberties) and relational rights (positive liberties) within an expanded framework of citizenship and territorial sovereignty that makes the case for animals as political citizens. Three civic designations are submitted for inclusion in the social contract: (1) domesticated animal citizens, (2) contact zone denizen political subjects, and (3) wild sovereign communities. The bridge from polis to zoopolis lies in a "social membership" theory of citizenship that departs from the traditional liberal construct of citizens as autonomous rational subjects who deliberate, voluntarily consent to, and function within a formal contractual environment. Citizenship is defined as membership in a particular community shaped by shared territorial, social, cultural, and historical identities and recognized as a sovereign entity. Unlike universal rights cosmopolitanism, which lacks sufficient political grounding, citizenship rights are grounded in a substantive, sovereign, territorial community.[92]

What kind of citizens are animal citizens? They are participants in democratic agency and popular sovereignty. But how? Drawing on feminist, disability, children's, and human rights theory and law, Donaldson and Kymlicka develop a working model of relational, interdependent agency that fits the life circumstances of many humans and animals around the world. Domesticated animals exhibit a type of "dependent agency" defined as assisted, collaborative, and facilitative participation in their social world. They express themselves in forms of embodied, nonverbal communication that can be translated through a variety of enabling "trust" models of codependent, intersubjective action.[93] It is an anthropocentric prejudice to assume that animals do not have a sense of their own good, cannot communicate this good, do not comply with social norms, and do not have a sense of justice. Animals have agency and are participants in the communities they live in.[94] Thus, they can make legitimate claims to co-citizenship status and qualify for zoopolis membership.

Since citizenship is as much about identity, residency, community, and territoriality as it is about agency, consent, and rights, status is a function of three distinct types of human-animal relations—domestic, wild, and liminal. Domestics qualify as co-citizens with respect to agency capacities, identity, and territorial location. Wild animals occupy distinct territories where they "govern" in the sense that they live within the boundaries of established social structures; defend their territory from intruders; have a sense of "property"; recognize forms of authority within and between species communities; and have historical claims to the land, sea, and air they live in. Thus, they have reasonable claims to sovereignty rights. As for contact zone animals, they can make claims to co-residency but not to citizenship or sovereignty, since they have the weakest territorial, identity, and community claims.

Donaldson and Kymlicka make their case empirically, not simply as a theory, and in great detail. In the case of domestic animals, while they are unwilling to put forth a bill of rights and obligations, they come up with a list of "presuppositions of citizenship" needed to put domestic animals on the path to co-citizenship. The main issues that need to be renegotiated are (1) mutual resocialization into a much more "mixed human-animal political community" that does not rely simply on general species norms but on socialization "adaptable to individual and contextual factors," which implies more involved training and retraining;[95] (2) greater "freedom of movement and the sharing of public space," which means ending old ways of physical restraint ("crates and cages, fenced runs, chains, leashes, etc."), offering greater public access ("public spaces, businesses, beaches, parks, public transportation, or even city limits in the case of agricultural animals"), and establishing other "mobility rights";[96] (3) stronger laws and enforcement protecting animals against deliberate harm, negligence, killing, and predation by other animals;[97] (4) eliminating meat from our diet and placing greater restrictions on the use and commercialization of most animal products;[98] (5) eliminating animal labor exploitation yet allowing forms of nonexploitative animal labor;[99] (6) a right to health care and veterinary procedures;[100] (7) balancing greater autonomy regarding sex and reproduction with population control;[101] (8) shifting domestics to a vegan diet;[102] and (9) effective political representation in the form of official advocates, trustees, ombudsmen, constitutional changes, and formal political and bureaucratic offices and office holders.[103]

As for wild animals, we need to understand them as living in sovereign communities "whose relations to sovereign human communities should be regulated by norms of international justice."[104] While not dependent on humans to survive like domestics, they are vulnerable to human colonization and violence. Therefore, we have a dual obligation (negative and positive duties) to leave them alone and to intervene, protect, and assist, depending on the situation. The main issue is habitat loss and the right of wild animals to have control over their homeland territory. The appropriate model here should be "animal sovereignty" rather than "environmental stewardship." The sovereignty model is much stronger in that it stands for collective "self-regulation" within a "territorial-based community," while the stewardship model operating in most parks, refuges, and sanctuaries treats wild animals as dependent "wards of the state" and not independent agents and citizens.[105]

Emancipating animals from the straitjacket of globalized industrial modernity does not mean abandoning the political paradigm of modern sovereignty. We do, however, need to modify it by emphasizing higher "moral purposes" over "legal forms" and developing a set of hybrid legitimizing criteria that are part human and part nonhuman.[106] Sovereignty for animals does not require an "institutionally distinct legal order."[107] Wild animals already have a set of attributes that qualify them for sovereign status—identifiable territorial communities, social organizations, individual and collective agency, authority structures and norms, self-regulation, and an "interest in autonomy."[108] They "govern" themselves and have done so for hundreds, thousands, and millions of years. Thus, they should be recognized as having sovereignty rights to their historical communities. Animal sovereignty is defined as a secure, demarcated, and legally recognized space that protects "community autonomy" and "community flourishing" within a stateless, socially organized territory.[109]

Translating the ideal of wild animal sovereignty into political reality requires addressing questions of how territorial boundaries should be drawn and recognized as well as what "fair terms of cooperation" between human and animal sovereign communities would be. With respect to "fair allocation of territory," we need to start with the "facts on the ground," the occupied, territorialized, modern sovereign world as it exists, which includes "existing settlement and use patterns."[110] Our approach should also be "forward-looking." Historical injustices should be acknowledged, but they have been "superseded by circumstances," and therefore reparations and restitutive justice should not be the primary focus of wild animal sovereignty.[111] Donaldson and Kymlicka endorse a fourfold policy that has radical implications.[112] First, all habitats not currently settled or developed by humans should be legally designated as sovereign animal territory. Second, there should be a moratorium on human settlement and development that includes logging, mining, and grazing. Third, decolonization over time should be pursued, which includes phasing out large livestock farming, downsizing monocultural crop farming, and rewilding land and sea habitats. Fourth, there should be closer monitoring and control over human development and modernization practices. We need to build smarter and upward, not outward.

While animal sovereignty is a principle of territorial autonomy and protection from foreign aggression, it also includes a duty to assist and intervene. We should not intervene in the natural processes of predation and food cycles, but we have a duty to assist for the "greater good," in the case of such catastrophes as mass famines, poaching, and the protection of species facing extinction. Our interventions should ideally be small-scale and benign, but large-scale assistance is legitimate if needed.[113] The drawing of lines and boundaries should not be like that of a national park but rather should reflect "a more multilayered conception of sovereignty which can account for (a) ecological viability, (b) the multidimensionality of territory, (c) the facts of human and animal mobility, and (d) the possibilities for sustainable and cooperative parallel co-habitations."[114] Cooperation between sovereign human and animal communities should be defined in terms of fair risk assessment and distribution, which includes making the case that "the imposed risks are genuinely necessary to achieve some legitimated interest, and are proportional to that benefit," that the risks and benefits "are equitably shared overall," and that "society compensates, where possible, the victims of inadvertent harm."[115]

I agree with Donaldson and Kymlicka that animals—domestic, wild, and liminal—should be members of our social contract. Yet I conceptualize the next social contract in posthumanist terms, not as an extension of the modern liberal social contract. I also do not justify my idea of an archipelago in terms of modern sovereignty. And while I identify animals as co-citizens, I do not regard them as political citizens in a modern liberal sense. Social membership is crucial, yet the practical feasibility of realizing legal citizen status for domestic animals is so limited that it undermines the moral and political idea of animal citizenship by in effect narrowing the qualified applicants to a select few. I further disagree with the idea that domestic animals qualify for citizenship while contact zone animals are merely residents. I place denizens on equal par with domestics. They are not second-class citizens. Of the three civic designations, Donaldson and Kymlicka make the strongest case for the sovereignty of wild animals.

Donaldson and Kymlicka's idea of animal citizens includes all domesticated animals as long as they meet the criteria of liberal democratic agency and are adaptable with respect to their nine areas of human-animal relations. As a practical and political matter of implementation, I see a number of problems. While all domestic animals may be eligible, what we really are talking about are companion animals that are capable of being rights-bearing citizens and complying with their duties and responsibilities. This narrows down the field to primarily dogs, which make up most of the examples of animal citizenship. At the same time, owners of all kinds of exotic species as well as exotic pet businesses will lobby for special citizenship status for their deer, monkeys, parrots, kangaroos, camels, foxes, raccoons, chimpanzees, and even some reptiles. Interest groups will seek to redefine what a "domestic animal" is and propose a tiered classification system. The political result will likely be the establishment of a stratified order of animal citizens very similar to the one proposed by Steven Wise, which is based on a hierarchy of cognitive capacities and practical autonomy. This result takes us back to square one.

Dogs are the most likely candidates for co-citizenship. But what about cats? Donaldson and Kymlicka admit that they are a "unique challenge" and do not feel completely confident that cats would make good zoopolis citizens.[116] I agree, and this is, in part, why I like cats. They are highly independent, carnivorous, aggressive, and skillful predators; breed prolifically; and often vote with their feet, changing habitat and location (and therefore their status) from domestic to stray to feral and back. The line between domestic and liminal is often blurred. Cats are Foucaultian, dissenting citizens skilled at resistance politics. They are not liberal democratic citizens like many dogs. Cats have become the most populous companion and contact zone species. They outnumber dogs and therefore are the majoritarian species in the zoopolis.

Clare Palmer has identified two key issues that render cats a major challenge as domestic co-citizens—routine sterilization and outdoor access. Cats are "*not* reproductively self-regulating," and from an animal welfare position, they need to be spayed and neutered; otherwise, their numbers would overwhelm community capacity.[117] Donaldson and Kymlicka appeal to the civic responsibility of feline citizens. It is in their best interest and the community's to be part of a population-control program. Birth control is a minor individual harm that yields a greater community benefit. From a utilitarian as well as a communitarian perspective, this belief makes sense. But from a rights perspective, this belief is not sufficient. Donaldson and Kymlicka justify breeding management "if it is of benefit to future animals, and operates under conditions that respect the rights of the breeding pair (as to whether and when they mate)."[118]

Cats not only want to have sex and reproduce; they want the freedom to roam, to establish their territory, to investigate the world, and to hunt. Yet precisely because of their nature, it is the human norm to keep them confined indoors. Palmer rightly admits, "There are deep disagreements about what constitutes a 'good life' for a cat."[119] I would add this question is the case with many animals. From a human-centered, paternalistic, welfarist, pet perspective, many domestic cats are living a very good life, as well cared for as residents of five-star hotels. Most cats adjust to indoor confinement quite easily, so it is not a big problem. But from an animal citizen–rights and a species-flourishing perspective, they are living in a white-collar prison with several of their rights violated. As for their duties and responsibilities to a zoopolis, from the cats' perspective, they are good citizens doing what comes naturally to them.

Cats are a worthy challenge, and no simple model can accommodate them. I agree with Palmer that there cannot be "a universal prescription."[120] Donaldson and Kymlicka remind us that as citizens, cats, like other domestic animals, have negative and positive liberties, individual protections, and community responsibilities. Therefore, it is reasonable to balance their rights to sex, reproduction, and mobility with a biopolitics of population control. And with regard to their carnivorous nature and the dilemma of feeding them cat food produced by factory farms, cats should be put on a vegan diet.[121] Other animal rights advocates go further and recommend spaying and neutering all domestic and feral cats out of existence, which solves the problem over the long term.[122] There is no easy, simple solution. As a posthumanist communitarian, I view this issue as one in which the behavior of all community members is subject to a prudent mixture of protection and regulation and in which cats are one of many constituents in the community. This approach requires a pluralistic and negotiated balancing act that involves multiple individual lives and species, including humans. The problem, of course, is that humans are the final arbiters in most if not all of these decisions, unless we begin to view our relationship to animals as one of coevolutionary and communitarian mutual accommodation. Domestic, stray, or feral, cats are highly adaptable and in many cases willing to negotiate with humans the terms of their community membership. They are shrewd bargainers and in this sense seem to have an intuitive sense of the reality of the social contract.

The challenges faced by animal advocates in securing sovereignty for wild animals are similar to those faced today by existing hunter-gatherer, pastoralist, and traditional village-farming peoples in securing title to their aboriginal and historical homelands. These people have always lived outside or on the peripheral borderlands of modern sovereign territories and institutions. Their conceptions of home are not modern, and their habitats, like those of animals, are an archipelago of spaces, places, networks, and corridors that reflect the reality of historical social ecologies. Yet aboriginal peoples are increasingly making claims for customary rights of occupancy and access, which requires defining boundaries in terms of habitats that include networks, corridors, and buffer zones between human and animal neighbors. The result is an archipelago of overlapping territories that are part sovereign and part shared.

Donaldson and Kymlicka back off from devising a "detailed blueprint," "institutional mechanism," or "new scheme of representation."[123] Yet this is the most challenging aspect of wild animal sovereignty, because it requires confronting the reality of national and international politics and testing whether modern sovereignty can, in fact, be rehabilitated. What kinds of models and scenarios are we looking at? What is the current world order willing to accept? The general working model I propose reflects the values and purposes of posthumanist communitarianism, coevolution, and the archipelago. It endorses a confederal, horizontal form of sovereignty, not a vertical, federal, or unitary model typical of modern sovereignty. And what is "sovereign" in an animal community is not a particular species or social ecology but rather the entire interspecies community.

As a functioning entity, the posthumanist sovereign community would consist of several geographic zones. The core homeland would be the largest zone and off limits to humans, with the exception of a small cadre of monitoring observers with special clearance status. The core would be protected by natural barriers and armed patrols. A buffer zone would surround the core habitat and provide access to several corridors that would connect to allied homelands. These three zones—core, buffer, and corridors—would be near exclusively nonhuman sovereign spaces. A semiperiphery zone would consist of small communities of local inhabitants and reinhabitants pursuing sustainable agriculture. The outer periphery would consist of natural and human barriers as well as the corridors, which would allow animals to travel within and without their homeland. There would be no invasive tourism, but there could be some outer visitor observation areas. The goal is to build a more autonomous animal community, not a wildlife preserve, refuge, or park. Interventions would require a majority vote from three main groups—wildlife experts, local inhabitants, and specially selected animal advocates. What is needed is one pioneering attempt to take hold, and then I believe more would follow. It could be sponsored by a national government, by a transnational effort, through the United Nations, by a group of nongovernmental organizations, or as a public-private partnership. Ideally, it would be part of a new regionalism that distinguishes itself from the old nation-state sovereignty model and the new neoliberal corporate model.

Extending rights, citizenship, and territorial sovereignty to animals can be viewed as a retrofitting of the old modernity of the liberal democratic state and nation-state system that is out of step with the current world order. The world today is more globalized, postmodern, postliberal, transnationally corporate, and anthropocentric in its biopolitical control over life. Human sovereignty has taken on a new form and apparatus of rule, a globalized imperium with multiple national, regional, and transnational centers deploying their power within an overlapping elite consensus on the sovereign principle of imperial right.[124] Unable to fully break free of modern liberalism, Donaldson and Kymlicka's zoopolis ends up as a new form of liberal neocolonialism, with the planet as a global zoo. Even if this is not their intention, as a practical political outcome, this is what the current world order would likely sanction at best. Donaldson and Kymlicka admit that while modern Western societies have made some progress in passing stronger animal welfare measures, "global trends are truly catastrophic, dwarfing the modest victories achieved through animal welfare reforms, and there is no sign that these trends will change."[125] Thus we are faced with the sobering reality that the new world order has rendered liberal democracy a more limited, reactive, and peripheral force.

For Wadiwel, "the biopolitical nature of sovereignty" in the zoopolis "remains intact."[126] Territorial status is linked to sovereignty and citizenship. While the zoopolis strives to be an emancipatory biopolitics, it exerts sovereign population management. The sexuality, reproduction, and diet of domestics are controlled, wild animals conform to modern sovereign norms, and liminal animals have neither citizen nor sovereign rights, because they lack a clearly defined homeland territory and therefore are like refugees, migrant workers, and illegal immigrants. From a Foucaultian perspective, every new liberal right contains within it new forms of disciplinary and biopolitical power. The liberal zoopolis is a new model of modern biopolitics. For Wadiwel, the problem is human sovereignty itself. Rather than asking which animals should be granted sovereignty and citizenship rights, we should be asking why sovereignty should continue to exist in its modern form. We should call into question the legitimacy of the modern social contract. Not only is the contract based on historical and institutional violence against animals; it is also grounded in "epistemic violence":[127]

The injustice of our war on animals is that this presumption of sovereignty is always one-sided: humans are always in the position of declaring their own right to dominion, explicitly and implicitly, upon no established basis, and simultaneously denying any similar claim to those they exclude through this very declaration.[128]

I agree that we need a new social contract, yet at the same time, one cannot escape biopolitics. To be human is to live within a socially constructed world and institutional reality that is woven into the cultural evolutionary fabric of our species. We live within webs of biopower and structures of biopolitics. To deny biopolitics is to attempt the impossible feat of ontological and ethical autonomy and purity beyond the bounds of institutional reality. This utopian imperative usually ends up fostering a dystopian politics. We begin to believe in the complete dedomestication of animals, ending most human relations with animals and animal relations with humans, and long for a future vegan planet where predatory carnivorous species have become extinct and the biosphere is inhabited by herbivores.

The real question is, what kind of biopolitics? Wadiwel proposes a Foucaultian resistance strategy ("counter-conduct") and acts of "desertion" in the "war against animals."[129] This radical refusal of modern biopolitics is best exemplified in veganism as "a perfect example of a contemporary model of counter-conduct."[130] He also recommends a "day of truce," a twenty-four-hour cease-fire in the institutional machinery of animal production, killing, and processing to allow the world to reflect on the systemic violence inflicted on animals.[131] Even if it is an impossible task to achieve, attempting such an event would build stronger animal advocacy alliances and raise consciousness around the world. Surely as a Foucaultian, Wadiwel realizes that veganism is also a form of disciplinary power, with its own regime of ethical policing. In the war against animals, desertion, disarmament, and vegan conscientious objection are all worthy strategies. Wadiwel concludes, "Thus, I give up the spear!"[132] Perhaps we should also "take up arms" and join animals in their struggles to resist human domination. Perhaps we should "arm bears" so they can better defend themselves.

## The Posthumanist Archipelago

I envision the next social contract as an archipelago of *humanimal* households, niches, nodes, contact zones, enclaves, cultures, communities, social networks, corridors, and passages. An archipelago is a chain of islands neighboring a large landmass. The large mass of our time is late-modern civilization. The posthumanist archipelago is not conceived as a determinate collection of separate territorial islands. It is more decentralized, pluralistic, and network-based, a loose confederation of local and regional actor networks and spaces that serve as the principal mediums of social exchange and change. It is part vision, part empirical reality, and part work in progress. In defining my own particular nodal point in the archipelago and next social contract, I acknowledge the influence of the mutual aid and anarchocommunitarian vision of Petr Kropotkin, the bioregional reinhabitory ethos of poet Gary Snyder, and the ecocommunitarianism of Bill McKibben.

The archipelago exists on the periphery of late modernity. An alternative culture and society are best nurtured and defended on the periphery of the dominant civilizational order. I do not mean the physical periphery, although this is the case to some degree. One can be on the periphery of the dominant order of things while still living and working for its core institutions. Being on the periphery is part and parcel of taking one's stand with animals, which occupy a precarious dual existence. For the most part, animals are central to human civilization as objects of use yet on the periphery of this society in terms of value and existence. The idea of "the periphery" can also be used in a larger historical sense as it pertains to human social evolution. One of the lessons of human history is that while the core of civilization strives to accumulate as much power as it can, its imperial overextension and relative exhaustion are inevitable. The periphery over time develops the resources to outflank increasingly outmoded institutions.

In volume 1 of his three-volume work on human social evolution from the Neolithic to 1945, *The Sources of Social Power* (1986), historical sociologist Michael Mann offers a compelling explanation of how humans have evolved as a social animal. First, societies are best understood as "constituted of multiple overlapping and intersecting sociospatial networks of power."[133] Humans are social but not necessarily "societal animals."[134] We have no fundamental disposition to "create a society, a bounded and patterned social totality."[135] Social life is decentralized, flexible, and messy and functions within loosely connected actor networks. We tend to think of societies in terms of "clear, fixed, confined social and territorial boundaries" because of the way the state has been employed as a "social cage" to demarcate spaces of inclusion and exclusion.[136] Furthermore, human social and political evolution has been much more discontinuous, cyclical, and spatial than linear and progressive. History is not a developmental process where "each successive form of social cooperation emerged immanently from the potentialities of its predecessor toward 'higher,' or at least to more complex and powerful, social organization."[137] To the contrary, history consists of multiple cycles of evolution, devolution, and stasis.

One of his more provocative propositions is that the advent of civilization was an anomaly. Sustained, general social evolution occurred during the late Paleolithic and early Neolithic. During the Paleolithic, small band and larger tribal hunter-gatherer societies were established. During the Neolithic, pastoral and agricultural village societies emerged. These social formations occurred throughout the world, yet no general social evolution occurred beyond the early Neolithic. Attempts to create more hierarchical and permanent authority structures were rare and unsustainable. The centralized organization employed by Megalithic societies to erect monuments was temporary. For several thousand years, there was no movement toward civilization or state societies. Social evolution effectively stopped.[138]

The advent of civilization was a deviation from relative Neolithic social stasis. Mann rejects the standard account that civilization evolved in a gradual cumulative process across the world. Rather, it occurred in only a few places and in most instances as a reaction to problems unique to river valley societies. The earliest civilizations to emerge were Sumerian, Egyptian, Minoan, Indus, Chinese, Olmec, and Inca. Five of these were river valleys that faced problems of flooding and control over water and soil that accompany alluvial agriculture. Their responses involved the centralized construction of dikes, dams, and large-scale irrigation projects. Increased agricultural surpluses, trading networks, and populations resulted in a decentralized network of city-states.[139]

The big question is not the emergence of civilization but rather its persistence, its ability to become the dominant social formation for the past four thousand to five thousand years. "How did some acquire permanent power over the material life chances of others?" and "how did social authority become permanently lodged in centralized, monopolistic, coercive powers in territorially defined states?"[140] The answer lies in organized warfare. The origins of centralized rather than decentralized civilization lie in the military state, which was invented to defend against foreign attack and as an instrument of domination used by the victors to control resources, put the defeated to work, and put down revolts. The ancient military state over time became routinized and diversified to perform more pacific tasks and govern by forced consent or "compulsory cooperation."[141] The social contract was born.

A key driver of civilizational evolution is the tensional relationship that develops over time between a dominant core complex and its adjacent frontiers and hinterlands. Centralization/decentralization and core/periphery dynamics have been played out again and again throughout history. Two key defining features of state-centered civilizations are their social caging drive to contain and control more resources and territory and "the logistical impossibility of maintaining collective control over them."[142] Peripheral social networks resist, innovate, and outflank domineering core institutions, which ultimately slip into a pattern of imperial overreach. Civilizational core-periphery conflict sends into motion a new pattern of social evolution that is cyclical and developmental. Civilizational cores dominate, cage, and overextend. Peripheries resist, innovate, outflank, and often become the new cores.

A key defining feature of the posthumanist archipelago is pluralism, but not in the sense of either modern liberal or postmodern pluralism. Modern liberal pluralism envisions the geography of the modern *polis* empirically and normatively as a space of diverse human social and economic interests organized into interest groups that lobby governmental agencies. Organized interests compete within an arena whose structural dynamics ensure an equilibrium of power relations that underwrite and legitimize modern representative democracy. Of course, the reality of interest-group politics is a highly stratified power environment. Postmodern pluralism portrays the public sphere as a dynamic space where performances of identity and difference shape the terms of political engagement. The agonistic contest of diverse conceptions of the good and encounters with "Others" define the public sphere. This belief reflects a postmodern view of society as a world of multiple, overlapping, and intersecting social networks where individual and group identities are constructed.[143]

Posthumanist pluralism portrays the world as a geography of diverse habitats occupied by human and nonhuman actors. Social networks and group dynamics extend far beyond humans to other life-forms and are populated by diverse sentient life-forms capable of agency. In this respect, posthumanist pluralism is similar to actor-network theory (ANT).[144] Agency is a function of actor networks, which include humans, animals, and physical entities and processes. We often speak of organizational agency, because institutions take on the attributes of agentic behavior. Agency is the achievement of diverse interactions of humans, nonhuman life, and social machines. Its principal location is neither in discrete subjects nor objects but in networks that are material and semiotic rather than simply symbolic and discursive.

The next social contract also embraces what sociologist Hartmut Rosa refers to as a "politics of deceleration." This approach involves slowing down the fast-paced, mass-consumption way of life of late-modern capitalist technoculture. Slow living calls into question the belief that the "fast life" is the good life. In *Social Acceleration: A New Theory of Modernity* (2013), Rosa argues that we find ourselves today living in "acceleration societies," where social reality is continually "temporally reconstructed" in the interest of a fast-forwarding system.[145] One sees this evolution in technologically driven social change and in the daily pace of life. Social acceleration is driven by three different yet interrelated engines: (1) the economic motor that drives technology innovation, (2) the functional differentiation that drives social change, and (3) the "shortening" and increasing "scarcity of time resources" attributable to social-structural changes that have in turn radically altered "time horizons and expectations," resulting in a lifeworld defined in terms of an "unfulfilled life project."[146] Individuals are squeezed between the promise of infinite expectations and the reality of the disappearance of time, increased temporal imperatives, timelines, and deadlines. The result is heightened frustration and the difficulty of realizing any deep, identity-constituting projects.

The scope and rate of innovation and change, largely driven by digital and virtual technologies, result in a "contraction of the present" and continual redefinition of what is "contemporary."[147] The present shrinks culturally and structurally, becoming smaller and affecting horizons of individual expectations and decision making. This radical morphing of the present in turn leads us to redefine what the relevant past and future are. At the level of the individual lifeworld, accelerated life has objective and subjective components. Objectively, we increasingly operate on shorter time budgets. Subjectively, we experience a feeling of lost time, of being unable to keep up, and of lacking control over our temporal world.

Rosa identifies "islands" and "oases" of deceleration that provide a limited countervailing effect.[148] Many natural (geophysical and biological) limits to speed are in the process of being overcome by technology. Modernity by definition represents the aggressive re-engineering of nature by technology, yet built into the logic of acceleration are unintended side effects that slow things down, such as traffic jams, delays, and waiting times. Rosa also acknowledges "ideological decelerating movements" that are opposed to fast modernity, from neo-Luddites to deep ecology to slow-food and slow-life movements.[149] Most people develop strategies of "selective deceleration" in which they slow down aspects of their lives, keep parts of their lifeworlds on pace, and in some cases speed things up. Deceleration does not mean absolute rejection or dropping out but rather a commitment to holding greater control over one's lifeworld.[150]

The posthumanist archipelago is shaped by the desire to foster a culture of coevolutionary communitarianism. One of the earliest and best expressions of this ideal can be found in the thoughts of the Russian scientist and "anarchist prince" Kropotkin, in particular in his two masterpieces, *Mutual Aid* and *Fields, Factories and Workshops*. *Mutual Aid: A Factor in Evolution* (1902) was published as a compilation of articles Kropotkin wrote between 1890 and 1896 with the goal of correcting the "abuse of Darwin's terminology" and "popular misconceptions of the Darwinian theory" developed by social Darwinian, Hobbesian, and Nietzschean interpreters of Charles Darwin's original theory.[151] One of Kropotkin's main targets is Thomas H. Huxley's view of nature as "a gladiator's show" and "Hobbesian war of each against all."[152] As Stephen Jay Gould points out, while Kropotkin believes in natural selection, he finds glaring limitations in the theory and in "British Darwinism" as the cultural expression of the English national character. Kropotkin questions Malthusian population theory, Darwin's view of ecology, and the language of Darwinism, which reflected an urban-industrial, bourgeois individualist, and competitive England and the modern doctrines of liberalism and market economics.[153]

Darwin's main focus in *Origin* is on the competitive struggle between individual organisms for limited resources, especially within species. Kropotkin argues this focus is a reflection in both Darwin's work and that of Alfred Russel Wallace of their field experience and empirical evidence, which came largely from tropical ecosystems where numerous species inhabited dense environs. Darwin's view of ecosystems is crowded habitats saturated with species and organisms and with limited resources and space. Competitive struggle is a logical explanation. Yet in Kropotkin's experience, most of Russia was characterized by a "paucity of life—under-population—not over-population" and more extreme environmental conditions.[154] Furthermore, it was neither urban-industrial nor culturally individualistic. Kropotkin spent time in eastern Siberia and northern Manchuria from 1862 to 1866 as a military officer, government bureaucrat, and scientist conducting research in geography, geology, and zoology. His research findings indicated that organisms and species primarily struggle against their physical environmental circumstances and secondarily against members of their own species. Living things search for and/or construct niches that reduce competition and enhance coexistence.

Kropotkin's theory of mutual aid as a central factor in biological and human sociocultural evolution takes the form of three main arguments:

1. In *Origin*, Darwin overemphasizes and overgeneralizes natural selection as one of competitive struggle between individual organisms for limited resources (especially within species), employing such phrases as "the struggle for existence" and "survival of the fittest" as well as Malthusian population theory. To the contrary, evolutionary struggle primarily occurs in organisms and species adapting to their physical environments and to a much lesser degree as one-on-one struggles against members of their own species or societies.

2. Evolutionists have underestimated the relevance of Darwin's insights in *The Descent of Man*. Here, he argues that social cooperation is the key to the development of higher intellectual and moral faculties in animals. Yet we need to widen Darwin's theory

of social cooperation as the key to evolutionary adaptation. Mutual aid occurs at all levels of life, not merely among "higher" evolved mammal and bird species. Also "no progressive evolution of the species can be based upon such periods of keen competition."[155]

3. The Hobbesian/social Darwinian view of human nature and history—that without authority and sovereign, centralized institutions of coercion humans would resort to "savagery" and war, and that morality is the creation and cultural overlay of civilized existence—is an inaccurate representation of the facts of nature as well as human prehistory and history.

Kropotkin justifies these propositions with reference to a rich array of empirical evidence from biology, zoology, archaeology, paleontology, anthropology, history, and political sociology. He documents the wide range of social cooperation among invertebrates, especially eusocial ants, termites, and bees, and the diverse hunting, fishing, and mutual defense associations among more solitary and small family-oriented species, such as big cats and birds of prey.[156] He also identifies only a very small number of truly unsocial species, such as tigers, bears, wolverines, and weasels. And even here, he argues that part of this behavior has to do with human predation and habitat alteration. Human evolutionary pressures and extermination practices have to a significant degree shaped their now-solitary existence.[157]

Combining an ambitious vision with erudite scholarship, Kropotkin develops an alternative account of human sociocultural evolution that places mutual-aid institutions and cultural practices center stage and that also contradicts modern bourgeois European anthropology and historiography. He examines available Paleolithic and Neolithic archaeological evidence as well as anthropological and ethnographic accounts of "primitive" aboriginal peoples and develops two themes: (1) the centrality of the social unit of the tribe in the lives of precivilized humans and (2) the misunderstood and underestimated complexity of tribal social organization and the highly developed nature of tribal morality. *Homo sapiens* "did not begin its life in the shape of small isolated families" but in "societies, bands, or tribes."[158] The family, "far from being a primitive form of organization," is "a very late product of human evolution."[159] Paleolithic and Neolithic habitation "stations" reveal "numberless" concentrated quantities of stone tools, flint implements, spear points, pottery, and workshops of tool production.[160]

Unlike modern "state of nature" scenarios, early humans were not rational choice, self-maximizing individualists or private propertarians, nor did they live in solitary nobility. One identified one's "own existence with that of his tribe," and "each of their acts, however insignificant, was considered a tribal affair."[161] The "idea of the clan is always present in his mind, and self-restriction and self-sacrifice in the interest of the clan are of daily occurrence."[162] Kropotkin lambasts "West European men of science" and "moral Europeans" on their superficial understandings and bigoted characterizations of the "savage's conception of justice," "infanticide," "parricide," "blood revenge," and "head-hunting."[163] All are evolutionary adaptations to preserve the tribe that furthermore can be found in modern society in more violent forms. Modern Europeans "have in some measure extended [their] ideas of solidarity—in theory, at least—over the nation, and partly over other nations as well," yet they "have lessened the bonds of solidarity within [their] own nations, and even within [their] own families."[164]

Kropotkin's historical reconstruction of Western civilization focuses on three mutual-aid institutions: (1) the Germanic village community of late antiquity, which replaced the collapsed institutions of the Western Roman Empire and formed the foundation of medieval feudalism; (2) the free medieval city of the High Middle Ages, with its guilds, universities, and self-governing institutions; and (3) modern industrial labor unions.[165] A proper and balanced history of the West should focus on its "two dominant currents"—"the self-assertion of the individual or groups of individuals, in their struggle for superiority" and "mutual aid."[166] The focus of most historians and philosophers has been on the former current, yet the latter current is what most people rely on as "the necessary foundation of every-day life."[167]

In *Fields, Factories and Workshops, or, Industry Combined with Agriculture and Brain Work with Manual Work* (1898), Kropotkin works out his model of anarchocommunitarianism in great statistical and empirical detail (the book includes twenty-five appendices). It is a vision of cooperative communities capable of integrating smaller-scale agriculture and industry, manual and mental work, and science and traditional handicrafts. Kropotkin likens this vision to a modern reinvention of the free towns and cities of the High Middle Ages. He detects a trend in industrial globalization whereby nations are moving toward greater internal diversification and production for their consumer markets, not simply for the world market. He believes that "each region will become its own producer and its own consumer of manufactured goods."[168] Second, scientific and technical knowledge is becoming more decentralized.[169] Kropotkin believes the era of electricity and electric-powered machinery will facilitate a more decentralized industrial base and economy. Third, the focus on industrialization has resulted in the neglect of agriculture and the estrangement of agriculture and industry, rural and city life.[170] Yet he is optimistic about innovations in agriculture occurring at the local level.

Kropotkin documents "the possibilities of agriculture" in his detailed analysis of experimental farms, intensive agriculture, market gardening, raised-bed gardening, horticultural research, and intensive fields integrated with local industries. He cites example after example of how small and medium-sized farms, orchards, and gardens dedicated to intensive methods outproduce large "mammoth farms."[171] Iowa small and medium-sized farms hold their own with Great Plains and Far West farms in America.[172] Belgium and Denmark are more productive agriculturally than other European nations.[173] He cites the prevalence of "glasshouse culture" (greenhouses) and urban market gardening.[174] Kropotkin notes the great strides in agricultural innovation and yields taking place in densely populated urban areas. He concludes that the future of agriculture lies neither in small family farms of one to five acres nor in vast corporate farms but rather in mid-sized one-hundred-acre to two-hundred-acre farms organized in a more cooperative fashion and more integrated with local industries and artisan workshops.[175]

As an alternative to the industrial capitalism of his day—one of big cities, big factories, big agriculture, a specialized and segmented division of labor, low-skill proletarians as extensions of machines, and export-oriented imperialist nation-states—Kropotkin proposes the parallel development of associational agricultural-industrial villages or "garden cities."[176] Their main features would include intensive horticulture and market gardening; smaller-scale shops, businesses, and factories; skilled craftsmen and apprentices; community gardens and workshops; and craft and household production oriented toward community needs and local economies. The goal is better balance and integration of agricultural and industrial labor, manual and brain work, science and handicraft, urban and rural life. He admits that "oceanic steamers cannot be built in village factories," but "our big factories are nothing else but agglomerations under a common management of several distinct industries."[177] Today, many large structures (i.e., new skyscrapers) are being manufactured in several component-part industries and assembled on the spot. Kropotkin also wants to empower the common worker with "integral education," which combines a general scientific education with a hands-on technical education.[178]

His ultimate ideal is a community of worker-farmer-citizens who aspire to integrate and balance industrial work, farming and gardening, civic activity, and leisure. All workers and families should have a small plot of land as well as access to community gardens and workshops. He refers to this structure as the "social economy" and distinguishes it from modern political economy with its highly specialized division of labor, which translates into a highly segmented social life.[179] Kropotkin's vision would not come to pass in his day. Corporate capitalism and the state would join forces to institute and monopolize mass production, distribution, and consumption economies of scale. Yet his communitarian ideal is more promising today, as people seek out smaller "green" cities and "town-country" living.

Another coevolutionary communitarian is the poet and essayist Gary Snyder, whose way of life combines East Asian and Native American culture, Zen Buddhist practices, deep ecology, upper Paleolithic studies, and back-country reinhabitation. One of Snyder's most-often-cited statements is: "As a poet I hold the most archaic values on earth. They go back to the upper Paleolithic: the fertility of the soil, the magic of animals, the power-vision in solitude, the terrifying initiation and rebirth, the love and ecstasy of the dance, the common work of the tribe."[180] He advocates reconnection to place informed by a bioregional ethos, research into the depth ecology and evolu-tionary history of one's habitat, and the restoration of native environs. Snyder implores us to learn everything about our habitats and neighbors, recognizing that they are not simply human. The human world is a surface community, the tip of the iceberg. Our real community consists of all the animals, trees, plants, rivers, mountains, watersheds, geology, and processes of evolution of our bioregions. This constitutes "the practice of the wild."[181]

Snyder employs the term "reinhabitation" in a twofold sense. It refers to not only those "persons who come out of industrial societies (having collected or squandered the fruits of eight thousand years of civilization) and then start to turn back to the land, back to place" but also those "actual inhabitants—peasants, paisanos, paysan, peoples of the land" who have developed "local ecosystem habitation styles."[182] To become "reinhabitory," one not only com-mits to a place and develops "a direct sense of relation to the "land" but also makes "common cause" with the actual inhabitants of the land, which include animals and plants.[183] Snyder's preferred place of reinhabitation is the back-country, land that is typically undeveloped, not easily accessible to the public, and in need of rehabilitation due to human exploitation. Snyder defines the posthumanist archipelago in terms of "bioregions" and "watersheds."[184] A bio-region is a geographic area that shares a similar topography, plant and animal life, and human culture and history organized around watersheds.

Snyder's home state of California consists of six distinct bioregions—the central coast from Point Mugu to Monterey Bay, the great Central Valley, the Sierra Nevada, the Modoc plateau and volcano country in the northeast cor-ner, the northern coast Klamath region up to Trinidad Head, and in the "coastal valleys and mountains south of the Tehachapis, with natural connec-tions onto into Baja."[185] He redefines citizenship in terms of bioregional iden-tity. Snyder considers himself a citizen of Turtle Island (the Native American name for North America) and the Sierra Nevada bioregion.[186] The appropriate economic and political unit becomes that of "the watershed/bioregion/ city-state model," not the modern nation-state.[187] I consider Snyder's management of his one-hundred-acre homestead in the wilderness of the Sierra foothills to be an instructive model of contact zone applied ethics.

Bill McKibben believes that the era of centralized modernity—big bureaucracies, transnational corporations, and megamachine technological projects—is in its twilight. While old modernity did a lot of good, it also did a lot of damage, especially to the planet and its living inhabitants. It is not that modernity failed per se; rather, it succeeded too well, and its global religion of aggressive growth economics and individualistic high consumption has become more destructive than creative. The reality of contemporary capitalism is less that of Adam Smith and John Maynard Keynes and more Thorstein Veblen's conspicuous consumption on steroids, which is not sustainable. As an alternative to neoliberalism, McKibben proposes that we strengthen the "deep economy" of local communities and their social ecology, social capital, and sustainable economic infrastructures.[188] We need to "back off," "hunker down," "dig in," and build new communities that will serve as small-scale pilot projects for a new model of civilization.[189]

Our top priority should be reconstruction, which requires strategic dispersal rather than greater centralized concentration. The era of Hamiltonian "big-money, big-government schemes" should yield to a more neo-Jeffersonian approach. We have been left "with a big national government and smaller national purposes."[190] Hypermodernity, which is a form of culturally adolescent bigger-is-better thinking, needs to be replaced with a politics of maturity. In the aftermath of "a long period of frenetic growth, we're suddenly older."[191] We should start acting our age. To fully emphasize the scope of the changes we face, McKibben no longer refers to our planet as Earth but rather as "Eaarth." We are currently living in the early period of "a tough new planet."[192] This new Eaarth is the Anthropocene.

Big Agriculture and Big Energy are our biggest roadblocks. McKibben argues that Big Ag has peaked and, with global warming intensifying, has entered a vicious cycle from which it is unlikely to prevail. Hotter temperatures, larger and longer drought zones, and more extreme weather translate into more crop damage, a greater number of more resilient insects, and weaker and smaller crop yields with lower protein and iron content.[193] More energy, more chemical fertilizers, more genetically modified organisms (GMOs), and more corporate centralization and control (i.e., Monsanto) will be needed to keep Big Ag going, which will in turn favor cheaper, dirtier, bigger, corporate-controlled energy sources—oil, coal, and fracked natural gas. Big

Ag, Big Fossil Fuel, and Big Mining form a triumvirate of late-modern dinosaur economics. They have turned rural America into a vast, neofeudal landscape under the dominion of corporate overlords, federal agencies and agents, and the petty fiefdoms of small-town mayors and county commissioners.

McKibben's alternative is a form of postmodern farming that combines the smaller organic model with new high-tech and permaculture methods.[194] We need an agriculture that is more intensive, more people-oriented, environmentally lighter, and more integrated into community and household life; that cares more about animals; and that is more local and regional than world market–oriented. We need a part-time farmers' movement, more community organic gardens, and more farmers markets. We also need to change our diets from high meat and processed food to more vegetarian and locavore. By reducing our reliance on the middlemen in Big Ag—transportation, storage, advertising, special packaging, big supermarkets—through communitarian networks, we could end up with better-quality foods at comparatively cheaper prices, better health, less animal agriculture controlled by concentrated animal feeding operations (CAFOs), animals being more integrated into our communities, and a better environment.[195]

Moving beyond Big Ag is currently underway at the local community level. Moving beyond Big Energy is a greater challenge. McKibben is not an advocate of replacing big, corporate fossil fuels with big, corporate renewable energy (giant wind and solar farms), yet this direction is where we are headed. A community-based model would feature microgrids and "distributed energy" that the average individual would have access to. As costs come down, small-scale solar and wind generation as well as home battery systems will become more feasible and simpler to set up by average citizens. While admitting that the trend is toward more fossil fuels and nuclear energy as well as big corporate green energy, he sides with community-based models of distributed renewable energy.[196]

The call for a return to local, small, self-sufficient, democratic communities and a slower life is the classic Rousseauian solution to the Leviathan of modernity. Yet this path can easily lead to our being cut off from modernity and result in a bunker survivalist mentality, Ludditism, group conformity, and cultural stultification. In McKibben's mind, the Internet saves us from a neofeudal and New Age social regression. Digital technology and worldwide Web culture, with its decentralized, populist-based information sharing and solutions, create a condition of "glocality." This high-tech interconnection of the local and global "can wean us into the next world."[197] The goal here is not antimodernity but a transition away from big modernity toward a more postmodern communitarianism.

Some, likely many, will argue that Kropotkin's vision of industrial-agrarian, mutual-aid villages; Snyder's deep-ecology, reinhabitory communitarianism; and McKibben's deep-economy ecocommunitarianism are romantic and fringe attempts to make a radical break with modernity. This is a fair criticism. Neo-Hobbesian modernity is alive and well and will be well into the future. These alternative models are key nodal points in the archipelago, but they are not complete replacements for modernity. They are parallel institutions and cultures. The social-contract-as-archipelago model approaches the issue of habitation and community from a posthumanist perspective. The central question is what the best model is for human-animal coexistence and coevolution in the time of the Anthropocene. What is best for animals living with and among humans in late-modern/postmodern times? It is not what the best social contract is for humans that treats animals as second-class citizens.

Posthumanist communitarianism has no illusions of replacing large-scale global bureaucratic and corporate institutions and systems with bioregional communities. It rather represents an alternative that limits our dependence on late modernity and offers a buffer zone to help protect us from aggressive techno-neoliberalism. Decentralized networks capable of providing resources and social capital serve as checks and balances on resource streams controlled by bureaucratic and corporate systems. With respect to food, there is no comparison in taste and quality between well-grown local fruits, vegetables, and eggs and supermarket produce. Modern systems of resource allocation and expertise continue to be accessed but are filtered through posthumanist networks to help ensure that they are the means and not ends of *humanimal* relations.

One can see today the growing signs of the next social contract in a number of social trends. Veganism is growing among millennials and generation Z, while the hobby-farm movement is growing among baby boomers and retirees. Many nouveau farmers maintain a homestead and microecosystem that embodies sustainable agriculture, land stewardship, and animal welfare. A postmodern microfarm typically consists of vegetable, berry, and forest gardens; a mini-orchard of fruit trees; chickens; a few goats; bioswales and "hugel" (mound) garden beds; solar panels; a greenhouse; and woodlands where contact zone animals can feel safe. Postmodern farming is not a replay of the 1970s back-to-the-land movement, which embraced voluntary primitivism, communalism, and living off the grid. It is more an exurban communitarianism that combines appropriate technologies, renewable energy, digital connectivity, and land reclamation. Postmodern homesteads also serve as safe havens for contact zone animals, complete with signs such as "Animals welcome, humans by appointment only."

One of the great challenges faced by posthumanist communitarianism is the role of domestic animals in mixed *humanimal* communities as co-laborers working with humans. Can there be such a thing as nonexploitative, cooperative domestic animal work? This is also closely tied to the issue of the use of animal products not only for private household and community consumption but also as a commercial economic resource. Most domestic animals have been bred to work for humans. The problem is that they mainly have been bred to work for us as slaves, not alongside us as companions, co-laborers, and fellow community members. While at some point in the future we may embark on the phased dedomestication of animals, in the short term, we should redomesticate them to take on different roles as members of our communities. How we do this and where we draw lines in terms of exploitative and nonexploitative labor are functions of politics. And the "we" is a function of community, of which animals are community members.

There is the need for a debate on what nonexploitative, cooperative human-animal labor would look like. This definition would develop in tandem with an animal labor politics that compares and contrasts the working conditions of animals; their working relations with humans; whether the work is truly cooperative or exploitative, mutually rewarding or instrumental; and which social experiments have succeeded and which have failed. This evaluation already occurs in the world of pets and farm animals. The difference is that it is largely one-sided and weighed in human terms. The debate on cooperative human-animal labor should be framed by a more posthumanist and communitarian approach.

The fact that individual households and communitarian networks work with animals in diverse ways using different models and norms in effect creates a communications network and political dynamic throughout the archipelago that allows for information sharing and, I hope, fosters better labor relations and a more equitable division of labor between humans and animals. With continued advances in AATs, the need for animal labor will be further reduced. However, even in the absence of necessary labor, many domesticated animals and humans enjoy working with each other as much as they enjoy playing with each other. While we have bred them to behave as compliant laborers, nonetheless many animals find great emotional satisfaction in a variety of working behaviors, such as guarding, herding, tracking, retrieving, riding, competing, rescuing, alerting, and assisting.

Donaldson and Kymlicka address the question of what nonexploitative relations between human and farmed animals might look like outside the model of industrial farming in their article "Farmed Animal Sanctuaries: The Heart of the Movement?" They develop the idea of intentional interspecies communities (IICs) and contrast it with the current model of farm animal sanctuaries (FASes). The sanctuary movement has been touted by many animal advocates as paving the way toward the creation of new interspecies societies. Animal sanctuaries include a variety of models, missions, and community members ranging from rescued farm animals to working animal rescue and rehabilitation centers to feral animal communities, wild animal rehabilitation centers, exotic animal refuges, laboratory animal sanctuaries, and companion animal rescues.

Donaldson and Kymlicka's central thesis is that in their present form, animal sanctuaries do not represent the best model for moving to the next phase of the animal advocacy movement, which is building new, more integrated, nonexploitative human-animal communities. They identify several problems that render the current animal sanctuary model limited (a) as an advocacy model of animal liberation; (b) institutionally as a permanent, "forever home" for rescued, abandoned, and abused farm animals; and (c) as a bridging model toward creating new mixed, interspecies communities.[198] They conclude that animal sanctuaries are neither "the heart of the (animal advocacy) movement" nor the model of the future. I largely agree with their assessment and am particularly supportive of how their vision of creating intentional interspecies communities moves beyond the animal rights liberalism of their original zoopolis model toward a more communitarian outlook on the future of human-animal relations.

As an advocacy model, they question the "visitor experience" that typifies many public animal sanctuaries.[199] Guests, mostly urbanites and suburbanites, visit a rural traditional family farm setting; are given a tour complete with a sobering presentation of factory farming and a strong pro-vegan message; and are encouraged to become part of the sanctuary "family" as donors, volunteers, and advocates. The goal is individual conversion to animal rights veganism. Donaldson and Kymlicka question the idealized family farm versus factory farm frame, which presents a narrow and somewhat simplistic view of the plight of animals today; the way animals are presented as more like members of a zoo than an animal community; the identification of universal veganism as the benchmark of ethical legitimacy; and the overemphasis on individual change, which tends to downplay or ignore the larger political-institutional challenges of animal politics as well as the communitarian alternative.

At the institutional level, sanctuaries resemble "total institutions" and operate more like retirement homes, disabled veterans homes, homeless shelters, orphanages, and asylums.[200] The care is highly paternalistic; the animals are sequestered and segregated; there is a ban on reproduction; there is little "freedom of association" among individuals as well as species, little real inter-species community life, and little attempt to integrate the farm with the surrounding ecosystem; and everyday life tends to be boring, with opportunities to socialize, play, work, and roam very limited.[201] Any type of "work" or "useful" activity is regarded as exploitation. Donaldson and Kymlicka stress the importance of "physical accomplishment" and cooperative activity in the lives of domestic animals as being part of their biosocial good. They are highly social and curious, and they often enjoy participating in group activities.[202] They conclude that the animals tend to suffer from excessive paternalism, limited rights, and diminished opportunities.

They also contrast the core operating principles and ethical commitments of many farm sanctuaries with their own principles of an animal community. Sanctuary goals include providing "a safe, healing environment," "support for species-typical flourishing," "recognition of individuality," "non-exploitation," "non-perpetuation," and "awareness and advocacy" with animals as "public ambassadors."[203] Donaldson and Kymlicka's principles include "belonging" (a more integrated, interspecies community), "absence of fixed hierarchical relationships" (social relations more "multiple, fluid, and egalitarian" and less guardian-ward), "self-determination" (not confining animals to "pre-determined roles or conceptions of well-being" and allowing them to explore their own "individualized script"), "citizenship" (animals as participatory agents involved in human-animal shared decision making), "dependent agency" (animal agency "enacted through relationship with others who are responsive to what they communicate about their needs and desires"), and "scaffolded choices and reconfigured spaces" (starting with the basics and building toward greater animal empowerment).[204]

The idea of an intentional community involves a small group of people who deliberately come together to "found" a specific goal-oriented community, engage in social experimentation, and foster a transitional social alternative to mainstream society that can be sustained multigenerationally. This type of community is reminiscent of those intentional "utopian" communities—Shaker villages, New Harmony, Oneida, Amana, Aurora—established as a result of the western pioneering movement in nineteenth-century America. Donaldson and Kymlicka focus on modeling their ideal on examples of disability communities.[205] Ideally, the IIC should be on the periphery of mainstream society but not cut off from it. It should have a sufficient bounded space of experimentation yet be socially and economically connected to the region and maintain a "creative tension" with modern society.[206]

The idea of developing communities whose main focus is nurturing mixed human-animal cooperative societies that can grow spatially and temporally fits my ideas of posthumanist communitarianism, coevolutionary ethics, and the archipelago. My main reservation with Donaldson and Kymlicka's approach is that it relies too much on viewing domestic animals as dependent agents that resemble people with disabilities. Animals, even domestics, should not be conceptualized and classified as analogous to people with cognitive or severe intellectual disabilities (SIDs). This also goes for liminal animals, which should not be viewed as illegal immigrants, migrants, or resident aliens. This kind of neohumanist projection does not capture what animals are. They are agents, but they are not dependent agents any more than any human being is dependent in part on others. Animals may require the help of humans in functioning and participating in human-designed communities, but so do most humans. All agency, human and animal, is varying degrees of interdependent agency.

I would add that existing towns and cities can also move in the direction of declaring themselves to be "animal sanctuary cities" as an exercise in democratic animal politics. They could put local laws, policies, and social norms in place that ensure greater protections for all domestic, contact zone, and wild animals; establish more open and wild spaces and buffer zones for animals; move toward no-kill shelters; establish broader, more community-based sanctuaries and rescues; require nonlethal methods in dealing with human-animal problems; establish more safety corridors for animal travel; lower speed limits; and establish collaborative networks with other sanctuary cities.

Where do contact zone and wild animals fit into the posthumanist archipelago? As mentioned in this and previous chapters, posthumanist communitarianism prioritizes the contact zone as ground zero of the Anthropocene biopolitics. I believe it is the largest and fastest-growing realm of *humanimal* relations. It is also the most misunderstood, underappreciated, undervalued, and undertheorized realm of animal ethics and politics. And it is sustained largely by informal networks. In many ways, it best represents the archipelago model. It is where everyday residents, human and animal, of urban, suburban, exurban, sprawl, and rural habitats work out relations of coexistence. It is where neighbors, government authorities, and civic associations interact, clash, negotiate, and compromise.

And where do wild animals fit into the next social contract? Here, bioregionalism, reinhabitation, rewilding, assisted migration and colonization, and sovereign animal communities all take center stage. Developed in the 1990s, rewilding is a conservation model designed to remedy the serious problems of wild habitat and biodiversity loss, ecosystem destabilization and fragmentation, and species extinction by deploying three interrelated strategies referred to as "cores, corridors, and carnivores."[207] The first goal is the greater protection and restoration of core wilderness areas by expanding the size and number of national parks and wildlife refuges. Second, protected corridors (a natural freeway system) need to be developed to connect core wilderness areas. These corridors would enable animals with larger ranges and migratory routes to travel more freely from human interference and connect isolated habitats to core areas. Finally, some damaged predator-prey relations must be restored to keep ecosystems healthy and sustainable. Another strategy involves "assisted colonization" "or "managed relocation." Plant and animal species that have been pushed out of their habitats by human development and climate change and are slow adapters are helped to gradually move to viable adjacent ranges and habitats.[208]

Rewilding can also be applied to humans in the form of bioregional reinhabitation. It is a conscious attempt to seek out animal habitats, reinhabit the land, and build coevolutionary communities. One can think of the posthumanist vision as a constellation of networks and nodal points consisting of diverse habitat/plant/animal/human assemblages. Bioregions and watersheds range across urban, suburban, rural, backcountry, and wild landscapes. The posthumanist archipelago is not simply a "back to the land" movement or a form of neorural utopianism; it is an urban and suburban phenomenon as well. The development of neourban prairies, farmlands, community gardens, and wildlife habitats is also part of the posthumanist biopolitical contract, as are diverse suburban habitats and contact zones.[209]

Jamie Lorimer contends that our rewilding policies and experiments in the twenty-first century need to be much wilder. Despite its limitations as "a young and immature concept," "terminological deficiencies," and "awkward genesis," the "diagnosis of the Anthropocene is revolutionary" and "shocking," especially for the future of planetary wildlife.[210] To mitigate this looming tsunami in terms of public policy (especially conservation policy), we are going to need a bold and radical biopolitics—"a *cosmopolitics for wildlife*."[211] Lorimer's biopolitical agenda shares common ground with posthumanist ethics and communitarian archipelago politics. Four practices in particular stand out: (1) a new ontology of wildlife, (2) moving beyond species-centrism, (3) wilder rewilding experiments, and (4) preserving "brownfields" as protected ecologies for urban wildlife.

We need a new ontology (understanding of worldliness), epistemology (model of science), and biopolitics (conservation biology) attuned to a biosphere that is immanently and visibly more fluid, hybridized, and novel, with less wilderness and more "wildness." Lorimer enlists the help of Bruno Latour (ANT), Isabelle Stengers (science as cosmopolitics; a creative, constructivist, ecology of practices), Gilles Deleuze and Félix Guattari (assemblage theory),

Foucault (biopower and biopolitics), Donna Haraway (hybridity), and Sarah Whatmore (hybrid geographies). The result is a wildlife ontology organized around the core ideas of multinatural ecologies, hybridity, difference, nonhuman agency, affective logics, nonhuman charisma, topology, and biopolitics.[212] Bounded organisms and environments do not really exist, if they ever did. Nearly all animals and habitats are mixed natural/social assemblages of human and nonhuman, biological, cultural, and technological processes, overlapping and shifting between human-designated "wild" contact and bounded sovereign spaces. This condition of hybrid, fluid ecologies requires new network topological geographies that better reflect multiple, overlapping, fragmented, cut-off, and highly compressed as well as dispersed Anthropocene animal habitats.

With respect to the practice of conservation itself, field biologists need to open themselves up to "multispecies processes of 'learning to be affected' by the world," by the experience of animals as affective agents whose lifeworlds exude corporeal, aesthetic, and ecological charisma.[213] Affect is "a set of energies that flow between bodies" that give rise to an "affective logic" as "a particular mode of engaging with, knowing, and feeling toward wildlife."[214] An advocate of *umwelt* ethology, Lorimer urges us to take off our phenomenological blinders and be more receptive to the "visceral and emotional epiphanies" of up-close animal encounters;[215] to experience the *jouissance* (sensual joy) of wildness (allowing oneself to become wild as a participant-observer);[216] to see beauty in all animals, not simply charismatic megafauna and flagship species; to work through our "biophobias" against snakes, rodents, insects, and "the popular incarnation of aliens as insects";[217] and to recognize the distinctive "anatomical, geographical, and temporal properties" of animals that constitute their ecological charisma[218] as well as their *jizz* ("the unique combination of properties of an organism that allows its ready identification and differentiation from others").[219]

At the policy level, conservation needs to move away from its overreliance on "species" as the basic norm and unit for quantifying biodiversity and determining action plans. To be "conserved," animals must have a taxonomic identity classification and be evaluated as worthy of prioritization and action.[220] While "species" is the dominant concept in taxonomy, it is a highly contested unit, for it distorts as much as clarifies the reality of life in the biosphere.[221] Since biopolitics is about population management, and wildlife conservation is a form of biopolitics, conservation in the Anthropocene should employ an approach that accords equal weight to species, habitats, ecological processes and delivery, genetics, individual animals, and animal cultures. This approach helps remove species bias, taxonomic bias, and bias toward particular species and taxonomic groups, which currently favor mammals and birds, to the detriment of many invertebrates and plants.[222] Regardless of our approach, we must conclude that different "ways of cutting up wildlife result in different modes of conservation."[223]

The most controversial and yet promising of the new conservation practices are what Lorimer identifies as "wild experiments." Unlike a conventional scientific experiment conducted under controlled laboratory or field conditions, a wild experiment is distinguished by several key properties: (1) the experimental site is "found" not "made" and selected for its "wildness," the wilder the better; (2) gaining access to the site, the authority to conduct the experiment, and the ongoing experiment itself involve multiple authorities, constituencies, and publics, which make the process as political as it is scientific; (3) a high level of agency is accorded to the animal experimental subjects as well as to the site's ecological processes; (4) the lack of control over the experiment is viewed as a virtue leading to surprises; and (5) given the scope of the Anthropocene, the experiments are much larger and therefore have larger consequences, thereby increasing the risk factor and potential for controversy.[224]

The case Lorimer profiles, the Oostvaardersplassen (OVP) experiment conducted in the Netherlands under the supervision of ecologist Frans Vera, represents an attempt to recreate late Pleistocene ecological conditions and introduce grazing animals with the intent of dedomesticating them over time.

The OVP land parcel north of Amsterdam was originally scheduled for industrial development, but when this plan fell through, it was colonized by geese and other bird species to become a novel Anthropocene ecosystem. Vera and Dutch land management and forestry authorities decided to use the site to test Vera's scientific hypothesis—that postglacial European ecosystems were not "high-forest" ecologies (high, closed canopy forests) but rather "wood-pasture" ecologies dominated by large Pleistocene herbivores, such as red deer, bison, aurochs, and tarpans. The experiment was an exercise in pre-Holocene, pre-Neolithic domestication and ecological restoration. It was also an experiment in dedomestication, since domesticated cattle and horses were introduced as grazing populations that over time would re-create Pleistocene-like habitats. The OVP experiment represents a trend among some environmentalists who advocate wilder rewilding projects that include dedomestication.[225]

Vera's OVP experiment was designed as an attempt to resurrect late Pleistocene ecology. It was not undertaken to explore what a post-Anthropocene, posthumanist ecosystem might look like. Its goal was rewilding an Anthropocene anthrome into a pre-Anthropocene, not post-Anthropocene ecology. What also stands out is the politics of the experiment, as multiple segments of the public intervened, most notably animal welfare groups. The cattle and horses introduced were regarded as test subjects, "grazing tools," means to a greater ecological end. And despite the fact that the animals were domestic, they were designated as experimentally "wild." With little active management and no animal welfare plan, many ended up starving and dying.[226] The animals were treated no differently from laboratory research animals, yet as domestic animals they required assistance, since they were essentially dependent on humans, abruptly deposited in a simulated wild environment, and arbitrarily deemed independent or dedomesticated when, in fact, they were not. They were treated as objects and not adequately transitioned into dedomesticated agents. The experiment, therefore, was not posthumanist at all but rather a form of radical Anthropocene environmentalism.

Finally, it is important to understand that the contact zone of the twenty-first-century Anthropocene is as much an urban as it is a suburban phenomenon, with well-established species populations and ecologies as well as new arrivals carving out their residencies. Cities around the world and urban ecologists promote the "greening" of urban spaces—more greenbelts, green neighborhoods, green infrastructures, corridors, community gardens, emerald networks, and living roofs. But what about the role of "brownfield sites" in urban ecologies?[227] These closed and abandoned industrial, commercial, and residential blocks and neighborhoods, deteriorated and overgrown with vegetation, are bemoaned as eyesores that lower property values and are potentially hazardous. The typical response to brownfields is clean them up, "greenwash" them, and put them back in the economic development pipeline as viable real-estate properties.

But to urban wildlife, they are thriving ecosystems, invertebrate utopias. These "deadwoods" are alive with vegetation and insects. Why not preserve some of them as protected wildlife spaces? The problem, critics remind us, is that they attract not only plants and insects but also snakes, mice, rats, feral cats, coyotes, and other more problematic animals. This challenge seems to fit the agenda of posthumanist communitarianism. Can future-oriented, sustainable towns and cities see value in not only urban gardens and greenbelts but also managed brownfields and deadwoods? Can we build posthumanist urban communities around unconventional urban wildlife spaces? Do plants and invertebrates deserve our ethical and political commitments the way vertebrates do? Since posthumanism is a coevolutionary, biocentric, *umwelt* ethics, plants and insects have as much "right" to moral consideration as mammals and birds. They are members of the next social contract.

We must also neither forget nor ignore the darker side of the posthumanist archipelago. It too lies on the periphery of human civilization. It is a world of roadside and traveling menageries, puppy mills, dog- and cockfighting rings, the pet trade, exotic animal owners, and hoarders. It is a world of drug traffickers, reactionary survivalists, doomsday preppers, fringe religious cults, white supremacists, and gun rights constitutionalists. It is a world of illegal black markets, animal traffickers and poachers, and criminal gangs. The illegal wildlife trade is the third-largest black market after guns and drugs. It is a world of elephant ivory, rhino horns, bear bile, gorilla-hand ashtrays, turtle shells, shark fins, and millions of animal skins. Nearly every part of every species is sought after by humans and rationalized in bizarre ways. It is also a world of websites and blogs filled with conspiracy theories, hate speech, and, unfortunately, too many self-righteous animal rights liberationists and vegans outing the impure of thought and deed in the advocacy movement. It is a world that cuts across all social classes, cultures, and spaces of human habitation from urban to suburban to rural to the backcountry.

The next social contract stands as a biopolitical artifact entered into by diverse subject-citizens dedicated to the preservation of animals in the Anthropocene. It exists as a network of archipelagos, a patchwork and mosaic of locales, actor networks, and activities involved in the daily round of promoting the greater posthumanist good. It is evident in a wide variety of people and practices—from habitat preservation and land reinhabitation to rewilding and species reintroduction; in the new animal welfarism as well as in the abolition movement; in animal sanctuaries and rescues; in antiextinction efforts worldwide; in postmodern farming; in vegans, vegetarians, and ethical omnivores; in bioregionalists; in sustainability, climate change, and environmental justice activists; in subirdias, community gardens, and urban prairies; and in animal shelter volunteers and reformers. It is present in all animal lovers and advocates who regard animals as our kin, members of our community, subjects of justice and special protections, and fellow inhabitants of the next social contract.

# CONCLUSION

_____

## ANIMALS, THE ANTHROPOCENE, AND BIOPOLITICS

_____

### *A Labor of Sisyphus*

Life in the Anthropocene is too strange to be human and afforded
rights. It is too social and multiple to be objectified and given a
price. And it is too feral to be pure or risky to be liberated in the
wilderness.

— JAMIE LORIMER, *Wildlife in the Anthropocene*

## Biopolitics in the Twenty-First Century

In the narrative of evolution, every "age" is the age of a dominant life-form.
The current Anthropocene is a small blip on the evolutionary radar screen.
The age of the dinosaurs was a much greater story. They dominated the
planet for more than 150 million years, and just as the plant and animal remains of their time are now fuel for our modern civilization, our future remains will likely be a resource for the next dominant species. We could not
have done it without the help of other animals and plants. Since the Great
Domestication, we have depended on a small but essential number of species.
We have also hastened the extinction of numerous other species. Planetary
evolution is indifferent to a looming mass extinction largely of our own making. The planet will heat up and eventually go into another Ice Age. Existing
species will vanish, and new species will come into being.

Just as "sustainability" was the mantra of late twentieth-century environmentalism, "resiliency" is the buzzword of twenty-first-century climate change.
As global warming heats the planet, animals and plants have read the news and
are moving to more hospitable habitats. The vacuum is being filled by new
invasive species moving into these destabilized habitats. Life everywhere is on
the move, seeking better environs. Humans are also thinking more seriously
about the viability of their own civilization. If human evolution—perhaps all
of evolution—experiences critical thresholds of optimal adaptation only when

on the brink, when on the precipice of a crisis, then this is our moment, this is our century.

In *The Fate of Species* (2012), Fred Guterl identifies six major threats facing humans in the twenty-first century: (1) superviruses, (2) species extinction, (3) climate change, (4) ecosystemic collapse, (5) synthetic biology, and (6) artificial intelligence (AI). Four of these challenges are playing out currently—superviruses, species extinction, climate change, and ecosystemic disruption. Biotech Frankenstein monsters, malignant designer diseases, and fully autonomous AI and robots are no longer the stuff of science fiction. Robots and synthetic life-forms will be mainstream by the twenty-first century's end. Guterl is a "techno-optimist," a believer in human high-tech ingenuity.[1] He rejects what he regards as the twin extremes of megatechnological geoengineering and environmentalist calls for a return to a simpler life.[2] He recommends carbon sequestration, changing farming methods, more genetically modified foods, shifting from annual to perennial crops, bioengineering synthetic meats from stem cells, and "reengineering wild animals that can live in the world as we've changed it."[3] He concludes: "Humanity is a bold assertion, a derisive snort at nature. We've beaten the odds so far. To continue beating them will take every good idea."[4]

As I have maintained throughout this book, I remain skeptical of the ability of our late-modern civilization to meet the challenges of the Anthropocene. The fact that "humanity is a bold assertion" and has defined its identity in terms of "a derisive snort at nature" is precisely the problem. I believe that techno-liberalism will not be enough to save us. Yet the key to this statement lies in the "us." Who are the "we" likely to beat the odds? For most anthropocentric liberals, it is civilized humanity. Yet for posthumanists, the "we" is the biosphere and its living inhabitants. From the perspective of animal life, the odds are not that good. Humans will adapt and survive, but at what cost to other species?

Jedediah Purdy shares Guterl's liberal optimism when it comes to the Anthropocene, yet his source of hope and inspiration is not humanity's technological cleverness but rather the American "environmental imagination" and our ability throughout our history to translate this into an effective politics and progressive legislation. Of course, this ability has not been without great struggle, but each major era of American history has resulted in not only a new democratic politics of nature but also a new paradigm of environmental law that has served the country well. In *After Nature: A Politics for the Anthropocene* (2015), Purdy reconstructs four historical versions of the American environmental imagination in the buildup to a fifth vision we need to forge today in response to the challenge of our time, the Anthropocene.

Purdy's conception of politics, historiography, and the environment revolves around his idea of imaginative lawmaking:

> From the beginning, as noted in the Prologue, there has been a link
> between how Americans have acted toward the natural world and
> how they have imagined it—as a wilderness designed by God to
> become a garden, as a piece of symbolic art with the power to bring
> spiritual insight, as a storehouse of essential resources for national
> wealth.[5]

> Law is a circuit between imagination and the material world. Laws
> choreograph human action in a thousand ways[.][6]

> Laws play out the logic of competing versions of environmental imag-
> ination.[7]

> Law is the warp and weft that bind the two, shaping the material
> landscape, guiding human action on it, by translating ideal images of
> people and nature into concrete regimes of power.[8]

What then should be the next environmental imagination and legal regime
for the Anthropocene? To sum up Purdy's vision in one sentence, we need a
"democratic Anthropocene" capable of reining in the "neoliberal Anthropocene" and addressing the "paradigmatic problems" of "food, the treatment of
animals, and climate change."[9] This vision requires establishing a new farming
and food system; addressing "the unsettling perception that we do not know,
maybe cannot know, the ethical status, meaning, or experience of another living thing that stands in front of us"; and developing "new standards of success"
with respect to climate change.[10]

Three issues addressed by Purdy speak directly to the concerns of this
book: (1) the treatment of animals, (2) posthumanism, and (3) democracy in
the Anthropocene. He acknowledges the animal welfare/rights divide. Both
sides care deeply about animals, develop reasonable arguments, and cannot
resolve their differences. He also is unable, or unwilling, to reconcile this
impasse. However, he believes that both sides share an overconfidence in
claiming to "know" animals and what they want. They underestimate "the
difficulty of interpreting animal experience."[11] For Purdy, "not knowing
another's consciousness" leaves us in a condition of "uncanniness" and "offers
an ethics of uncertainty, a pause before judgment."[12] We "simply do not know
what is behind another pair of eyes, and what is projection from behind our

own."[13] We are in the infancy of animal studies and need more data, more legal discovery.

One attempt at illuminating the lifeworld of animals is posthumanism, which calls for, among other things, "leveling the hierarchical divide between human and nonhuman by blurring the boundary."[14] The basis of value is shifted from the prevailing norm of anthropocentric humanism to biocentric "autopoesis." We are a more complex emergent order of self-organizing matter "among other emergent orders."[15] Humans are not the only agents in the world. It is more accurate to view the world not in terms of agents and nonagents but in terms of "actants" (borrowing Jane Bennett's term).[16] Humans, animals, plants, biotic entities, and ecological processes all act on each other in complex cause-and-effect networks. This "new animism" extends the principle of equality of valuation to all life-forms. Purdy believes that posthumanism has the potential to initiate "a Copernican revolution in ethical imagination."[17]

The chief threat to our future is neoliberalism, with its corporate-centered view of the planet as a quantifiable standing reserve of consumable resources, its strategies of globalization, and free-market and megatechnological solutions to all problems, including global warming and biodiversity. Purdy regards this model of planetary management as antipolitical and antidemocratic. Since he believes that our current crisis is ultimately political, politics must lead us out of this neoliberal dead end. Yet what kind of politics? Purdy advocates a new vision of democracy capable of providing the underpinnings and structure for a new environmental imagination and era of environmental lawmaking. A democracy "open to post-human encounters with the living world would be more likely to find ways to restrain its demands and stop short of exhausting the planet."[18]

Purdy's vision of posthumanist democracy and a new environmentalism is grandiose, noble, and presented in eloquent, inspirational, poetic prose. His optimism is a reaffirmation of American liberal environmentalism. I agree with his characterization of the Anthropocene as a powerful framing concept for understanding our time; critiquing neoliberal globalization; and identifying our food system, the plight of animals, and climate change as our great challenges. Yet I find his vision of a new Anthropocene politics unconvincing. Purdy's conception of politics is liberal, legalistic, and idealistic. He acknowledges that "the public language and legal forms of modern liberalism is a poor sort of knowledge" and "palpably artificial."[19] We need a more imaginative dimension to mainstream liberalism. Yet in the end it is law that defines politics, an idealistic view of law as the cause rather than the effect of change, as the connective tissue between the ideal images of people and institutional reality rather than as the handmaiden of powerful material interests, and in the more Platonic sense of an ideal form that shapes reality rather than in the Weberian sense of the routinization and legitimation of power.

This conception of politics informs his idea of Anthropocene democracy, which is painted in very speculative and broad brushstrokes. Purdy admits that democracy in the world "has not been doing well." I would contend that it has been effectively outflanked by neoliberal globalization and technocracy. Democracy in the Anthropocene is dedicated to equality; is highly discursive and driven by active citizens (your voice and vote count); is "exemplary, or prophetic"; "less beholden to money"; "capable of self-restraint"; and posthumanist.[20] How all of these key features come together as a working model is unknown. For Purdy, democracy in the Anthropocene is largely a set of attitudes, an ethos capable of generating a new environmental imagination. How this new democratic imaginary is translated into environmental law that is able to effectively rein in our neoliberal Anthropocene is not developed.

As for the promise of posthumanism as a candidate for a new environmental imagination, following his position on the animal welfare/rights debate, Purdy resists making "the choice between the post-human position and the humanist riposte, and instead adopt(s) both." Let's "learn from both," he says.[21] In the end, he is a modern liberal humanist who believes that humans are qualitatively different from all other forms of life. We are not assemblages of matter like other life-forms. We are distinctive *zoon politikon*. Posthumanism is "just another name for an enriched humanism."[22] We should be open to posthumanist experiences, but posthumanism cannot translate into anything other than an intuition and feeling for the nonhuman world. While in principle we may believe in interspecies equality, in "liberal society and legalistic culture," it is impossible to implement this ethical ideal into a politics and laws, because we fundamentally cannot "know" animals, and therefore they cannot be represented in human councils.[23] We should admit that "we don't know what an animal's life means, to it or to us."[24] The best we can do is to approximate their lifeworld through anthropomorphic projection.

I take issue with this rather superficial view of animals. The case I make for posthumanism as a coevolutionary, biocentric, lifeworld-based ethics refutes this. We can know animals if we make them central to our lives as members of our community. One can turn Purdy's view of animals toward humans. Do we really "know" human beings in some deep existential, embodied sense? Has advanced liberal capitalism not rendered most of our experiences and knowledge of our fellow human beings superficial and instrumental? Furthermore, for Purdy, the question of animals is essentially a stand-in for "the larger issue of how to see nature."[25] The challenges facing animals in the Anthropocene are enormous, complex, ethical, and biopolitical questions of life and death. His response to the question of animals in the Anthropocene is essentially a new version of the old animal welfarism.

As this century literally heats up and Anthropocene trends intensify, our species will redouble its efforts to protect its civilization from an ever-increasing set of challenges and resiliency tests. The list is long and growing longer—extreme weather incidents, coastal deterioration, habitat loss and fragmentation, ecosystem disruption, infrastructure disintegration and breakdowns, population pressures, mega-urbanization, overconsumption, displaced populations, refugee migrations, pandemic breakouts, resource production and allocation bottlenecks, cascade effects, system-capacity overloads, and technological overreach. The human race will become even more human-centered as it pulls out all the stops to ensure not its survival, which is not in critical jeopardy, but rather its current standard of living. This goal will come at the expense of the majority of life on planet Earth—the world's poorest human populations, the world's animals, and the biosphere.

The institutional logic of advanced modernity is weighed heavily toward policy responses that leverage "big modernity"—a plethora of global initiatives and international agreements, mega-engineering projects, and technocracy. The same mind-set that inaugurated the Anthropocene will be called on to tame and control it. This policy orientation represents an even stronger tightening of the ideology of anthropocentrism. Civilization will circle the wagons under the banner of "resilience"—human resiliency, or, more precisely, the resiliency of its power elites and their propertied resources.

Where Earth is headed geologically and biologically beyond this century is not fully known to us. What we do know is that the planet will continue to warm up, altering land, sea, and air environments and thus the conditions within which evolution takes place. We will have a much better sense of our planet's future at the end of this century. If trends continue, we will be much farther down the road toward triggering a mass sixth extinction. Environmentally, the Anthropocene will begin to replicate conditions that existed on Earth during the early Eocene epoch fifty-six million to forty-nine million years ago. The Eocene began ten million years after the last mass extinction wiped out most of the dinosaurs and ended the great age of large reptiles. This cleaned the evolutionary slate for the rise of mammals. Eocene translates as "dawn of new fauna" (i.e., mammals). The genesis of this new epoch was a major global-warming event that played out over several thousand years and kept Earth in warm greenhouse conditions for seven million years—the Paleocene-Eocene Thermal Maximum (PETM).

If the Anthropocene re-creates Eocene-like conditions on Earth over the next two to three centuries, then what will the biosphere look like? In general, we can expect major mass migrations of life from old to new ecosystems, which will send both into disequilibrium. Ecologically, the planet will become more homogenized, and biologically more and more species will become invasive. The result will be simple ecosystems, which translates into less biodiversity. There will likely be fewer species within a habitat, but they will be more dominant, predatory, and spread throughout the general population. In short, expect more turbulent habitats and more competition within and between species. Expect a more visible and pronounced struggle for existence.

A warmer planet is likely to be beneficial to many plant species, since carbon-dioxide levels and temperatures will be higher, creating better conditions for photosynthesis. As for the oceans, expect the disappearance of many coral reefs; fewer fish and sea mammals; rising extinction rates; and more mass migrations, infestations, and deaths. Expect much higher levels of algae, which will compromise and kill off even more marine species. Our blue planet will become blue-green. Expect a golden age of jellyfish. Expect a global surge in insect populations and larger insects. Expect environments dominated by swarms of larger and more aggressive mosquitoes. Infectious diseases take hold and spread in warmer, more humid environments. Thus, expect malaria, dengue, and Zika virus belts to expand. Expect more and larger reptiles, especially snakes. Overall, expect a world with fewer mammals, birds, amphibians, and fish; less ocean life; and more plants, insects, and simpler life-forms. Therefore, expect more bacteria, spores, fungi, parasites, moss, millipedes, ants, termites, spiders, lizards, snakes, and, of course, humans. Over the next few centuries, what we will likely witness is the devolution of "higher," more complex life-forms combined with the punctuated evolution of simpler life-forms.

## A Labor of Sisyphus

In *The Myth of Sisyphus* (1942), Albert Camus defines the human condition as "absurd." We confront a universe largely unfathomable and indifferent to our existence, yet it is in our nature to find a purpose or reason for our place in the world. The search for meaning is fundamental to our existence. It is the consequence of having a large, complex brain that produces surplus consciousness. We are overly conscious busybodies. For Camus, the world itself is not absurd; rather, our efforts to understand it are. Two predominant types of answers have been given to us by the world's great thinkers and salvationists—religion and reason. Yet the metaphysical hope provided by traditional religion and the systems of logical empiricism developed by modern philosophy and science are insufficient. Religion, philosophy, and science come up short.[26]

Camus maintains that the fundamental contradictions of life must be lived and worked through in the realm of action. The experience of life cultivates in us a tragic awareness of the human condition. There is no escape or exit from our fate, yet rather than give ourselves over to despair, resignation, nihilism, or false utopias, we should adopt the perspective of conscious revolt.[27] This rebellion is not ontological. It is not a revolt against existence itself. It is a revolt against the concrete injustices of this world. In *The Rebel* (1951), Camus utters his famous reversal of Descartes—"I revolt, therefore we exist."[28] It is through our commitment to action, not in the abstract but to specific causes, that we find our place in the world and solidarity with others. In the end, Camus leaves us with two models. *The Myth of Sisyphus* represents the model of the individual in revolt. *The Plague* offers us a model of a community in revolt.

For Camus, the ancient Greek myth of Sisyphus exemplifies his response to the human condition. Sisyphus's fame comes not from his exploits among his fellow humans but from his defiance of the gods, not once but twice. Condemned to Hades by Zeus, Sisyphus outwits Thanatos (death) and imprisons him in his home. Ares, the god of war, frees Thanatos and delivers Sisyphus to Zeus. Before his descent to Hades, Sisyphus subverts the accustomed funeral rituals and appeals to the goddess Persephone that he needs to return to Earth for three days to arrange a proper burial and funeral. She allows him to go home. Once free from Hades, he refuses to return and lives a long life until he dies an old man. For his crimes against the gods and cosmic order, Sisyphus is sentenced by Zeus to roll a huge boulder up a hill only to have it roll back again. It is his labor for all eternity.

Sisyphus is Camus's "absurd hero." He respects his passionate embrace of life in all of its contradictions and identifies with his scorn of the gods. Yet ultimately he valorizes how he accepts his fate, owns it, and transforms it through Stoic rebellion: "His fate belongs to him. His rock is his thing."[29] What most interests Camus is "that pause" as Sisyphus "watches the stone rush down in a few moments toward that lower world whence he will have to push it up again toward the summit":[30]

> I leave Sisyphus at the foot of the mountain. One always finds one's burden again. But Sisyphus teaches the higher fidelity that negates the gods and raises rocks. He too concludes that all is well. This universe henceforth without a master seems to him neither sterile nor futile. Each atom of that stone, each mineral flake of that night-filled mountain, in itself forms a world. The struggle itself toward the heights is enough to fill a man's heart. One must imagine Sisyphus happy.[31]

In *The Plague* (1947), a fictional account of the response of the inhabitants of Oran, Algeria, to the onset of bubonic plague, Camus works out his model of a community in revolt. The plague appears mysteriously, is indifferent to human suffering and death, and disappears as mysteriously as it appears. All the main characters represent different types of what existentialists refer to as authentic and inauthentic ways of life. Father Paneloux, the doctrinaire Catholic priest, explains the plague as divine punishment for our sins. Jean Tarrou, the son of a public prosecutor, has come to Oran to heal his troubled conscience and seek moral redemption. He views the world as being in the grip of rational murderers. Disgusted with the machinery of modern justice, he aspires to be an "innocent murderer." Raymond Rambert, a journalist on assignment from Paris, regards the plague as not his problem and does all he can to convince local bureaucrats to allow him to go home to his happy bourgeois world. Grand, a lonely civil servant, lives in a bipolar world of mundane routines and grandiose fantasies. Dr. Bernard Rieux, a doctor and Camus's Sisyphean hero, fights the plague day by day with Stoic dedication.

In dealing with the plague, Camus's characters overcome their personal estrangements through action and solidarity. Through his characters, Camus expresses his personal, philosophical, and artistic beliefs and commitments. Father Panaleoux's first sermon exemplifies all that Camus despises in official religion. However, his arrogant faith in God's cosmic justice is shaken by the agonizing death of Judge Othon's child, and his second sermon expresses a more humane humility.[32] Through Tarrou, Camus communicates his belief that moral purity is impossible. We all have blood on our hands.[33] As for Dr. Rieux, he embodies Camus's ideal of being-in-the-world. He is world-weary but resilient. He befriends all the main characters and listens to their stories in a nonjudgmental way. He is lacking in moral self-righteousness but is firmly dedicated to fighting cruelty and relieving suffering. Fighting the plague is an act of common decency, not heroism. He confesses to Tarrou that he feels "more fellowship with the defeated than with saints. Heroism and sanctity don't really appeal to me, I imagine. What interests me is being a man."[34] And as the plague subsides, he realizes that "plague," a metaphor for all the concrete social evils of the world, never really dies but is reborn in a new and different form with each new generation.[35]

The labor of Sisyphus and the community in revolt against injustice are compelling models of being-in-the-world. One discovers clarity of purpose in one's commitment to a course of action carried out with Stoic determination. One takes up a cause knowing full well that one's preferred or expected outcome is neither guaranteed nor likely. The historical context of Camus's thinking, writing, and politics was World War II and the Holocaust. Our time is one of climate change and the holocaust facing animals. The Anthropocene is our "plague." Camus's challenge was the human condition. Our challenge is the posthumanist condition. In my own mind, adopting an evolutionary worldview renders the world meaningful. Life evolves, adapts, and coevolves. The first two processes are facts of life, occurring regardless of whether we are fully conscious of them. The third piece of the puzzle, coevolution, allows for conscious agency in a limited sense.

Carrie Packwood Freeman characterizes humans "as social animals who are uniquely prone to excess, explaining the biological need for humanity's complex ethical systems."[36] I agree that humans are prone to excess, but they are not unique in this regard. All animals—indeed, all living things—have an evolutionary drive toward excess displayed in different ways to ensure survival by optimizing adaptability. An optimal survival strategy is to proliferate and dominate. The difference is that most nonhuman animal excess is checked by environmental pressures. Most living organisms and populations live within the boundaries of larger ecological forces. What is unique about human excess is our ability to overcome environmental checks and balances. We are good at manufacturing excessive excess.

Modernity today is a juggernaut that has shifted into radical hyperdrive. As the human race becomes more fully modern, animals become more critically endangered. The odds are stacked against many animals. The human desire for animal meat is increasing as the world's middle class mushrooms. The world's oceans are overfished. CAFOs are growing globally. Climate change is radically altering habitats, and human terraforming continues to eliminate and fragment animal habitats. Many charismatic megafauna as well as the smallest of species will be gone if not ecologically extinct by century's end. Shelters, zoos, and sanctuaries cannot accommodate all the abandoned, abused, and surplus animals.

The task is so formidable and daunting that our interventions become Sisyphean labors. In most circumstances, the plight of animals today can be reasonably comprehended and acted on only by adopting a calibrated form of triage biopolitics.

One can, however, be fortified by the knowledge that all evolution is local. The basis of macroevolution is microevolution. So it is with coevolution. It is here that we can cultivate a modest Sisyphean optimism. The next social contract will be shaped by the efforts of a diverse array of inhabitants of the posthumanist archipelago. I hope they will be equipped with an awareness and knowledge of the challenges facing nonhuman animals and humans in the Anthropocene, with a critical citizen's eye on the legitimacy deficits of late-modern civilization, and with a posthumanist ethics and sense of justice.

Posthumanism is about up-close, real-world engagement with nonhuman animals as coevolutionary coinhabitants. On a personal level, I recommend that you do some serious homework. Be patient. Know the risks, the dangers, and your limitations. See the nobility in what are often mundane labors. Be prepared for adversity, frustration, defeat, and loss. Reach out to others. Since you are a culturally productive learning animal, if you take the time, you will find that your fellow animals are much smarter, reasonable, sophisticated, adaptable, and intuitive than you think. You can learn a lot from them. Go to where animals are and build communities around them. Making common cause with the plight of animals is a worthy calling. In doing so, you will discover that the lives of animals make life worth living.

# NOTES

## CHAPTER 1

1. Paul J. Crutzen and Eugene F. Stoermer, "The Anthropocene," *Global Change Newsletter* 41 (2000): 17–18; Paul J. Crutzen, "Geology of Mankind," *Nature* 415 (2002): 23.

2. Jan Zalasiewicz, Mark Williams, Will Steffen, and Paul Crutzen, "The New World of the Anthropocene," *Environmental Science and Technology* 44, no. 7 (2010): 2228–2231. Also see Jan Zalasiewicz and Mark Williams, *The Goldilocks Planet: The Four Billion Year Story of Earth's Climate* (Oxford, UK: Oxford University Press, 2012), chap. 9, "Birth and Death of the Holocene," 199–227, and chap. 10, "The Anthropocene Begins," 229–267.

3. For an excellent summary of the geological debate to date on the Anthropocene, see Simon L. Lewis and Mark A. Maslin, "Defining the Anthropocene," *Nature* 519 (2015): 171–180.

4. See Elizabeth Kolbert, *The Sixth Extinction: An Unnatural History* (New York: Holt, 2014), chap. 5, "Welcome to the Anthropocene," 92–110. Also see the collection of essays in *Thinking about Animals in the Age of the Anthropocene*, ed. Morten Tonnessen, Kristin Armstrong Oma, and Silver Rattasepp (Lanham, MD: Lexington Books, 2016). Three scientific journals also deal directly with the Anthropocene—*The Anthropocene, Anthropocene Review*, and *Elementa*.

5. Lewis and Maslin, "Defining the Anthropocene."

6. Adrian Franklin, "Ecosystem and Landscape: Strategies for the Anthropocene," in *Animals in the Anthropocene: Critical Perspectives on Non-human Futures*, ed. Human Animal Research Network Editorial Collective (Sydney, Australia: Sydney University Press, 2015), 65.

7. Niles Eldredge, *Dominion* (Berkeley: University of California Press, 1997), xiv.

8. Jedediah Purdy, *After Nature: A Politics for the Anthropocene* (Cambridge, MA: Harvard University Press, 2015), "Introduction," 17–21.

9. Ibid., chap. 7, "Environmental Law in the Anthropocene," 228–255.

10. Jamie Lorimer, *Wildlife in the Anthropocene: Conservation after Nature* (Minneapolis: University of Minnesota Press, 2015), "Introduction," 1–18.

11. Richie Nimmo, "Apiculture in the Anthropocene: Between Posthumanism and Critical Animal Studies," in *Animals in the Anthropocene*, 195.

12. See Patrick Gerland et al., "World Population Stabilization Unlikely in This Century," *Science* 346, no. 6206 (2014): 234–237.

13. Jack A. Goldstone, "The New Population Bomb: Four Megatrends that Will Change the World," *Foreign Affairs*, January/February 2010, 31–43.

14. See John Bongaarts, "Human Population Growth and the Demographic Transition," *Philosophical Transactions of the Royal Society: Biological Sciences* 364 (2009): 2985–2990.

15. Goldstone, "The New Population Bomb," 32–33.

16. See Laurence C. Smith, *The World in 2050: Four Forces Shaping Civilization's Northern Future* (New York: Dutton, 2010), chap. 2, "A Tale of Teeming Cities," 29–50.

17. See Mike Davis, *Planet of Slums* (London: Verso, 2006); Tommy Firman, "Post-suburban Elements in Asian Extended Metropolitan Region: The Case of Jabodetabek (Jakarta Metropolitan Area)," in *International Perspectives on Suburbanization: A Post-Suburban World*, ed. N. A. Phelps and F. Wu (New York: Palgrave Macmillan), 195–209; Benjamin Marx, Thomas Stoker, and Tavnett Suri, "The Economics of Slums in the Developing World," *Journal of Economic Perspectives* 27, no. 4 (2013): 187–210.

18. In the United States, the Regional Plan Association has put forth "America 2050," which has identified eleven megaregions and a proposal to link them by high-speed rail. They are the Northeast, Great Lakes, Piedmont Atlantic, Florida, Gulf Coast, Texas Triangle, Front Range, Arizona Sun Corridor, Southern California, Northern California, and Cascadia. See www.america2050.org/megaregions.html.

19. See the World Bank Data Catalog 2012 GDP ranking table, available at http://data.worldbank.org/data-catalog/GDP-ranking-table. Also see "Sober Look: Goldman's World GDP Projections for 2050," available at http://soberlook.com/2012/11/goldmans-gdp-projection-for-2050.html.

20. See the 2013 United Nations Human Development Report, "The Rise of the South: Human Progress in a Diverse World," available at http://hdr.undp.org/en/content/human-development-report-2013.

21. See Global Footprint Network at www.footprintnetwork.org.

22. See the International Energy Association (IEA) World Energy Outlook at www.worldenergyoutlook.org; U.S. Energy Information Administration at www.eia.gov.today inenergy; "Prediction of Energy Consumption World-wide" at http://timeforhcange.org/preduction-of-energy-consumption; Smith, *The World in 2050*, chap. 3, "Iron, Oil, and Wind," 51–81; and Daniel Yergin, *The Quest: Energy, Security, and the Remaking of the Modern World* (New York: Penguin Press, 2011).

23. See Larua Paskus, "A Place in the Sun," photographs by Dave Lauridsen, *Nature Conservancy*, October/November 2014, 30–41.

24. See Marianne Lavelle, "Fracking for Methane," photographs by Mark Thiessen, *National Geographic*, December 2012, 90–109; Edwin Dobb, "The New Oil Landscape," photographs by Eugene Richards, *National Geographic*, March 2013, 29–59; and "5 NEW ENERGY BOOMS Every Investor Should See Right Now," available at www.popularresistance.org/oil-industry-not-done-raping-the-plane.

25. Erle C. Ellis et al., "Anthropogenic Transformation of the Biomes, 1700 to 2000," *Global Ecology and Biogeography* 19 (2010): 589–606.

26. Michael L. Rosenzweig, "The Four Questions: What Does the Introduction of Exotic Species Do to Diversity?" *Evolutionary Ecology Research* 3 (2001): 361–367.

27. George Newcombe and Frank M. Dugan, "Fungal Pathogens of Plants in the Homogocene," in *Molecular Identification of Fungi*, ed. Y. Ghervawy and K. Voight (Berlin: Springer-Verlag, 2010), 3–34.

28. The Mauna Loa Observatory registered 400 parts per million (PPM) of atmospheric carbon-dioxide concentration in May 2013. The monthly average in January 2013 was 395.54, and in January 2014 it was 397.80. See Justin Gillis, "Heat-Trapping Gas Passes Milestone, Raising Fears," *New York Times*, May 10, 2013, available at www.nytimes.com/2013/05/11/science/earth/carbon-dioxide-level-passes-long-feared-milestone.html; Earth System Research Laboratory, "Trends in Atmospheric Carbon Dioxide," www.esrl.noaa.gov/gmd/ccgg/trends; and Bruce Melton, "Climate Change 2013: Where We Are Now—Not What You Think," *Popular Resistance*, December 27, 2013, www.popularresistance.org/climate-change-2013.

29. The Intergovernmental Panel on Climate Change (IPCC) released the first part of its Fifth Assessment Report (AR5) compiled by Working Group 1, "Climate Change 2013: The Physical Science Basis," in September 2013. It was followed by other reports in 2014—"Impacts," "Adaptation and Vulnerability," "Mitigation of Climate Change," and "Synthesis Report." See www.ipcc.ch/report/ar5/wg1.

30. "Carbon Dioxide: Projected Emissions and Concentrations," IPCC Data Distribution Centre, www.ipcc-data.org.

31. See NRC Climate Stabilization Targets, "Future of Climate Change," www.epa.gov/climate-change-science.

32. See Robert Kunzig, "World without Ice," photographs by Ira Block, *National Geographic*, October 2011, 90–109.

33. Eric Rignot et al., "Widespread, Rapid Grounding Line Retreat of Pine Island, Thwaites, Smith and Kohler Glaciers, West Antarctica, from 1992 to 2011," *Geophysical Research Letters* 4, no. 10 (2014): 3502–3509.

34. On the effects of climate change on global sea levels, see Peter Ward, *The Flooded Earth: Our Future in a World without Ice Caps* (New York: Basic Books, 2010). Ward projects into the future estimated global atmospheric carbon-dioxide levels and posits likely scenarios from 2030 (420 ppm) to 2135 (800 ppm) to 2214 (1,300 ppm).

35. See Benjamin I. Cook, Toby R. Ault, and Jason E. Smerdon, "Unprecedented 21st-Century Drought Risk in the American Southwest and Central Plains," *Science Advances* 1, no. e1400082 (2015): 1–7.

36. "Policy Implications of Warming Permafrost," United Nations Environment Programme 2012, www.unep.org/pdf/permafrost/pdf. Also see Michael D. Lemonick, "Nearing a Tipping Point on Melting Permafrost?" *Climate Central*, February 21, 2013, www.climatecentral.org/news/nearing-a-tipping-point-on-melting-permafrost-15636.

37. See Paul D. Taylor, ed., *Extinctions in the History of Life* (Cambridge, UK: Cambridge University Press, 2004); Fred Guterl, *The Fate of Species: Why the Human Race May Cause Its Own Extinction and How We Can Stop It* (New York: Bloomsbury, 2012), chap. 2, "Extinction," 28–49; and Kolbert, *The Sixth Extinction*.

38. See John Alroy, "Accurate and Precise Estimates of Origination and Extinction Rates," *Paleobiology* 40, no. 3 (2014): 374–397.

39. See Stuart Pimm, "The Extinction Puzzle," www.project-syndicated.org/commentary/the-extinction-puzzle; Jeremy B. C. Jackson, "Ecological Extinction and Evolution in the Brave New Ocean," *Proceedings of the National Academy of Sciences* 105 (2008): 11458–

11465; and Luke Gibson et al., "Near-Complete Extinction of Native Small Mammal Fauna 25 Years after Forest Fragmentation," *Science* 341 (2013): 1508–1510.

40. See Carl Zimmer, "How Many Species? A Study Says 8.7 Million, but It's Tricky," *New York Times*, August 23, 2011, available at www.nytimes.com/2011/08/30/science/30 species.html.

41. For a more detailed account of the extinction risk of known species, consult the International Union for Conservation of Nature (IUCN) Red List. More than seventy-one thousand species have been assessed and classified as extinct, extinct in the wild, critically endangered, endangered, vulnerable, near threatened, least concern, data deficient, and not evaluated; see www.iucn.org. Also see Richard Monastersky, "Life—A Status Report," *Nature* 516 (2014): 159–161.

42. William J. Ripple et al., "Collapse of the World's Largest Herbivores," *Science Advances* 1, no. e1400103 (2015): 1–12.

43. Monastersky, "Life—A Status Report," 161.

44. See Corey J. A. Bradshaw and Barry W. Brook, "Human Population Reduction Is Not a Quick Fix for Environmental Problems," *Proceedings of the National Academy of Sciences* 111, no. 46 (2014): 16610–16615.

45. See David Harvey, *A Brief History of Neoliberalism* (Oxford, UK: Oxford University Press, 2005).

46. See Freeman J. Dyson, "Warm-Blooded Plants and Freeze-Dried Fish," *Atlantic*, November 1997, available at www.theatlantic.com/past/docs/issues/97nov/space.htm.

47. See Paul J. Crutzen, "Albedo Enhancement by Stratospheric Sulfur Injections: A Contribution to Resolve a Policy Dilemma," *Climate Change* 77 (2006): 211–219.

48. See Leslie Paul Thiele, *Indra's Net and the Midas Touch: Living Sustainably in a Connected World* (Cambridge, UK: Massachusetts Institute of Technology Press, 2011).

49. Ray Kurzweil, *The Singularity Is Near: When Humans Transcend Biology* (Oxford, UK: Oxford University Press, 2005).

## CHAPTER 2

1. See Annalee Newitz, *Scatter, Adapt, and Remember: How Humans Will Survive a Mass Extinction* (New York: Doubleday, 2013), pt. 1, "A History of Mass Extinctions," 13–60.

2. Anthony D. Barnosky et al., "Has the Earth's Sixth Mass Extinction Already Arrived?" *Nature* 471 (2011): 51–57.

3. Anthony D. Barnosky et al., "Assessing the Causes of Late Pleistocene Extinctions on the Continents," *Science* 306, no. 5693 (2004): 70–75.

4. For a summary of the main theories of the late Pleistocene megafauna extinctions, see Todd A. Surovell, "Extinctions of Big Game," *Encyclopedia of Archaeology* 2 (2008): 1365–1374.

5. See Ted Goebel, Michael R. Waters, and Dennis H. O'Rourke, "The Late Pleistocene Dispersal of Modern Humans in the Americas," *Science* 319 (2008): 1497–1502; Michael Marshall, "Was America First Colonized by Two Cultures at Once?" *New Scientist*, July 12, 2012; and Jennifer Viegas, "First Americans Were Not Alone," *Discovery News*, November 27, 2012.

6. See Richard Firestone, Allen West, and Simon Warwick-Smith, *The Cycle of Cosmic Catastrophes: How a Stone-Age Comet Changed the Course of World Culture* (Rochester, VT: Bear, 2006); Richard Firestone et al., "Evidence for an Extraterrestrial Impact 12,900 Years Ago that Contributed to the Megafaunal Extinctions and the Younger Dryas Cooling,"

NOTES TO CHAPTER 2 **191**

*Proceedings of the National Academy of Sciences* 104, no. 41 (2007): 16016–16021; and D. J. Kennett et al., "Nanodiamonds in the Younger Dryas Boundary Sediment Layer," *Science* 323, no. 5910 (2009): 94.

7. Barnosky et al., "Assessing the Causes of Late Pleistocene Extinctions on the Continents," fig. 1, tab. 1.

8. See Tim Flannery, *The Future Eaters: An Ecological History of the Australasian Lands and Peoples* (New York: Grove Press, 2002).

9. Barnosky et al., "Assessing the Causes of Late Pleistocene Extinctions on the Continents," fig. 1, tab.1.

10. Ibid.

11. Morten Erick Allentoft et al., "Extinct New Zealand Megafauna Were Not in Decline before Human Colonization," *Proceedings of the National Academy of Sciences* 111, no. 13 (2014): 4922–4927.

12. See Joel Greenberg, *A Feathered River across the Sky: The Passenger Pigeon's Flight to Extinction* (London: Bloomsbury, 2014).

13. See Peter Gwin, "Rhino Wars," photographs by Brent Stirton, *National Geographic*, March 2012, 106–123.

14. See Caroline Alexander, "A Cry for the Tiger," photographs by Steve Winter, *National Geographic*, December 2011, 62–87; and George B. Schaller, "Politics Is Killing the Big Cats," *National Geographic*, December 2011, 88–91. On the growing practice of tiger farming in China to produce tiger parts and products for its wealthy bourgeois elites, see J. A. Mills, *Blood of the Tiger: A Story of Conspiracy, Greed, and the Battle to Save a Magnificent Species* (Boston: Beacon Press, 2015).

15. P. J. Bishop et al., "The Amphibian Extinction Crisis—What Will It Take to Put the Action into the Amphibian Conservation Action Plan?" *S.A.P.I.E.N.S.* 5, no. 2 (1012): 97–111.

16. Ibid., sec. 2, "What Is Causing Amphibian Declines," 100–102.

17. See Cheryl J. Briggs, Roland A. Knapp, and Vance T. Vredenburg, "Enzootic and Epizootic Dynamics of the Chytrid Fungal Pathogen of Amphibians," *Proceedings of the National Academy of Sciences* 107 (2010): 9695–9700.

18. See Douglas J. McCauley et al., "Marine Defaunation: Animal Loss in the Global Ocean," *Science* 347, no. 6219 (2015): 641–647.

19. Ibid.

20. See Charles Sheppard, Simon K. Davy, and Graham M. Pilling, *The Biology of Coral Reefs* (Oxford, UK: Oxford University Press, 2009); Kent E. Carpenter et al., "One-Third of Reef-Building Corals Face Elevated Extinction Risk from Climate Change and Local Impacts," *Science* 321 (2008): 560–563; and J. E. N. Veron, "Is the End in Sight for the World's Coral Reefs?" *e360 Online*, December 6, 2010.

21. As Elizabeth Kolbert explains in *The Sixth Extinction*, chap. 6, "The Sea around Us," 114, "Like the Richter scale, the pH scale is logarithmic, so even such a small numerical difference represents a very large real-world change. A decline of .1 means that the oceans are now thirty percent more acidic than they were in 1800."

22. See Ralph F. Keeling, Arne Kortzinger, and Nicholas Gruber, "Ocean Deoxygenation in a Warming World," *Annual Review of Marine Science* 2 (2010): 199–229.

23. The State of World Fisheries and Aquaculture 2014 (SOFIA), Food and Agriculture Organization of the United Nations, www.fao.org/fishery/sofia.

24. See Charles J. Moore, "Choking the Oceans with Plastic," *New York Times*, August 25, 2014.

25. See Joel K. Bourne Jr., "How to Farm a Better Fish," photographs by Brian Skerry, *National Geographic*, June 2014, 93–111.

26. Victoria Braithwaite, *Do Fish Feel Pain?* (Oxford, UK: Oxford University Press, 2010), 180–183.

27. See Bryan Walsh, "The Pacific Bluefin Tuna Is Going, Going . . . ," *Time*, January 11, 2013.

28. See "How Many Sharks Are Actually Killed Each Year?" *SHARKPROJECT*, www .sharkproject.org/haiothek/index_e.php?site=gefahr_10.

29. Bret A. Muter et al., "Australian and U.S. News Portrayal of Sharks and Their Conservation," *Conservation Biology* 27, no. 1 (2012): 187–196.

30. See "Information about Sea Turtles: Why Care?" *Sea Turtle Conservancy*, www .conserveturtles.org/seaturtleinformation.php?page=whycareaboutseaturtles.

31. Lisa-ann Gershwin, *Stung! On Jellyfish Blooms and the Future of the Ocean* (Chicago: University of Chicago Press, 2013), chap. 4, "Jellyfish: The Basics," 80–83.

32. Ibid., chap. 15, "The Rise of Slime," 343.

33. Ibid., chap. 5, "Overview of Ecosystem Perturbations," 106.

34. See Tom Philpott, "Obama's 5 Biggest Sellouts to the Meat Industry," *Mother Jones*, November 5, 2013.

35. See Frances M. Ufkes, "Building a Better Pig: Fat Profits in Lean Meat," in *Animal Geographies: Place, Politics, and Identity in the Nature-Culture Borderlands*, ed. Jennifer Wolch and Jody Emel (London: Verso, 1998), 241–255.

36. These estimates were compiled from referencing "Farm Animal Statistics: Slaughter Totals," Humane Society of the United States (HSUS), www.humanesociety.org; "Animal Death Statistics," Farm Animal Rights Movement (FARM), http://farmusa.org/statistics11 .html; and "The Animal Kill Counter," Animals Deserve Absolute Protection Today and Tomorrow (ADAPTT), www.adaptt.org/killcounter.html.

37. More than three hundred million acres of federal and state lands are leased for live-stock grazing well below private-market rates through permits that have been bought up and monopolized by large corporate entities, to the detriment of an overgrazed and damaged environment, exterminated animals, and small ranchers. See George Wuerthner and Mollie Matteson, eds., *Welfare Ranching: The Subsidized Destruction of the American West* (Wash-ington, DC: Island Press, 2002).

38. See Erik Marcus, *Meat Market: Animals, Ethics, and Money* (Boston: Brio Press, 2005), chap. 2, "Farmed Animal Lives," 34–48.

39. See Hal Herzog, *Some We Love, Some We Hate, Some We Eat: Why It's So Hard to Think Straight about Animals* (New York: HarperCollins, 2010), chap. 6, "In the Eyes of the Beholder: The Comparative Cruelty of Cockfights and Happy Meals," 167–170; Mark Hawthorne, *Bleating Hearts: The Hidden World of Animal Suffering* (Winchester, UK: Changemakers Books, 2013), chap. 1, "Bleating Hearts: Animals Use for Food," 5–22.

40. Marcus, *Meat Market*, chap. 2, "Farmed Animal Lives," 27–34.

41. See Cynthia F. Hodges, "Detailed Discussion of the Humane Methods of Slaugh-ter Act," Michigan State University College of Law, Animal Legal and Historical Center, 2010, Summary, www.animallaw.info/article/detailed-discussion-humane-methods-slaughter-act#id-1.

42. Ibid., sec. 3, "Acceptable Methods of Slaughter."

43. Ibid., sec. 5, "Limitations of the HMSA," under "B. Ritual Slaughter Exemption."

44. Ibid., sec. 2, "Animals Covered under HMSA."

45. Ibid., sec. 5, "Limitations of the HMSA," under "A. Exclusion of Certain Species."

46. Ibid.

47. Ibid., sec. 4, "Provisions for Nonambulatory Livestock."

48. See David J. Wolfson and Mariann Sullivan, "Foxes in the Hen House: Animals, Agribusiness, and the Law: A Modern American Fable," in *Animal Rights: Current Debates and New Directions*, ed. Cass R. Sunstein and Martha Nussbaum (Oxford, UK: Oxford University Press, 2004), 205–233.

49. See Karen Davis, "The Need for Legislation and Elimination of Electrical Immobilization," *United Poultry Concerns*, www.upc-online.org/slaughter/report.html.

50. See "McDonald's: Animal Health and Welfare—How Do We Know If We're Doing Better?" *McDonalds.com*, www.aboutmcdonalds.com/mcd/sustainability/sourcing/animal-health-and-welfare.html.

51. See North American Meat Institute, www.animalhandling.org.

52. See Temple Grandin, "Livestock Handling Systems, Cattle Corrals, Stockyards, and Races," http://grandin.com/design/design.html; Temple Grandin, "Recommended Stunning Practices," http://grandin.com/humane/rec.slaughter.html; Grandin Livestock Handling Systems, Inc., www.grandinlivestockhanldingsystems.com; and Temple Grandin and Mark Dessing, *Humane Livestock Handling: Understanding Livestock Behavior and Building Facilities for Healthier Animals* (North Adams, MA: Storey Publishers, 2008).

53. Temple Grandin, "Animal Welfare Audits for Cattle, Pigs, and Chickens that Use the HACCP Principles of Critical Control Points with Animal Based Outcome Measures (Updated July 2013)," www.grandin.com/welfare.audit.using.haccp.html.

54. See James McWilliams, "Why the Meat Industry Loves Temple Grandin," *Daily Pitchfork*, January 30, 2015, http://dailypitchfork.org/?p=536.

55. Timothy Pachirat, *Every Twelve Seconds: Industrialized Slaughter and the Politics of Sight* (New Haven, CT: Yale University Press, 2011), chap. 1, "Hidden in Plain Sight," 4.

56. Ibid.

57. Ibid., 17–18.

58. Ibid., chap. 2, "The Place Where Blood Flows," 20–37.

59. Ibid., chap. 3, "Kill Floor," 38–84, and chap. 6, "Killing at Close Range," 140–161.

60. Ibid., chap. 1, nn2–3.

61. Ibid.

62. Marcus, *Meat Market*, chap. 6, "Creating a Dismantlement Movement," 79.

63. Ibid., chap. 9, "The Militancy Question," 109–110.

64. Ibid., chap. 6, 84.

65. Gary Francione identifies what I regard as the "new welfarism" in *Rain without Thunder: The Ideology of the Animal Rights Movement* (Philadelphia: Temple University Press, 1996).

66. See the Gary Francione–Erik Markus debate, which took place on February 25, 2007, www.gary-francione.com/francione-markus-debate.html.

67. See Anna L. Peterson, *Being Animal: Beasts and Boundaries in Nature Ethics* (New York: Columbia University Press, 2013), chap. 8, "Being Animal," 161–172.

68. John M. Marzluff, *Welcome to Subirdia: Sharing Our Neighborhoods with Wrens, Robins, Woodpeckers, and Other Wildlife* (New Haven, CT: Yale University Press, 2014), chap. 2, "Finding Subirdia," 15–17.

69. Ibid., chap. 3, "A Child's Question," 31–41.

70. Ibid., chap. 5, "The Fragile Nature of Subirdia," 85.

71. Ibid., chap. 8, "Beyond Birds," 156–161.

72. Ibid., 174.

73. Ibid., chap. 9, "Good Neighbors," 182–188.

74. Ibid., 189.

75. Ibid., 191–194.

76. Ibid., 194–204.

77. See Jonathan Franzen, "Emptying the Skies," *New Yorker*, July 26, 2010; and "Last Song," photographs by David Guttenfelder, *National Geographic*, July 2013, 60–89.

78. Jim Sterba, *Nature Wars: The Incredible Story of How Wildlife Comebacks Turned Backyards into Battlegrounds* (New York: Crown Publishers, 2012), pt. 1, "Forest People," 1–4.

79. Ibid., chap. 2, "An Epidemic of Trees," 19–45, and chap. 3, "Sprawl," 46–52.

80. Ibid., chap. 4, "The Fifty-Pound Rodent," 75.

81. Ibid., chap. 5, "The Elegant Ungulate," 87.

82. Ibid., 117.

83. Ibid., "Epilogue," 275–293.

84. Ibid., chap. 11, "Feathered Friends," 233.

85. Ibid., chap. 8, "Teddies," 161–165.

86. See Stephen S. Ditchkoff et al., "Wounding Rates of White-Tailed Deer with Traditional Archery Equipment," *Proceedings of the Annual Conference of the Southeast Association of Fish and Wildlife Agencies* 52 (1998): 244–248; Rocco Murano, "Reducing Wounding Losses," *South Dakota Game, Fish, and Parts*, https://gfp.sd.gov/hunting/waterfowl/wounding-losses.aspx.

87. Sterba, *Nature Wars*, chap. 12, "Feral Felines," 260.

88. Ibid., 256–263.

89. Clare Palmer, *Animal Ethics in Context* (New York: Columbia University Press, 2010), 66.

90. Sue Donaldson and Will Kymlicka, *Zoopolis: A Political Theory of Animal Rights* (Oxford, UK: Oxford University Press, 2011), chap. 7, "Liminal Animal Denizens," 211.

91. Palmer, *Animal Ethics in Context*, chap. 3, "Capacities, Context, and Relations," 44–62.

92. Ibid., 54–57.

93. Ibid., 48.

94. Ibid., chap. 4, "Wildness, Domestication, and the Laissez-faire Intuition," 63–76.

95. Ibid., 66–67.

96. Donaldson and Kymlicka, *Zoopolis*, chap. 7, 216–226.

97. Ibid., 239–250.

98. Kelsi Nagy and Phillip David Johnson II, *Trash Animals: How We Live with Nature's Filthy, Feral, Invasive, and Unwanted Species* (Minneapolis: University of Minnesota Press, 2103), "Introduction," 1–27.

99. Palmer, *Animal Ethics in Context*, chap. 6, "Past Harms and Special Obligations," 102–106.

100. Ibid., 104.

101. Ibid., 105.

102. Ibid., 103.

103. Ibid., 104.

104. Ibid., 105.

105. Ibid., chap. 8, "Puzzling through Some Cases," 152–158.

106. Ibid., 154.

107. Ibid., 155–156.

108. Ibid., 157–158.

109. Ibid., 158.

### CHAPTER 3

1. See Cary Wolfe, *What Is Posthumanism?* (Minneapolis: University of Minnesota Press, 2010), "Introduction: What Is Posthumanism?" xi–xxxiv.

2. See Keith Ansell Pearson, *Viroid Life: Perspectives on Nietzsche and the Transhuman Condition* (London: Routledge, 1997); and Joel Garreau, *Radical Evolution: The Promise and Peril of Enhancing Our Minds, Our Bodies—and What It Means to Be Human* (New York: Random House, 2005).

3. Gary Snyder, "The Rediscovery of Turtle Island," in *A Place in Space: Ethics, Aesthetics, and Watersheds* (Berkeley: Counterpoint, 1995), 236.

4. John Searle maintains that humans create institutional reality through collective intentionality and social agreements (i.e., social contracts). Linguistic declarations (speech acts) create and sustain social reality. Institutional reality and social facts, however, are grounded in the ontologically objective reality of the brute facts of the physical world. Human social constructs have an ontological and epistemological status dependent on the real world of physical reality, which is ontologically objective, and the sociolinguistic world of intersubjective understanding, which lays claim to epistemological objectivity through collective intentionality. Searle distinguishes his social constructionist theory from postmodernism, which he argues conceives of social reality as radically relativistic ontologically and epistemologically. See John R. Searle, *The Construction of Social Reality* (New York: Free Press, 1995), chap. 1, "The Building Blocks of Social Reality," chap. 2, "Creating Institutional Facts," chap. 3, "Language and Social Reality," 1–78; *Freedom and Neurobiology: Reflections on Free Will, Language, and Political Power* (New York: Columbia University Press, 2007), chap. 2, "Social Ontology and Political Power," 79–109; and *Making the Social World: The Structure of Human Civilization* (Oxford, UK: Oxford University Press, 2010), chap. 5, "The General Theory of Institution and Institutional Facts: Language and Social Reality," 90–122.

5. See Wayne Gabardi, *Negotiating Postmodernism* (Minneapolis: University of Minnesota Press, 2001), 87.

6. Hal Herzog, *Some We Love, Some We Hate, Some We Eat: Why It's So Hard to Think Straight about Animals* (New York: Harper Perennial, 2010), "Introduction," 11.

7. Charles Darwin, *The Descent of Man, and Selection in Relation to Sex* (1871), in *From So Simple a Beginning: The Four Great Books of Charles Darwin*, ed. Edward O. Wilson (New York: Norton, 2006), chap. 3, "Comparison of the Mental Powers of Man and the Lower Animals—Continued," 823.

8. Ibid., 837.

9. Ibid., chap. 2, "Comparison of the Mental Powers of Man and the Lower Animals," 802–816.

10. Ibid., chap. 3, 819–825.

11. Ibid., 818.

12. Ibid., 826–830.

13. Ibid., 834–835.

14. Ibid., 818. Also see Denis L. Krebs, *The Origins of Morality: An Evolutionary Account* (Oxford, UK: Oxford University Press, 2011), chap. 4, "Darwin's Theory of the Origin of Morality," 40–56.

15. Darwin discusses group selection in his tribal scenario in *The Descent of Man*, chap. 5, "On the Development of the Intellectual and Moral Faculties during Primeval and Civilized Times," in *From So Simple a Beginning*, 868–872.

16. See Stuart A. West, Ashleigh S. Griffin, and Andy Gardner, "Social Semantics: How Useful Has Group Selection Been?" *Journal of Evolutionary Biology* 21 (2008): 374–385.

17. See David Sloan Wilson and Elliot Sober, *Unto Others: The Evolution and Psychology of Unselfish Behavior* (Cambridge, MA: Harvard University Press, 1998); and David Sloan Wilson, *Darwin's Cathedral: Evolution, Religion, and the Nature of Society* (Chicago: University of Chicago Press, 2002).

18. William D. Hamilton, "The Evolution of Social Behavior," *Journal of Theoretical Biology* 7 (1964): 1–52.

19. Robert L. Trivers, "The Evolution of Reciprocal Altruism," *Quarterly Review of Biology* 46 (1971): 35–57.

20. See Denis L. Krebs, *The Origins of Morality*, chap. 11, "The Evolution of Cooperation," 124–142; and Kim Sterelny et al., eds., *Cooperation and Its Evolution* (Cambridge, MA: MIT Press, 2013).

21. Patricia S. Churchland, *Braintrust: What Neuroscience Tells Us about Morality* (Princeton, NJ: Princeton University Press, 2001), chap. 2, "Brain-Based Values," 12–26.

22. Ibid., chap. 3, "Caring and Caring For," 27–62.

23. Ibid., 28–29.

24. Ibid., 33–46.

25. Ibid., 48–53.

26. Ibid., 46–48.

27. Ibid., chap. 4, "Cooperating and Trusting," 71–81.

28. Frans de Waal critically contrasts his Darwinian view of evolutionary ethics with the view of morality as a cultural overlay or veneer in the writings of Thomas Hobbes and Thomas Huxley in Frans de Waal et al., *Primates and Philosophers: How Morality Evolved*, ed. Stephen Macedo and Josiah Ober (Princeton, NJ: Princeton University Press, 2006), pt. 1, "Morally Evolved: Primate Social Instincts, Human Morality, and the Rise and Fall of Veneer Theory," 1–22. On the evolutionary origin and function of morality, see Frans de Waal, *The Bonobo and the Atheist: In Search of Humanism among Primates* (New York: Norton, 2013), chap. 8, "Bottom-Up Morality," 223–240.

29. De Waal, *Primates and Philosophers*, pt. 1, 42–49.

30. Ibid., 21–42; Frans de Waal, *The Age of Empathy: Nature's Lessons for a Kinder Society* (New York: Harmony Books, 2009), chap. 3, "Bodies Talking to Bodies," 78–83.

31. Frans de Waal, *The Ape and the Sushi Master: Cultural Reflections by a Primatologist* (New York: Basic Books, 2001). Also see William C. McGrew, "The Nature of Culture: Prospects and Pitfalls of Cultural Primatology," in *Tree of Origin: What Primate Behavior Can Tell Us about Human Social Evolution*, ed. Frans B. M. de Waal (Cambridge, MA: Harvard University Press, 2001), 229–254; and Kevin N. Laland and Bennett G. Galef, eds., *The Question of Animal Culture* (Cambridge, MA: Harvard University Press, 2009).

32. Frans B. M. de Waal and Peter L. Tyack, eds., *Animal Social Complexity: Intelligence, Culture, and Individualized Societies* (Cambridge, MA: Harvard University Press, 2004), "Preface," ix–x.

33. De Waal, *Primates and Philosophers*, "The Tower of Morality," 161–181.

34. De Waal, *The Bonobo and the Atheist*, chap. 8, 232–235.

35. Dale Peterson, *The Moral Lives of Animals* (New York: Bloomsbury Press, 2011), chap. 4, "Structures," 62–83.

36. Ibid., chap. 1, "Words," 18.

37. Ibid., 20.

38. Mark Rowlands, *Can Animals Be Moral?* (Oxford, UK: Oxford University Press, 2012), chap. 1, "Animals, Emotions, and Moral Behavior," 32–35, and chap. 3, "Moral Agents, Patients, and Subjects," 71–98.

39. Ibid., chap. 4, "The Reflection Condition: Aristotle and Kant," 99–123.

40. Ibid., chap. 8, "Moral Reasons and Practice," 191–123.

41. See Sarah El Mcfarland and Ryan Hediger, eds., *Animals and Agency: An Interdisciplinary Exploration* (Leiden, Netherlands: Brill, 2009); and Virginia Morell, *Animal Wise: The Thoughts and Emotions of Our Fellow Creatures* (New York: Crown Publishers, 2013).

42. The famous "is-ought" passage appears in *A Treatise of Human Nature*, bk. 3, "Of Morals," pt. 1, "Of Virtue and Vice in General," sec. 1, "Moral Distinctions Not Derived from Reason," para. 27. See David Hume, *A Treatise of Human Nature*, ed. David Fate Norton and Mary J. Norton (Oxford, UK: Oxford University Press, 2000), 302. Also see H. O. Mounce, *Hume's Naturalism* (London: Routledge, 1999), chap. 7, "Reason and Morality," 77–98; and David Fate Norton, "The Foundations of Morality in Hume's Treatise," in *The Cambridge Companion to Hume*, 2nd ed., ed. David Fate Norton and Jacqueline Taylor (Cambridge, UK: Cambridge University Press, 2009), 270–310.

43. On the influence of Hume on animal studies, see Tom L. Beauchamp, "Hume on the Nonhuman Animal," *Journal of Medicine and Philosophy* 24 (1998): 322–335; Gary Steiner, *Animals and the Moral Community: Mental Life, Moral Status, and Kinship* (New York: Columbia University Press, 2008), chap. 3, "An Associationist Model of Animal Cognition," 57–88; Julia Driver, "A Humean Account of the Status and Character of Animals," in *The Oxford Handbook of Animal Ethics*, ed. Tom L. Beauchamp and R. G. Frey (Oxford, UK: Oxford University Press, 2011), 144–171; and Angela Coventry and Avram Hiller, "Hume on Animals the Rest of Nature," in *Animal Ethics and Philosophy: Questioning the Orthodoxy*, ed. Elisa Aaltola and John Hadley (London: Rowman and Littlefield, 2015), 165–184.

44. David Hume, *A Treatise of Human Nature*, bk. 1, "Of the Understanding," pt. 1, "Of Ideas, Their Origin, Composition, Connection, Abstraction, Etc.," sec. 4, "Of the Connection or Association of Ideas," 12–14. Also see David Owen, "Hume and the Mechanics of Mind: Impressions, Ideas, and Association," in *The Cambridge Companion to Hume*, 70–104.

45. David Hume, *An Enquiry Concerning Human Understanding: A Critical Edition*, ed. Tom L. Beauchamp (Oxford, UK: Clarendon Press, 2000), sec. 9, "Of the Reason of Animals," 79.

46. Ibid., 80.

47. Ibid., 81.

48. On natural and artificial virtues, see David Hume, *A Treatise of Human Nature*, bk. 3, "Of Morals," pt. 2, "Of Justice and Injustice," sec. 1, "Justice, Whether a Natural or Artificial Virtue?" 307–311; pt. 3, "Of Other Virtues and Vices," sec. 1, "Of the Origin of the Natural Virtues and Vices," 367–378.

49. David N. Stamos, *Evolution and the Big Questions: Sex, Race, Religion, and Other Matters* (Oxford, UK: Blackwell Publishing, 2008), chap. 1, "Evolution and Knowledge," 21–22, and chap. 7, "Evolution and Ethics," 156–158; and Michael Ruse, *Evolutionary Naturalism: Selected Essays* (London: Routledge, 1995), chap. 8, "Evolution and Ethics: The Sociobiological Approach," 256.

50. Ruse, *Evolutionary Naturalism*, chap. 8, "Evolution and Ethics: The Sociobiological Approach," 254.

51. Stamos, *Evolution and the Big Questions*, chap. 7, 155–175.

52. On the biological theory of coevolution, see Paul R. Ehrlich and Peter Raven, "Butterflies and Plants: A Study in Coevolution," *Evolution* 18 (1965): 586–608.

53. On the chimpanzee-human last common ancestor (CHLCA) theory, see Nick Patterson et al., "Genetic Evidence for Complex Speciation of Humans and Chimpanzees," *Nature* 441 (2006): 1103–1108.

54. See Tim D. White et al., "Ardipithecus Ramidus and the Paleobiology of Early Hominids," *Science* 326, no. 5949 (2009): 75–85; and Jamie Shreeve, "The Evolutionary Road," *National Geographic*, July 2010, 34–67.

55. Primatologist Richard Wrangham has developed the "cooking hypothesis" that the control of fire and the advent of cooking raw meat were major revolutions in human evolution. Cooking provided more metabolic energy to early hominids and led to physiological changes, resulting in a smaller digestive system, jaw, and teeth and a more flexible skull, all of which allowed for greater brain growth and rudimentary speech. See Richard Wrangham, *Catching Fire: How Cooking Made Us Human* (New York: Basic Books, 2009).

56. There are two theories regarding the takeoff of sustained human cultural evolution. The "human revolution" view places a more "sudden" flourishing of "modern" human traits fifty thousand to forty thousand years ago. The gradualist view locates the onset of cultural evolution as far back as one hundred thousand to seventy thousand years ago. See Richard G. Klein, "Anatomy, Behavior, and Modern Human Origins," *Journal of World Prehistory* 9, no. 2 (1995): 167–198; and Sally McBrearty and Alison S. Brooks, "The Revolution that Wasn't: A New Interpretation of the Origin of Modern Human Behavior," *Journal of Human Evolution* 39, no. 5 (2000): 453–463.

57. The old narrative of Neanderthals as simple brutes who could not successfully compete with more sophisticated *Homo sapiens* who arrived in Europe forty-six thousand years ago has been significantly revised. They were in many respects as "modern" as our species. See Annalee Newitz, *Scatter, Adapt, and Remember*, chap. 7, "Meet the Neanderthals," 77–88; and Dimitra Papagianni and Michael A. Morse, *The Neanderthals Rediscovered: How Modern Science Is Rewriting Their Story* (London: Thames and Hudson, 2013).

58. See Joseph Henrich and Richard McElreath, "The Evolution of Cultural Evolution," *Evolutionary Anthropology* 12 (2003): 123–135. Robert Boyd and Peter J. Richerson summarize their gene-culture coevolution research program in *The Origin and Evolution of Cultures* (Oxford, UK: Oxford University Press, 2005), "Introduction," 1–11. See also Boyd and Richerson, *Not by Genes Alone: How Culture Transformed Human Evolution* (Chicago: University of Chicago Press, 2005), chap. 1, "Culture Is Essential," 1–17.

59. The theory of the human mind as operating with a modular architecture and functionality is first developed by Jerry Fodor in *The Modularity of Mind: An Essay on Faculty Psychology* (Cambridge, MA: MIT Press, 1983).

60. Richard Dawkins introduces the idea of the meme in *The Selfish Gene* (Oxford, UK: Oxford University Press, 1976).

61. Kim Sterelny, *Thought in a Hostile World: The Evolution of Human Cognition* (Oxford, UK: Blackwell Publishing, 2003), chap. 9, "Heterogeneous Environments and Variable Response," 162–173, and chap. 10, "The Massive Modularity Hypothesis," 177–210.

62. Boyd and Richerson, *The Origin and Evolution of Cultures*, chap. 1, "Social Learning as an Adaptation," 19–34; Boyd and Richerson, *Not by Genes Alone*, chap. 4, "Culture Is an Adaptation," 108–126; Kim Sterelny, "The Evolution and Evolvability of Culture," *Mind and Language* 21, no. 2 (2006): 137–165; Sterelny, *The Evolved Apprentice: How Evolution Made Humans Unique* (Cambridge, MA: MIT Press, 2012); and Sterelny, "The Evolved Apprentice Model: Scope and Limits," *Biological Theory* 8 (2013): 37–43.

63. See Kim Sterelny, *Thought in a Hostile World*, chap. 7, "The Cooperation Explosion," 123–145.

64. Ibid., chap. 8, "The Self-Made Species," 146–161.

65. Heidegger's idea of dwelling is one of the key modalities of *Dasein*, human being-in-the-world. In the essay "Building Dwelling Thinking," he makes the case that dwelling and building are closely connected ontologically and linguistically. In classic Heidegger fashion, he takes the reader on a genealogical journey, revealing the "primal nature" of words that have fallen into "oblivion" and whose "true meaning" has been lost. Dwelling and building come from the old English *bauen* and German *baun*, which means to inhabit an abode and cultivate a space of habitation. Building is not the art or technique of physical construction per se but a way of being-in-the-world that creates a space where humans can dwell. Building is about "locations in space," determining where we should live and why. More than this, it connects and integrates the "fourfold" primal forces of Being—Earth, sky, divinities, and mortals. Dwelling and building bring "the fourfold" into presence. They therefore are fundamental ethical practices dedicated to the preservation of an abode of dwelling. Dwelling is finding one's home in the world, a world Heidegger believes under conditions of modernity is one of existential homelessness. See Martin Heidegger, *Poetry, Language, Thought*, trans. Albert Hoftstadter (New York: Harper, Colophon Books, 1971), "Building Dwelling Thinking," 143–161. Also see Leslie Paul Thiele, *Timely Meditations: Martin Heidegger and Postmodern Politics* (Princeton, NJ: Princeton University Press, 1995), chap. 7, "Saving the Earth: The Plight of Homelessness," 171–191.

66. The ancient Greek word *"phronesis"* translates as "practical wisdom." In book six of the *Nicomachean Ethics*, Aristotle classifies, defines, and analyzes the intellectual virtues of the soul—scientific knowledge (*episteme*); art, technical skill, and craftsmanship (*techne*); practical reason (*phronesis*); intelligence (*nous*); theoretical wisdom (*sophia*); understanding (*sunesis*); and judgment (*gnome*). Practical reasoning deals with the realm of action and conduct (*praxis*). It involves deliberation and judgment with regard to changing circumstances, applying knowledge and experience to things that are variable by nature. Practical wisdom concerns itself with particulars as well as universals. But knowledge of particulars can be attained only through experience, not through theoretical wisdom. Thus *phronesis* is a practical value-rationality that involves the application of principles and deliberative reasoning to context-dependent action-oriented situations to arrive at prudent decisions. It informs and guides how we act in particular situations. See *The Ethics of Aristotle*, trans. J. A. K. Thomson, rev. ed. (New York: Penguin Books, 1976), bk. 6, "Intellectual Virtues," 209–210.

67. Niche differentiation is one theory that has been developed to explain not only species coexistence and coevolution but also the fact that there are many similar species in nature. Other scientific theories that help explain coexistence and coevolution are the "neutral theory of biodiversity," which focuses on the rough equivalence of species in a habitat that do not outcompete each other, the idea of "self-organized similarity" among species within a niche, and the rate of new species introduction. See Martin Scheffer and Egbert H. van Nes, "Self-Organized Similarity: The Evolutionary Emergence of Groups of Similar Species," *Proceedings of the National Academy of Sciences* 103, no. 16 (2006): 6230–6235; and Tommaso Zillio and Richard Condit, "The Impact of Neutrality, Niche Differentiation, and Species Input on Diversity and Abundance Distributions," *Oikos* 116 (2007): 931–940.

68. On the different approaches of environmental and animal ethics and the idea of biocentric ethics as a way of reconciling both of these outlooks, see Anna L. Peterson, *Being Animal: Beasts and Boundaries in Nature Ethics* (New York: Columbia University Press, 2013).

69. Paul W. Taylor, *Respect for Nature: A Theory of Environmental Ethics* (Princeton, NJ: Princeton University Press, 1986), chap. 3, "The Biocentric Outlook on Nature," 101–116.

70. Ibid., 116–119.

71. Ibid., 118.

72. Ibid.

73. Ibid., 119–129.

74. Ibid., 120.

75. Ibid., 121.

76. Ibid., 120.

77. Ibid., 121.

78. Ibid., 119.

79. Ibid., 122.

80. Ibid.

81. Ibid., 123.

82. Ibid., 124.

83. Ibid., 129–135.

84. Ibid., 135–152.

85. Ibid., 129.

86. Ibid., 131.

87. Ibid., 155; emphasis original.

88. Ibid., 121n7.

89. Ibid., 123.

90. See Wayne Williams, "Enchanted Worlds and Animal Others," in Aaltola and Hadley, eds., *Animal Ethics and Philosophy*, 83–98.

91. Taylor, *Respect for Nature*, chap. 1, "Environmental Ethics and Human Ethics," sec. 3, "Formal Conditions for Valid Moral Principles," 27–33.

92. Ibid., chap. 3, 161–168.

93. Ibid., chap. 4, "The Ethical System," 169–218.

94. Ibid., 172–173. Taylor makes clear that the rule of nonmaleficence applies to only human moral agents. It does not apply "to the behavior of a nonhuman animal or the activity of a plant that might bring harm to another living thing or cause its death" (172).

95. Ibid., 174–175.

96. Ibid., 179–186.

97. Ibid., 187. Taylor acknowledges that "the detailed facts of each situation" would influence "what restitutive acts are called for," but we "can nevertheless formulate some middle-range principles of justice" that can help guide our decisions with regard to the three rules of nonmaleficence, noninterference, and fidelity." For example, with regard to doing no harm, the situation would be different if an organism were harmed and not killed, if a species-population was harmed or on the verge of extinction, or if an entire biotic community was harmed or destroyed by humans.

98. Ibid., chap. 6, "Competing Claims and Priority Principles," 263.

99. Ibid., 264–265.

100. Ibid., 270.

101. Ibid., 272.

102. Ibid., 280–291.

103. Ibid., 291–304.

104. Ibid., 304–306.

105. Ibid., chap. 1, sec. 7, "A Note on the Ethics of the Bioculture," 53–58.

106. Roberto Esposito, *Bios: Biopolitics and Philosophy*, trans. Timothy Campbell (Minneapolis: University of Minnesota Press, 2008), chap. 1, "The Enigma of Biopolitics," 13, and chap. 2, "The Paradigm of Immunization," 45–77.

107. Ibid., chap. 5, "The Philosophy of *Bios*," 191–194.

108. Ibid., 186.

109. Ibid., 186–187.

110. On Heidegger's philosophy of *Dasein* (being-in-the-world), see Thiele, *Timely Meditations*, chap. 2, "Heidegger's Vision: Being-in-the-World," 42–57; and Dana R. Villa, *Arendt and Heidegger: The Fate of the Political* (Princeton, NJ: Princeton University Press, 1996), chap. 4, "The Heideggerian Roots of Arendt's Political Theory," 113–143.

111. On Heidegger's postmetaphysical anthropocentrism, see Gary Steiner, *Anthropocentrism and Its Discontents: The Moral Status of Animals in the History of Western Philosophy* (Pittsburgh, PA: University of Pittsburgh Press, 2005), chap. 9, "Postmodern Conceptions of the Human-Animal Boundary," 204–214; and Matthew Calarco, *Zoographies: The Question of the Animal from Heidegger to Derrida* (New York: Columbia University Press, 2008), chap. 1, "Metaphysical Anthropocentrism: Heidegger," 15–53.

112. See Jonathan D. Singer, "The Flesh of My Flesh: Animality, Difference, and 'Radical Community' in Merleau-Ponty's Philosophy," in Aaltola and Hadley, eds., *Animal Ethics and Philosophy*, 99–116. Also see Maurice-Merleau Ponty, *Phenomenology of Perception*, trans. Colin Smith (New York: Routledge, 1989); and Maurice-Merleau Ponty, *The Visible and the Invisible*, ed. Claude Lefort and trans. Alphonso Lingis (Evanston, IL: Northwestern University Press, 1968).

113. Thomas Nagel, "What Is It Like to Be a Bat?" *Philosophical Review* 83 (1974): 435–450.

114. J. M. Coetzee, *The Lives of Animals* (Princeton, NJ: Princeton University Press, 1999), "The Poets and the Animals," 50–54.

115. See Jakob von Uexküll, *A Foray into the Worlds of Animals and Humans: With a Theory of Meaning*, trans. Joseph D. O'Neilo (Minneapolis: University of Minnesota Press, 2010); Jesper Hoffmeyer, *Biosemiotics: An Examination into the Signs of Life and the Life of Signs* (Scranton, PA: University of Scranton Press, 2008); and Donald Favareau, *Essential Readings in Biosemiotics* (Dordrecht, Netherlands: Springer, 2010).

116. See Morten Tonnessen and Jonathan Beever, "Beyond Sentience: Biosemiotics as Foundation for Animal and Environmental Ethics," in Aaltola and Hadley, eds., *Animal Ethics and Philosophy*, 47–62.

117. See Adolf Portmann, *New Paths in Biology* (New York: Harper and Row, 1964); Neil Evernden, *The Natural Alien: Humankind and Environment* (Toronto: University of Toronto Press, 1993); Kenneth Shapiro, "A Phenomenological Approach to the Study of Nonhuman Animals," in *Anthropomorphism, Anecdotes, and Animals*, ed. R. W. Mitchell, N. S. Thompson, and H. L. Miles (Albany: State University of New York Press, 1997), 277–295; Elizabeth Behnke, "Ghost Gestures: Phenomenological Investigations of Bodily Micro-movements and Their Intercorporeal Implications," *Human Studies* 20 (1997): 181–201; Traci Warkentin, "Interspecies Etiquette: An Ethics of Paying Attention to Animals," *Ethics and the Environment* 15, no. 1 (2010): 101–121; and Julie A. Smith and Robert W. Mitchell, eds., *Experiencing Animal Minds: An Anthology of Animal-Human Encounters* (New York: Columbia University Press, 2012).

118. See Traci Warkentin, "Thinking Like a Whale: Interdisciplinary Methods for the Study of Human-Animal Interactions," in Smith and Mitchell, eds., *Experiencing Animal Minds*, 129–141.

119. See Gala Argent, "Toward a Privileging of the Nonverbal: Communication, Corporeal Synchrony, and Transcendence in Humans and Horses," in Smith and Mitchell, eds., *Experiencing Animal Minds*, 114–115.

120. Ibid., 114.

121. See Partha S. Bhagavatula et al., "Optic Flow Cues Guide Flight in Birds," *Current Biology* 21, no. 21 (2011): 1794–1799.

122. Charles Darwin, *The Formation of Vegetable Mould, through the Action of Worms: With Observations on Their Habits* (London: J. Murray, 1882), Nineteenth Century Collections Online (NCCO): Science, Technology, and Medicine: 1780–1925. Also see Oliver Sacks, "The Mental Life of Plants and Worms, among Others," *New York Review of Books*, April 29, 2014, 4–8.

123. Ralph R. Acampora, *Corporal Compassion: Animal Ethics and Philosophy of Body* (Pittsburgh, PA: University of Pittsburgh Press, 2006), "Introduction: Somaesthetics and Animal Ethics," xiii–ix.

124. Ibid., chap. 1, "Interspecies Ethics and Phenomenology of Body: Precursors and Pathways," 23, and chap. 4, "Ethos and Leib: Symphysics of Transpecific Morality," 72–94.

125. Ibid., chap. 2, "Flesh-and-Blood Being-in-a-World: Toward a Transpecific Ontology of Somatic Society," 25–47.

126. Jean-Jacques Rousseau associates this feeling with *amour de soi* and our natural inclination toward goodness and compassion, all of which are innate impulses and dispositions that exist prior to reasoning. See N.J.H. Dent, *A Rousseau Dictionary* (Oxford, UK: Blackwell Publishers, 1992), 89.

127. Acampora, *Corporal Compassion*, chap. 3, "Appreciation of Animal Nature under the Aspect of Bodiment," 57–71.

128. Jean-Jacques Rousseau, "Discourse on the Origin and Foundations of Inequality among Men," in *Classics of Moral and Political Theory*, ed. Michael L. Morgan (Indianapolis, IN: Hackett Publishing, 2001), pt. 1, 727.

129. Cynthia Willett, *Interspecies Ethics* (New York: Columbia University Press, 2014), chap. 1, "Can the Animal Subaltern Laugh? Neoliberal Inversions, Cross-species Solidarities, and Other Challenges to Human Exceptionalism," 43–38.

130. Ibid., 48–59.

131. Ibid., 33–42, and chap. 3, "Affect Attunement: Discourse Ethics across Species," 80–81.

132. Ibid., chap. 5, "Reflections: A Model and a Vision of Ethical Life," 135.

133. Ibid., chap. 3, "Affect Attunement: Discourse Ethics across Species," 81–88.

134. Ibid., "Introduction," 10, 17–21.

135. Ibid., 18.

136. Coetzee, *The Lives of Animals*, "The Philosophers and the Animals," 23.

137. Ibid., "The Poets and the Animals," 52.

138. Ibid., 50–53.

139. Ibid., 53.

140. Ibid., 52.

141. Gary Snyder, *A Place in Space: Ethics, Aesthetics, and Watersheds* (Berkeley: Counterpoint, 1995), "Unnatural Writing," 169.

142. Ibid.

143. Ibid., 170.

144. Peter Singer summarizes his ethical outlook in *Practical Ethics*, 3rd ed. (Cambridge, UK: Cambridge University Press, 2011), chap. 1, "About Ethics," 1–15.

145. See Peter Singer, *Animal Liberation*, 2nd ed. (New York: Random House, 1990), chap. 1, "All Animals Are Equal . . . ," 1–23.

146. Singer, *Practical Ethics*, chap. 3, "Equality for Animals?" 53.

147. Ibid., chap. 5, "Taking Life: Animals," 101.

148. Ibid., 94–104.

149. Ibid., 104–122. Also see Singer's response to Coetzee in *The Lives of Animals*, 85–91.

150. Singer, *Practical Ethics*, chap. 3, 53–58.

151. Gary L. Francione, *Animals as Persons: Essays on the Abolition of Animal Exploitation* (New York: Columbia University Press, 2008), chap. 3, "Taking Sentience Seriously," 129–147.

152. Ibid., chap. 2, "Reflections on *Animals, Property, and the Law* and *Rain without Thunder*," 67–128.

153. See Steven M. Wise, "Animal Rights, One Step at a Time," in *Animal Rights: Current Debates and New Directions*, ed. Cass R. Sunstein and Martha C. Nussbaum (Oxford, UK: Oxford University Press, 2004), 19–50.

154. Gary Steiner, *Animals and the Moral Community: Mental Life, Moral Status, and Kinship* (New York: Columbia University Press, 2008), chap. 5, "The Idea of Cosmic Holism," 117–142, and chap. 6, "Cosmo-politics: Grounding Liberal Individualism in Cosmic Holism," 143–163.

155. Ibid., chap. 5, 132–142.

156. Ibid., chap. 6, 156–163.

157. Ibid., chap. 5, 121–125, 132–142.

158. Thomas Nagel, *Mind and Cosmos: Why the Materialist Neo-Darwinian Conception of Nature Is Almost Certainly False* (Oxford, UK: Oxford University Press, 2012), chap. 1, "Introduction," 3–12.

159. Ibid., chap. 2, "Antireductionism and the Natural Order," 16–17.

160. Ibid., chap. 4, "Cognition," 92.

161. Ibid., chap. 2, "Antireductionism and the Natural Order," 17.

162. Ibid., chap. 4, 85.

163. Ibid., 85–86.

164. Ibid., chap. 5, "Value," 97–126.

165. Matthew Calarco, *Thinking through Animals: Identity, Difference, Indistinction* (Stanford, CA: Stanford University Press, 2015), 24.

166. Jacques Derrida, *The Animal that Therefore I Am*, ed. Marie-Louise Mallet and trans. David Wills (New York: Fordham University Press, 2008); "'Eating Well,' or the Calculation of the Subject: An Interview with Jacques Derrida," in *Who Comes after the Subject?* ed. Eduardo Cadava, Peter Connor, and Jean-Luc Nancy and trans. Peter Connor and Avital Ronnell (New York: Routledge, 1991), 96–119; "Force of Law: The 'Mystical Foundation of Authority,'" *Cardozo Law Review* 2 (1989–1990): 920–1045; "Before the Law," trans. Avigtal Ronnell, in *Acts of Literature*, ed. Derek Attridge (New York: Routledge, 1992), 181–220; *Rogues: Two Essays on Reason*, trans. Pascale-Anne Brault and Michael Naas (Stanford, CA: Stanford University Press, 2005); and *The Beast and the Sovereign*, vol. 1, ed. Michel Lisse, Marie-Louise Mallet, and Ginette Michaud and trans. Geoffrey Bennington (Chicago: University of Chicago Press, 2009).

167. Wolfe, *What Is Posthumanism?* "Introduction," xxv.

168. Ibid., xxv–xxvi, and chap. 2, "Flesh and Finitude," 49–98.

169. Ibid., chap. 2, 74. Here Wolfe quotes Cora Diamond from her 2001 essay "Injustice and Animals," in *Slow Cures and Bad Philosophers: Essays on Wittgenstein, Medicine, and Bioethics*, ed. Carl Elliott (Durham, NC: Duke University Press, 2001), 118–148.

170. Matthew Calarco, "Toward an Agnostic Animal Ethics," in *The Death of the Animal*, ed. Paola Cavalieri (New York: Columbia University Press, 2009), 73–84.

171. See Gabardi, *Negotiating Postmodernism*, chap. 6, "Postmodern Strategies and Democratic Politics," 122–143.

172. Matthew Calarco, *Zoographies*, chap. 2, "Facing the Other Animal: Levinas," 55–77.

173. Gary Steiner, *Animals and the Limits of Postmodernism* (New York: Columbia University Press, 2013), chap. 3, "Later Here Signifies Never: Derrida on Animals," 77–131.

174. Gabardi, *Negotiating Postmodernism*, chap. 1, "The Modern-Postmodern Debate and Its Legacy," 3–16, and chap. 3, "The Idea of Critical Postmodernism," 43–65.

175. See Chloe Taylor, "Foucault and Critical Animal Studies: Genealogies of Agricultural Power," *Philosophy Compass* 8, no. 6 (2013): 539–551.

176. Cary Wolfe, *Before the Law: Humans and Other Animals in a Biopolitical Frame* (Chicago: University of Chicago Press, 2013), chap 2, 17–18.

177. Ibid., chap. 1, 3–10.

178. Ibid., chap8,, 103; emphasis original.

179. Ibid., 90.

180. Ibid., 94.

181. See Carol J. Adams, *Neither Man nor Beast: Feminism and the Defense of Animals* (New York: Continuum, 1994); Adams, *The Sexual Politics of Meat: A Feminist-Vegetarian Critical Theory*, 20th anniv. ed. (New York: Bloomsbury, 2010); Carol J. Adams and Josephine Donovan, eds., *Animals and Women: Feminist Theoretical Explorations* (Durham, NC: Duke University Press, 1995); Josephine Donovan and Carol J. Adams, eds., *The Feminist Care Tradition in Animal Ethics* (New York: Columbia University Press, 2007); Lori Gruen, *Ethics and Animals: An Introduction* (Cambridge, UK: Cambridge University Press, 2011); Gruen, *Entangled Empathy: An Alternative Ethic for Our Relationships with Animals* (New York: Lantern Books, 2014); Gruen, *Sister Species: Women, Animals, and Social Justice*, ed. Lisa Kemmerer (Champaign: University of Illinois Press, 2011); and Kari Weil, *Thinking Animals: Why Animal Studies Now?* (New York: Columbia University Press, 2012).

182. Kathy Rudy, *Loving Animals: Toward a New Animal Advocacy* (Minneapolis: University of Minnesota Press, 2011), chap. 1, "What's behind Animal Advocacy?" 26.

183. Ibid., 25.

184. Ibid., 2–8.

185. Ibid., 9–12.

186. Ibid., 22.

187. Ibid., chap. 2, "The Love of a Dog: Of Pets and Puppy Mills, Mixed Breeds and Shelters," 29–72.

188. Ibid., chap. 3, "The Animal on Your Plate: Farmers, Vegans, and Locavores," 73–110.

189. Ibid., chap. 4, "Where the Wild Things Ought to Be: Sanctuaries, Zoos, and Exotic Pets," 122–127.

190. See Marc Bekoff, *Why Dogs Hump and Bees Get Depressed: The Fascinating Science of Animal Intelligence, Emotions, Friendship, and Conservation* (Novato, CA: New World Library, 2013), pt. 8, "The Lives of Captive Creatures: Why Are They Even There?" 211–222; and Barbara J. King, *How Animals Grieve* (Chicago: University of Chicago Press, 2013), chap. 5, "Elephant Bones," 52–63.

191. Rudy, *Loving Animals*, chap. 4, 127–142.

192. Ibid., 142–152.

193. See Lauren Slater, "Wild Obsession: The Perilous Attraction of Owning Exotic Pets," photographs by Vincent J. Musi, *National Geographic,* April 2014, 96–119.

194. Rudy, *Loving Animals,* chap. 5, "From Object to Subject: Animals in Scientific Research," 169–185.

195. See Hal Herzog, *Some We Love, Some We Hate, Some We Eat: Why It's So Hard to Think Straight about Animals,* chap. 8, "The Moral Status of Mice: The Use of Animals in Science," 205–235.

196. Gary Steiner, "Kathy Rudy's Feel-Good Ethics," *Humanimalia: A Journal of Human/Animal Interface Studies* 3, no. 2 (2012): 130–135.

197. Rudy, *Loving Animals,* chap. 6, "Clothing Ourselves in Stories of Love," 193–201.

198. Steiner, *Animals and the Moral Community,* chap. 5, "The Ideal of Cosmic Holism," 129.

199. Calarco, *Thinking through Animals,* 39.

## CHAPTER 4

1. See Linda Kalof, *Looking at Animals in Human History* (London: Reaktion Books, 2007), chap. 1, "Prehistory, before 5000 BC," 1–10; Jim Mason, "Animals: From Souls and the Sacred in Prehistoric Times to Symbols and Slaves in Antiquity," in *A Cultural History of Animals in Antiquity,* vol. 1, ed. Linda Kalof (Oxford, UK: Berg, 2007), 24–25.

2. Susan Foster McCarter, *Neolithic* (New York: Routledge, 2007), chap. 5, "Animal Domestication," 73–74.

3. See Jeffrey Moussaieff Masson, *The Dog Who Couldn't Stop Loving: How Dogs Have Captured Our Hearts for Thousands of Years* (New York: Harper Collings, 2010).

4. Ibid., 74–75.

5. See Patrick F. Houlihan, *The Animal World of the Pharaohs* (London: Thames and Hudson, 1996), chap. 8, "The Royal Menagerie," 195–208.

6. Ibid., chap. 1, "The Divine Bestiary," 1–9.

7. Ibid., chap. 4, "The Pleasure of Pets," 80–90.

8. See Arthur O. Lovejoy, *The Great Chain of Being: A Study of the History of an Idea* (Cambridge, MA: Harvard University Press, 1936, 1964). Lovejoy traces the history of this metaphysical conception of existence from its origins in Plato to its height in late antiquity and the Middle Ages in the thought of Plotinus, Augustine, and Pseudo-Dionysus the Areopagite and Church doctrine to its modern reinvention during the eighteenth-century Enlightenment.

9. See John Marenbon and D. E. Luscombe, "Two Medieval Ideas: Eternity and Hierarchy," in *The Cambridge Companion to Medieval Philosophy,* ed. A. S. McGrade (Cambridge, UK: Cambridge University Press, 2003), 51–72.

10. See Joyce E. Salisbury, *The Beast Within: Animals in the Middle Ages* (New York: Routledge, 2nd ed., 2011), chap. 1, "Animals as Property," 10–33; Linda Kalof, *Looking at Animals in Human History,* chap. 3, "The Middle Ages, 500–1400," 40–45, 49, 52–56.

11. Joyce E. Salisbury, *The Beast Within,* "Introduction: What Is an Animal?" 1–9.

12. Ibid., chap. 4, "Animals as Human Exemplars," 81–107.

13. Ibid., chap. 6, "Humans as Animals," 122–124.

14. Ibid., 131.

15. Ibid., chap. 5, "Animals as Humans," 108–115.

16. Ibid., chap. 6, "Humans as Animals," 140–145. Also see Aleksander Pluskowski, *Wolves and Wilderness in the Middle Ages* (Suffolk, UK: Boydell and Brower, 2006); Mat-

thew Beresford, *The White Devil: The Werewolf in European Culture* (London: Reaktion Books, 2013).

17. See W. M. Denevan, *The Native Population of the Americas in 1492*, 2nd ed. (Madison: University of Wisconsin Press, 1992); A. W. Crosby, *The Columbian Exchange: Biological and Cultural Consequences of 1492*, 30-year ed. (Westpoint, CT: Praeger, 2003); C. C. Mann, *1491: New Revelations of the Americas before Columbus* (New York: Vintage, 2005); and Kent G. Lightfoot et al., "European Colonialism and the Anthropocene," *Anthropocene* 4 (December 2013): 101–115.

18. On the extermination of wolves, coyotes, and other competitor species in the colonization of North America as a cultural practice and not simply an economic policy, see Jody Emel, "Are You Man Enough, Big and Bad Enough? Wolf Eradication in the US," in *Animal Geographies: Place, Politics, and Identity in the Nature-Culture Borderlands*, ed. Jennifer Wolch and Jody Emel (London: Verso, 1998), 91–116. Also see Keith Miller, "The West: Buffalo Hunting and the Great Plains: Promoting One Society While Supplanting Another," http://historynewsnetwork.org/article/531; Linda Kalof, *Looking at Animals in Human History*, chap. 6, "Modernity, 1800–2000," 148–153; Carol Cartaino, *Myths and Truths about Coyotes: What You Need to Know about America's Most Misunderstood Predator* (Birmingham: Menasha Ridge Press, 2010).

19. See Michael Allen Gillespie, *The Theological Origins of Modernity* (Chicago: University of Chicago Press, 2008).

20. See Stephen Toulmin, *Cosmopolis: The Hidden Agenda of Modernity* (New York: Free Press, 1990).

21. See Max Weber, *Economy and Society: An Outline of Interpretive Sociology*, vol. 1, ed. Guenther Roth and Claus Wittick (Berkeley: University of California Press, 1978), chap. 1, "Basic Sociological Terms," 3–62, and chap. 2, "Sociological Categories of Economic Action," 63–221; *The Protestant Ethic and the Spirit of Capitalism*, trans. Stephen Kalberg (Chicago: Fitzroy Publishers, 2001). Also see Anthony Giddens, *Capitalism and Modern Social Theory: An Analysis of the Writings of Marx, Durkheim, and Max Weber* (Cambridge, UK: Cambridge University Press, 1971), chap. 9, "Max Weber: Protestantism and Capitalism," 119–132, and chap. 12, "Rationalisation, the World Religions, and Western Capitalism," 169–184; Alex Callinicos, *Social Theory: A Historical Introduction* (New York: New York University Press, 1999), chap. 7, "Weber," 146–178; Alan Sica, "Rationalization and Culture," in *The Cambridge Companion to Weber*, ed. Stephen Turner (Cambridge, UK: Cambridge University Press, 2000); William H. Swatos Jr. and Lutz Kaelber, *The Protestant Ethic Turns 100: Essays on the Centenary of the Weber Thesis* (Boulder, CO: Paradigm Publishers, 2005); Gianfranco Poggi, *Weber: A Short Introduction* (Cambridge, UK: Polity Press, 2006), chap. 4, "The Protestant Ethic and the Spirit of Capitalism," 59–74; Stephen Kalberg, *Max Weber's Comparative-Historical Sociology Today: Major Themes, Mode of Causal Analysis, and Applications* (Burlington, VT: Ashgate, 2002), chap. 1, "Max Weber's Types of Rationality: Cornerstones for the Analysis of Rationalization Processes in History," 13–42.

22. Ryan Gunderson, "The First-Generation Frankfurt School on the Animal Question: Foundations for a Normative Sociological Animal Studies," *Sociological Perspectives* 57, no. 3 (2014): 285–300.

23. Max Horkheimer and Theodor Adorno, *Dialectic of Enlightenment*, trans. John Cumming (New York: Seabury Press, 1972), chap. 1, "The Concept of Enlightenment," 3–5. Also see David Held, *Introduction to Critical Theory: Horkheimer to Habermas* (Berkeley: University of California Press, 1980), chap. 5, "The Critique of Instrumental Reason: Critical Theory and Philosophy of History," 148–174, and "Appendix: The Odyssey," 401–407.

24. Horkheimer and Adorno, *Dialectic of Enlightenment*, 3.

25. Ibid., 16.

26. Ibid., 28.

27. Ulrich Beck, *Risk Society: Toward a New Modernity* (London: Sage, 1992); *Ecological Politics in an Age of Risk* (Cambridge, UK: Polity Press, 1994); Ulrich Beck, Anthony Giddens, and Scott Lash, *Reflexive Modernization: Politics, Tradition, and Aesthetics in the Modern Social Order* (Stanford, CA: Stanford University Press, 1994).

28. Thomas Hobbes, *Leviathan*, ed. Richard Tuck (Cambridge, UK: Cambridge University Press, 1991), pt. 1, "Of Man," chap. 13, "Of the Natural Condition of Mankind, as Concerning Their Felicity and Misery," 89.

29. Ibid., chap. 14, "Of the First and Second Natural Laws, and of Contracts," 91–94.

30. David Hume, "Of the Original Contract," in *Social Contract: Essays by Locke, Hume, and Rousseau* (Oxford, UK: Oxford University Press, 1969), 151.

31. Ibid., 154.

32. Friedrich Nietzsche, *On the Genealogy of Morality*, ed. Keith Ansell-Pearson and trans. Carol Diethe (Cambridge, UK: Cambridge University Press, 1994), chap. 2, "'Guilt,' 'Bad Conscience,' and Related Matters," 38.

33. Ibid., 39–40.

34. Ibid., 40.

35. Ibid, secs. 201 and 202, "Supplementary Material on *On the Genealogy of Morality*," 158–162.

36. Martha Nussbaum, *Frontiers of Justice: Disability, Nationality, Species Membership* (Cambridge, MA: Belknap Press of Harvard University Press, 2006), chap. 1, "Social Contracts and Three Unsolved Problems of Justice," 14–22.

37. Mark Rowlands, *Animal Rights: A Philosophical Defence* (New York: St. Martin's Press, 1998), chap. 6, "Contractarianism and Animal Rights," 135–145.

38. Martha Nussbaum, *Frontiers of Justice*, chap. 1, "Social Contracts and Three Unsolved Problems of Justice," 9–95, and chap. 6, "Beyond Compassion and Humanity: Justice for Nonhuman Animals," 325–407.

39. See Hannah Arendt, *The Human Condition* (Chicago: University of Chicago Press, 1958); Melvyn A. Hill, ed., *Hannah Arendt: The Recovery of the Public World* (New York: St. Martin's Press, 1979); Dana R. Villa, *Arendt and Heidegger*, pt. 1, "Arendt's Theory of Political Action," 15–109; Martin J. Matustik, *Postnational Identity: Critical Theory and Existential Philosophy in Habermas, Kierkegaard, and Havel* (New York: Guilford Press, 1993); Chantal Mouffe, *The Return of the Political* (London: Verso, 1993).

40. Jürgen Habermas, *Legitimation Crisis*, trans. Thomas McCarthy (Boston: Beacon Press, 1975), pt. 1, "A Social-Scientific Concept of Crisis," 1–31.

41. Ibid., pt. 2, "Crisis Tendencies in Advanced Capitalism," 33–94.

42. Ibid., pt. 3, "On the Logic of Legitimation Problems," 95–143. On Habermas's theory of discourse ethics as the philosophical and ethical foundation of his model of deliberative or "discursive" democracy, see Jürgen Habermas, *Justification and Application: Remarks on Discourse Ethics*, trans. Ciarin P. Cronin (Cambridge, MA: MIT Press, 1994). On the application of discourse ethics to democratic and legal theory, see Jürgen Habermas, *Between Facts and Norms: Contributions to a Discourse Theory of Law and Democracy*, trans. William Rehg (Cambridge, MA: MIT Press, 1996). Also see David Ingram, *Habermas: Introduction and Analysis* (Ithaca, NY: Cornell University Press, 2010), chap. 5, "Discourse Ethics," 115–151, and chaps. 6–9, "Law and Democracy," pts. 1–5, 153–265.

43. See Thomas Piketty, *Capital in the Twenty-First Century*, trans. Arthur Goldhammer (Cambridge, MA: Belknap Press of Harvard University Press, 2014).

44. See the *2013 Report Card for America's Infrastructure*, American Society of Civil Engineers, www.infrastrastructurereportcard.org.

45. Michel Foucault, *Discipline and Punish: The Birth of the Modern Prison*, trans. Alan Sheridan (New York: Pantheon Books, 1997).

46. See Thomas L. Dumm, *Michel Foucault and the Politics of Freedom* (Thousand Oaks, CA: SAGE Publications, 1996), chap. 3, "Freedom and Disciplinary Society," 69–122; John S. Ransom, *Foucault's Discipline: The Politics of Subjectivity* (Durham, NC: Duke University Press, 1997), chap. 3, "Disciplines and the Individual," 26–58.

47. See Stewart R. Clegg, *Frameworks of Power*, chap. 7, "Post-Structuralism, Sovereign Power, and Disciplinary Power," 149–178.

48. Michel Foucault introduced his concepts of biopower and biopolitics in *The History of Sexuality, Volume I: An Introduction*, trans. Robert Hurley (New York: Vintage Books, 1980), pt. 5, "Right of Death and Power over Life," 135–145.

49. Michel Foucault, "Truth and Power," in *Power/Knowledge: Selected Interviews and Other Writings, 1972–1977*, ed. Colin Gordon and trans. Colin Gordon, Leo Marshall, John Mepham, and Kate Soper (New York: Pantheon Books, 1980), 121.

50. See Max Weber, *Economy and Society*, vol. 1, chap. 3, "The Types of Legitimate Domination," 212–307.

51. On the idea of resistance and its relationship to power, see Michel Foucault, *The History of Sexuality, Volume I: An Introduction*, 92–96; "The Subject and Power," in Hubert L. Dreyfus and Paul Rabinow, *Michel Foucault: Beyond Structuralism and Hermeneutics* (Chicago: University of Chicago Press, 1983), 211–213. Also see Gabardi, *Negotiating Postmodernism*, chap. 4, "Foucault's Presence," 69–79.

52. Albert O. Hirschman, *Exit, Voice, and Loyalty: Responses to Decline in Firms, Organizations, and States* (Cambridge, MA: Harvard University Press, 1970).

53. On Michel Foucault's concept of modern biopolitics, see *"Society Must Be Defended" Lectures at the College de France, 1975–76*, ed. Mauro Bertani and Alessandro Fontana and trans. David Macey (New York: Picador,2003), chap. 11, "17 March 1976," 239–264, and "Course Summary," 265–272.

54. de Waal, *The Bonobo and the Atheist*, chap. 8, "Bottom-up Morality," 226–235.

55. Marc Bekoff and Jessica Pierce, *Wild Justice: The Moral Lives of Animals* (Chicago: University of Chicago Press, 2009), chap. 1, "Morality in Animal Societies: An Embarrassment of Riches," 7.

56. Ibid., 8.

57. Ibid., 13.

58. Ibid., 19–21.

59. Marc Bekoff, *The Emotional Lives of Animals* (Novato, CA: New World Library, 2007), chap. 4, "Wild Justice, Empathy, and Fair Play: Finding Honor among Beasts," 88–89.

60. Ibid., chap. 1, "The Case for Animal Emotions and Why They Matter," 1–28.

61. Ibid., chap. 2, "Cognitive Ethology: Studying Animal Minds and Hearts," 28–41; Bekoff and Pierce, *Wild Justice*, chap. 2, "Foundations for Justice: What Animals Do and What It Means," 24–54.

62. Bekoff, *The Emotional Lives of Animals*, chap. 4, 89–90; Bekoff and Pierce, *Wild Justice*, chap. 5, "Justice: Honor and Fair Play among Beasts," 110–115.

63. Bekoff and Pierce, *Wild Justice*, chap. 5, 120–130.

64. Ibid., 121.

65. Ibid., 115.

66. Ibid., 131–135.

67. Ibid., chap. 2, "Foundations for Justice: What Animals Do and What It Means," 40–43.

68. Martha C. Nussbaum, *Frontiers of Justice: Disability, Nationality, Species Member-ship* (Cambridge, MA: Belknap Press of Harvard University Press, 2006), "Introduction," 1–8, and chap. 1, "Social Contracts and Three Unsolved Problems of Justice," 9–95.

69. See Martha C. Nussbaum, "Beyond Compassion and Humanity: Justice for Nonhuman Animals," in Sunstein and Nussbaum, *Animal Rights: Current Debates and New Directions*, 299–320.

70. Richard Sorabji, *Animal Minds and Human Morals: The Origins of the Western Debate* (Ithaca, NY: Cornell University Press, 1993), chap. 1, "The Crisis: The Denial of Reason to Animals," 7–16.

71. Gary Steiner, *Anthropocentrism and Its Discontents: The Moral Status of Animals in the History of Western Philosophy* (Pittsburgh, PA: University of Pittsburgh Press, 2005), chap. 3, "Aristotle and the Stoics: The Evolution of a Cosmic Principle," 76.

72. Catherine Osborne, *Dumb Beasts and Dead Philosophers: Humanity and the Humane in Ancient Philosophy and Literatures* (Oxford, UK: Clarendon Press, 2007), chap. 4, "On Language, Concepts, and Automata: Rational and Irrational Animals in Aristotle and Descartes," 64.

73. Ibid., 79–97.

74. Larry Arnhart, "The Darwinian Biology of Aristotle's Political Animals," *American Journal of Political Science* 38, no. 2 (May 1994): 465.

75. Ibid.

76. Ibid., 466.

77. Thomas Hobbes, *Leviathan*, ed. Richard Tuck (Cambridge, UK: Cambridge University Press, 1991), pt. 2, "Of Commonwealth," chap. 17, "Of the Causes, Generation, and Definition of a Common-wealth," 119–120.

78. Nussbaum, *Frontiers of Justice*, chap. 6, "Beyond 'Compassion and Humanity': Justice for Nonhuman Animals," 346–352.

79. Ibid., 325–327.

80. Ibid., chap. 1, "Social Contracts and Three Unsolved Problems of Justice," 92–95.

81. Ibid., chap. 6, 366–372.

82. Ibid., 357–366.

83. Ibid., 372–380.

84. Ibid., 352–356.

85. Cary Wolfe, *What Is Posthumanism?* (Minneapolis: University of Minnesota Press, 2010), 61–68; Gary Steiner, *Animals and the Limits of Postmodernism* (New York: Columbia University Press, 2013), 183–186; Sue Donaldson and Will Kymlicka, *Zoopolis: A Political Theory of Animal Rights* (Oxford, UK: Oxford University Press, 2011), 95–99; Dinesh Joseph Wadiwel, *The War against Animals* (Leiden, Netherlands: Brill Rodopi, 2015), chap. 7, "Capability," 229–234.

86. Nussbaum's list of the ten central human capabilities are life, bodily health, bodily integrity, senses, imagination, and thought, emotions, practical reason, affiliation, other species, play, and control over one's environment. She admits it is "open-ended" and "no doubt will undergo further modification in the light of criticism." See Nussbaum, *Frontiers of Justice*, 76–78.

87. Ibid., chap. 6, "Beyond "Compassion and Humanity": Justice for Nonhuman Animals," 392–401.

88. Ibid., 380–384.

89. See Alex J. Bellamy, *Global Politics and the Responsibility to Protect: From Words to Deeds* (London: Routledge, 2011); Ramesh Thakur and William Malley, eds., *Theorizing the Responsibility to Protect* (Cambridge, UK: Cambridge University Press, 2015).

90. Guidance Note of the Secretary-General: United Nations Approach to Transitional Justice, March 2010, www.unrol.org.files/TJ_Guidance_Note_March_2010FINAL .pdf.

91. Donaldson and Kymlicka, *Zoopolis*, chap. 2, "Universal Basic Rights for Animals," 19–49.

92. Ibid., chap. 3, "Extending Animal Rights via Citizenship Theory," 50–69.

93. Ibid., chap. 5, "Domesticated Animal Citizens," 103–108.

94. Ibid., 108–122.

95. Ibid., 123–125.

96. Ibid., 126–132.

97. Ibid., 132–134.

98. Ibid., 134–139.

99. Ibid., 139–142.

100. Ibid., 142–144.

101. Ibid., 144–149.

102. Ibid., 149–153.

103. Ibid., 153–154.

104. Ibid., chap. 6, "Wild Animal Sovereignty," 157.

105. Ibid., 170–171.

106. Ibid., 172–174.

107. Ibid., 174.

108. Ibid., 174–178.

109. Ibid., 172.

110. Ibid., 192–193.

111. Ibid., 195–196.

112. Ibid., 193–195.

113. Ibid., 179–187.

114. Ibid., 191.

115. Ibid., 198.

116. Ibid., chap. 5, 152.

117. Clare Palmer, "Companion Cats as Co-citizens? Comments on Sue Donaldson's and Will Kymlicka's *Zoopolis*," *Dialogue* 52, no. 4 (December 2013): 759–767; emphasis original.

118. Donaldson and Kymlicka, *Zoopolis*, chap. 5, 149.

119. Palmer, "Companion Cats as Co-citizens?" 765.

120. Ibid., 766.

121. Donaldson and Kymlicka, *Zoopolis*, chap. 5, 149.

122. This is the position of Francione and Steiner. Donaldson and Kymlicka (*Zoopolis*) disagree and reject the "abolitionist/extinctionist" approach. They regard domestication, as I do, as a coevolutionary adaptive social strategy prevalent in many species. Furthermore, ending all relations with domesticated animals would be a "strategic disaster" for the animal advocacy movement. Here I also agree. See chap. 4, "Domesticated Animals within Animal Rights Theory," 77–89.

123. Ibid., chap. 6, 209.

124. See Michael Hardt and Antonio Negri, *Empire* (Cambridge, MA: Harvard University Press, 2000).

125. Donaldson and Kymlicka, *Zoopolis*, "Introduction," 2.

126. Wadiwel, *The War against Animals*, chap. 7, "Capability," 246.

127. Ibid., 251.

128. Ibid.

129. Ibid., "Conclusion: Truce," 276–277.

130. Ibid., 278.

131. Ibid., 287–293.

132. Ibid., 296.

133. Michael Mann, *The Sources of Social Power, Volume I: A History of Power from the Beginning to A.D. 1760* (Cambridge, UK: Cambridge University Press, 1986), chap. 1, "Societies as Organized Power Networks," 1.

134. Ibid., 14.

135. Ibid.

136. Ibid., chap. 2, "The End of General Social Evolution: How Prehistoric Peoples Evaded Power," 38.

137. Ibid., 35.

138. Ibid., 38–70.

139. Ibid., chap. 3, "The Emergence of Stratification, States, and Multi-power-actor Civilization in Mesopotamia," 73–104, and chap. 4, "A Comparative Analysis of the Emergence of Stratification, States, and Multi-power-actor Civilizations," 105–129.

140. Ibid., chap. 2, "The End of General Social Evolution: How Prehistoric Peoples Evaded Power," 49.

141. Ibid., 53–63, and chap. 5, "The First Empires of Domination: The Dialectics of Compulsory Cooperation," 130–178.

142. Ibid., chap. 5, "The First Empires of Domination: The Dialectics of Compulsory Cooperation," 166.

143. See Mark Anthony Wenman, "What Is Politics? The Approach of Radical Pluralism," *Politics* 23, no. 1 (2003): 57–65.

144. See John Law and John Hassard, eds., *Actor Network Theory and After* (Oxford, UK: Wiley-Blackwell, 1999); Bruno Latour, *Reassembling the Social—an Introduction to Actor-Network-Theory* (Oxford, UK: Oxford University Press, 2005).

145. Harmut Rosa, *Social Acceleration: A New Theory of Modernity*, trans. Jonathan Trejo-Mathys (New York: Columbia University Press, 2013), "Introduction," 1–13.

146. Ibid., chap. 2, "What Is Social Acceleration?" 71–80.

147. Ibid., 76.

148. Ibid., 83.

149. Ibid., 85–87.

150. Ibid., 86–87.

151. Petr Kropotkin, *Mutual Aid: A Factor of Evolution* (New York: Garland Publishing, 1972), "Preface 1914 Edition."

152. Ibid., chap. 1, "Mutual Aid among Animals," 4.

153. Stephen Jay Gould, "Kropotkin Was No Crackpot," *Natural History* 106 (June 1997): 12–21.

154. Kropotkin, *Mutual Aid*, "Introduction," viii.

155. Ibid., ix.

156. Ibid., chap. 1, "Mutual Aid among Animals," 9–31.

157. Ibid., chap. 2, "Mutual Aid among Animals (Continued)," 38–75.

158. Ibid., chap. 3, "Mutual Aid among Savages," 79.

159. Ibid.

160. Ibid., 80–83.

161. Ibid., 111.

162. Ibid., 112.

163. Ibid., 101–111.

164. Ibid., 114.

165. Kropotkin, *Mutual Aid*, chap. 4, "Mutual Aid among the Barbarians," 115–152; chaps. 5 and 6, "Mutual Aid in the Medieval City," 153–222; and chaps. 7 and 8, "Mutual Aid amongst Ourselves," 223–292.

166. Ibid., "Conclusion," 295.

167. Ibid., 299.

168. Petr Kropotkin, *Fields, Factories, and Workshops or, Industry Combined with Agriculture and Brain Work with Manual Work* (London: Thomas Nelson and Sons, 1912), chap. 2, "The Decentralisation of Industries (Continued)," 78.

169. Ibid., chap. 3, "The Possibilities of Agriculture," 79–83.

170. Ibid., 89–96.

171. Ibid., 151.

172. Ibid., 150–156.

173. Ibid., 107–119.

174. Ibid., 124–130, and chap. 5, "The Possibilities of Agriculture (Continued)," 188–232.

175. Ibid., chap. 5, "The Possibilities of Agriculture (Continued)," 236–240.

176. Ibid., chaps. 6 and 7, "Small Industries and Industrial Villages," 241–362.

177. Ibid., chap. 7, "Small Industries and Industrial Villages," 352–353.

178. Ibid., chap. 8, "Brain Work and Manual Work," 363–370.

179. Ibid., "Preface to the First Edition," ix–x, and chap. 1, "The Decentralization of Industries," 18–25.

180. Gary Snyder, *Earth House Hold* (New York: New Directions Books, 1969), back cover, and chap. 12, "Poetry and the Primitive: Notes on Poetry as an Ecological Survival Technique," 117–130. Also see George Sessions," Gary Snyder: Post-modern Man," in *Gary Snyder: Dimensions of a Life*, ed. Jon Halper (San Francisco: Sierra Club Books, 1991), 365–370.

181. See Gary Snyder, *The Practice of the Wild* (San Francisco: North Point Press, 1990), chap. 1, "The Etiquette of Freedom," 3–24, and chap. 2, "The Place, the Region, and the Commons," 25–47.

182. Gary Snyder, "Reinhabitation," in *A Place in Space: Ethics, Aesthetics, and Watersheds* (Berkeley: Counterpoint Press, 1995), 190, 184–185.

183. Ibid., 185, 191.

184. Snyder, *A Place in Space*, "Coming into Watersheds," 225–231.

185. Ibid., 221–223.

186. Ibid., "The Rediscovery of Turtle Island," 236–251.

187. Ibid., "Coming into Watersheds," 233.

188. Bill McKibben, *Deep Economy: The Wealth of Communities and the Durable Future* (New York: Times Books, 2007), "Introduction," 1–4, and chap. 1, "After Growth," 5–45.

189. Bill McKibben, *Eaarth: Making a Life on a Tough New Planet* (New York: Times Books, 2010), chap. 3, "Backing Off," 103.

190. Ibid., 120.

191. Ibid., 123.

192. Ibid., chap. 1, "A New World," 1–46.

193. Ibid., chap. 4, "Lightly, Carefully, Gracefully," 151–159.

194. Ibid., 166–182.

195. McKibben, *Deep Economy*, chap. 2, "The Year of Eating Locally," 46–94, and chap. 3, "The Wealth of Communities," 129–176.

196. McKibben, *Eaarth*, chap. 4, 187–195.

197. Ibid., 196–204.

198. Sue Donaldson and Will Kymlicka refer to this as "the refuge + advocacy model." See "Farmed Animal Sanctuaries: The Heart of the Movement" A Socio-political Perspective," *Politics and Animals* 1 (Fall 2015): 51.

199. Ibid., 53–55.

200. Ibid., 55–57.

201. Ibid., 57–61.

202. Ibid., 61–63.

203. Ibid., 51–52.

204. Ibid., 63–64.

205. Ibid., 64–65.

206. Ibid., 65–66.

207. See Caroline Fraser, *Rewilding the World: Dispatches from the Conservation Revolution* (New York: Metropolitan Books, 2009).

208. See P. J. Seddon, D. P. Armstrong, and R. F. Maloney, "Developing the Science of Reintroduction Biology," *Conservation Biology* 21, no. 2 (2007): 303–312; Malcom L. Hunter Jr., "Climate Change and Moving Species: Furthering the Debate on Assisted Colonization," *Conservation Biology* 21, no. 5 (2007): 1356–1358.

209. See John Gallagher, *Revolution Detroit: Strategies for Urban Reinvention* (Detroit, MI: Wayne State University Press, 2013).

210. Jamie Lorimer, *Wildlife in the Anthropocene: Conservation after Nature* (Minneapolis: University of Minnesota Press, 2015), "Introduction," 1–3.

211. Ibid., "Conclusion: Cosmopolitics for Wildlife," 179–193; emphasis original.

212. Ibid., "Introduction," 1–18, and chap. 1, "Wildlife: Companion Elephants and New Grounds for Multinational Conservation," 19–34.

213. Ibid., chap. 2, "Nonhuman Charisma: Counting Corncrakes and Learning to Be Affected in Multispecies Worlds," 39.

214. Ibid.

215. Ibid., 51.

216. Ibid., 52–54.

217. Ibid., 48–49.

218. Ibid., 40.

219. Ibid., 42.

220. Ibid., chap. 3, "Biodiversity as Biopolitics: Cutting Up Wildlife and Choreographing Conservation in the United Kingdom," 59–66.

221. Ibid., 67–69.

222. Lorimer illustrates this with respect to the United Kingdom Biodiversity Action Plan (UKBAP). Ibid., 71–73.

223. "Conclusion: Cosmopolitics for Wildlife," 186.

224. See Jamie Lorimer and Clemens Driessen, "Wild Experiments at the Oostvaardersplassen: Rethinking Environmentalism in the Anthropocene," *Transactions of the Insti-*

*tute of British Geographers* 39 (2014): 169–181; Lorimer, *Wildlife in the Anthropocene*, chap. 5, "Wild Experiments: Rewilding Future Ecologies at the Oostvaardersplassen," 100–105.

225. Lorimer, *Wildlife in the Anthropocene*, chap. 5, 97–100.

226. Ibid., 106–107.

227. Ibid., chap. 8, "Spaces for Wildlife: Alternative Topologies for Life in Novel Ecosystems," 164–170.

## CONCLUSION

1. Fred Guterl, *The Fate of Species: Why the Human Race May Cause Its Own Extinction and How We Can Stop It* (New York: Bloomsbury, 2012), "Introduction," 4–5.

2. Ibid., "Ingenuity," 170–176.

3. Ibid., 177–182.

4. Ibid., 186.

5. Jedediah Purdy, *After Nature: A Politics for the Anthropocene* (Cambridge, MA: Harvard University Press, 2015), "Introduction," 22.

6. Ibid.

7. Ibid.

8. Ibid., chap. 7, "Environmental Law in the Anthropocene," 229.

9. Ibid., "Introduction," 48–50, and chap. 7, "Environmental Law in the Anthropocene," 230.

10. Ibid., chap. 7, "Environmental Law in the Anthropocene," 230, 246–249.

11. Ibid., 240.

12. Ibid., 241, 243.

13. Ibid., 244.

14. Ibid., chap. 8, "What Kind of Democracy?" 271.

15. Ibid., 272.

16. Jane Bennett, *Vibrant Matter: A Political Ecology of Things* (Durham, NC: Duke University Press, 2010).

17. Purdy, *After Nature*, chap. 8, "What Kind of Democracy?" 274.

18. Ibid., 278–280.

19. Ibid., 280–281.

20. Ibid., "Introduction," 49–50, and chap. 8, 268.

21. Ibid., chap. 8, 277.

22. Ibid., 288.

23. Ibid., 280.

24. Ibid., chap. 7, 244.

25. Ibid.

26. Albert Camus, *The Myth of Sisyphus and Other Essays*, trans. Justin O'Brien (New York: Knopf, 1964), "The Myth of Sisyphus," 3–65.

27. Ibid., 64. Camus writes, "Having started from an anguished awareness of the inhuman, the meditation on the absurd returns to the end of its itinerary to the very heart of the passionate flames of revolt. Thus I draw from the absurd three consequences, which are my revolt, my freedom, my passion."

28. Albert Camus, *The Rebel: An Essay on Man in Revolt*, trans. Anthony Bower (New York: Vintage Books, 1991), pt. 1, "The Rebel," 22.

29. Camus, *The Myth of Sisyphus and Other Essays*, "The Myth of Sisyphus," 123.

30. Ibid., 121.

31. Ibid., 123.

32. Albert Camus, *The Plague*, trans. Stuart Gilbert (New York: Vintage Books, 1991), 220–228.

33. Ibid., 243–257.

34. Ibid., 255.

35. Ibid., 308.

36. Carrie Packwood Freeman, "Embracing Humanimality: Deconstructing the Human/Animal Dichotomy," in *Arguments about Animal Ethics*, ed. G. Goodale and J. E. Black (Lanham, MD: Lexington Books, 2010), 11–30.

# BIBLIOGRAPHY

Aaltola, Elisa, and John Hadley, eds. *Animal Ethics and Philosophy: Questioning the Orthodoxy*. London: Rowman and Littlefield, 2015.

Acampora, Ralph R. *Corporal Compassion: Animal Ethics and Philosophy of Body*. Pittsburgh, PA: University of Pittsburgh Press, 2006.

Aristotle. *History of Animals*. Edited and translated by D. M. Balme. Cambridge, MA: Harvard University Press, 1991.

———. *Nicomachean Ethics*. Translated by J.A.K. Thomson. Rev. ed.. Harmondsworth, UK: Penguin Classics, 1976.

———. *Politics*. Edited and translated by Ernest Barker. Oxford, UK: Oxford University Press, 1958.

Barker, Sir Ernest. *Social Contract: Essays by Locke, Hume, and Rousseau*. Oxford, UK: Oxford University Press, 1969.

Barnosky, Anthony D. *Heatstroke: Nature in an Age of Global Warming*. Washington, DC: Island Press/Shearwater Books, 2009.

Barnosky, Anthony D., Paul L. Koch, Robert S. Feranec, Scott L. Wing, and Alan B. Shabel. "Assessing the Causes of Late Pleistocene Extinctions on the Continents." *Science* 306, no. 5693 (2004): 70–75.

Barnosky, Anthony D., Nicholas Matzke, Susumu Tomiya, Guinevere O. U. Wogan, Brian Swartz, Tiago B. Quental, Charles Marshall, Jenny L. McGuire, Emily L. Lindsey, Kaitlin C. Maguire, Ben Mersey, and Elizabeth A. Ferrer. "Has the Earth's Sixth Mass Extinction Already Arrived?" *Nature* 471 (2011): 51–57.

Beck, Ulrich, Anthony Giddens, and Scott Lash. *Reflexive Modernization: Politics, Tradition and Aesthetics in the Modern Social Order*. Stanford, CA: Stanford University Press, 1994.

Bekoff, Marc. *The Emotional Lives of Animals*. Novato, CA: New World Library, 2007.

———. *Why Dogs Hump and Bees Get Depressed: The Fascinating Science of Animal Intelligence, Emotions, Friendship, and Conservation*. Novato, CA: New World Library, 2013.

Bekoff, Marc, and Jessica Pierce. *Wild Justice: The Moral Lives of Animals.* Chicago: University of Chicago Press, 2009.

Best, Steven, and Douglas Kellner. *The Postmodern Adventure: Science, Technology, and Cultural Studies at the Third Millennium.* New York: Guilford Press, 2001.

Boyd, Robert, and Peter J. Richerson. *The Origin and Evolution of Cultures.* Oxford, UK: Oxford University Press, 2005.

Braithwaite, Victoria. *Do Fish Feel Pain?* Oxford, UK: Oxford University Press, 2010.

Calarco, Matthew. *Thinking through Animals: Identity, Difference, Indistinction.* Stanford, CA: Stanford University Press, 2015.

———. *Zoographies: The Question of the Animal from Heidegger to Derrida.* New York: Columbia University Press, 2008.

Camus, Albert. *The Myth of Sisyphus and Other Essays.* Translated by Justin O'Brien. New York: Knopf, 1964.

———. *The Plague.* Translated by Stuart Gilbert. New York: Vintage International, 1991.

Castricano, Jodey, ed. *Animal Subjects: An Ethical Reader in a Posthuman World.* Waterloo, Canada: Wilfrid Laurier University Press, 2008.

Cavalieri, Paola. *The Death of the Animal: A Dialogue.* New York: Columbia University Press, 2009.

Churchland, Patricia S. *Braintrust: What Neuroscience Tells Us about Morality.* Princeton, NJ: Princeton University Press, 2011.

Cochrane, Alasdair. *Animal Rights without Liberation.* New York: Columbia University Press, 2012.

———. *An Introduction to Animals and Political Theory.* Basingstoke, UK: Palgrave Macmillan, 2010.

Coetzee, J. M. *The Lives of Animals.* Princeton, NJ: Princeton University Press, 1999.

Connolly, William E. *The Ethos of Pluralization.* Minneapolis: University of Minnesota Press, 1995.

———. *Identity/Difference: Democratic Negotiations of Political Paradox.* Ithaca, NY: Cornell University Press, 1991.

Coyne, Jerry A. *Why Evolution Is True.* New York: Penguin Books, 2009.

Crutzen, Paul Jozef, and Eugene F. Stoermer. "The Anthropocene." *Global Change Newsletter* 41 (2000): 17–18.

Darwin, Charles. *From So Simple a Beginning: The Four Great Books of Charles Darwin.* Edited by Edward O. Wilson. New York: Norton, 2006.

Dawkins, Marian Stamp, and Roland Bonney, eds. *The Future of Animal Farming: Renewing the Ancient Contract.* Oxford, UK: Blackwell Publishing, 2008.

DeKoven, Marianne, and Michael Lundblad, eds. *Species Matters: Humane Advocacy and Cultural Theory.* New York: Columbia University Press, 2012.

DeMello, Margo. *Animals and Society: An Introduction to Human-Animal Studies.* New York: Columbia University Press, 2012.

Derrida, Jacques. *The Animal that Therefore I Am.* Edited by Marie-Louise Mallet. Translated by David Wills. New York: Fordham University Press, 2008.

Diamond, Cora. "The Difficulty of Reality and the Difficulty of Philosophy." In *Philosophy and Animal Life.* Edited by Stanley Cavell, Cora Diamond, John McDowell, Ian Hacking, and Cary Wolfe, 43–89. New York: Columbia University Press, 2008.

———. "Eating Meat and Eating People." In *Animal Rights: Current Debates and New Directions.* Edited by Cass R. Sunstein and Martha C. Nussbaum, 93–107. Oxford, UK: Oxford University Press, 2004.

Donaldson, Sue, and Will Kymlicka. "Farmed Animal Sanctuaries: The Heart of the Movement? A Socio-political Perspective." *Politics and Animals* 1 (2015): 50–74.

———. *Zoopolis: A Political Theory of Animal Rights.* Oxford, UK: Oxford University Press, 2011.

Dumm, Thomas L. *Michel Foucault and the Politics of Freedom.* Thousand Oaks, CA: SAGE Publications, 1996.

Eldredge, Niles. *Dominion.* Berkeley: University of California Press, 1995.

Esposito, Roberto. *Bios: Biopolitics and Philosophy.* Translated by Timothy Campbell. Minneapolis: University of Minnesota Press, 2008.

Flannery, Tim. *Here on Earth: A Natural History of the Planet.* New York: Atlantic Monthly Press, 2010.

Foucault, Michel. *"Society Must Be Defended" Lectures at the College de France, 1975–76.* Edited by Mauro Bertani and Alessandro Fontana. Translated by David Macey. New York: Picador, 2003.

Francione, Gary L. *Animals as Persons: Essays on the Abolition of Animal Exploitation.* New York: Columbia University Press, 2008.

Gabardi, Wayne. *Negotiating Postmodernism.* Minneapolis: University of Minnesota Press, 2001.

Gershwin, Lisa-ann. *Stung! On Jellyfish Blooms and the Future of the Ocean.* Chicago: University of Chicago Press, 2013.

Grandin, Temple, and Catherine Johnson. *Animals Make Us Human: Creating the Best Life for Animals.* New York: Houghton-Mifflin Harcourt, 2009.

Guterl, Fred. *The Fate of Species: Why the Human Race May Cause Its Own Extinction and How We Can Stop It.* New York: Bloomsbury, 2012.

Habermas, Jürgen. *Communication and the Evolution of Society.* Translated by Thomas McCarthy. Boston: Beacon Press, 1979.

———. *Legitimation Crisis.* Translated by Thomas McCarthy. Boston: Beacon Press, 1975.

Haraway, Donna J. *The Companion Species Manifesto: Dogs, People, and Significant Otherness.* Chicago: Prickly Paradigm Press, 2003.

———. *When Species Meet.* Minneapolis: University of Minnesota Press, 2008.

Hardt, Michael, and Antonio Negri. *Empire.* Cambridge, MA: Harvard University Press, 2000.

Harvey, David. *A Brief History of Neoliberalism.* Oxford, UK: Oxford University Press, 2005.

———. *The Condition of Postmodernity: An Enquiry into the Origins of Cultural Change.* Oxford, UK: Basil Blackwell, 1989.

Hawthorne, Mark. *Bleating Hearts: The Hidden World of Animal Suffering.* Winchester, UK: Changemakers Books, 2013.

———. *Striking at the Roots: A Practical Guide to Animal Activism.* Winchester, UK: O-Books, 2010.

Heidegger, Martin. *Basic Writings.* Translated by David Farrell Krell. New York: Harper and Row, 1977.

———. *Poetry, Language, Thought.* Translated by Albert Hofstadter. New York: Harper Colophon Books, 1975.

———. *The Question Concerning Technology and Other Essays.* Translated by William Lovitt. New York: Harper Torchbooks, 1977.

Herzog, Hal. *Some We Love, Some We Hate, Some We Eat: Why It's So Hard to Think Straight about Animals.* New York: Harper Perennial, 2010.

Hirschman, Albert O. *Exit, Voice, and Loyalty: Responses to Decline in Firms, Organizations, and States.* Cambridge, MA: Harvard University Press, 1970.

Homans, John. *What's a Dog For? The Surprising History, Science, Philosophy, and Politics of Man's Best Friend.* New York: Penguin Press, 2012.

Horkheimer, Max, and Theodor Adorno. *Dialectic of Enlightenment.* Translated by John Cumming. New York: Seabury Press, 1972.

Houlihan, Patrick F. *The Animal World of the Pharaohs.* London: Thames and Hudson, 1996.

Hoy, David Couzens, ed. *Foucault: A Critical Reader.* Oxford, UK: Blackwell Publishing, 1986.

Human Animal Research Network Editorial Collective. *Animals in the Anthropocene: Critical Perspectives on Non-human Futures.* Sydney, Australia: Sydney University Press, 2015.

Hume, David. *An Enquiry Concerning Human Understanding: A Critical Edition.* Edited by Tom L. Beauchamp. Oxford, UK: Clarendon Press, 2000.

———. *A Treatise of Human Nature.* Edited by David Fate Norton and Mary J. Norton. Oxford, UK: Oxford University Press, 2000.

Kalof, Linda. *Looking at Animals in Human History.* London: Reaktion Books, 2007.

King, Barbara J. *How Animals Grieve.* Chicago: University of Chicago Press, 2013.

Koch, Andrew M., and Amanda Gail Zeddy. *Democracy and Domination: Technologies of Integration and the Rise of Collective Power.* Lanham, MD: Lexington Books, 2009.

Kolbert, Elizabeth. *The Sixth Extinction: An Unnatural History.* New York: Holt, 2014.

Krebs, Denis L. *The Origins of Morality: An Evolutionary Account.* Oxford, UK: Oxford University Press, 2011.

Kropotkin, Petr. *Fields, Factories and Workshops: Or Industry Combined with Agriculture and Brain Work with Manual Work.* London: Thomas Nelson and Sons, 1912.

———. *Mutual Aid: A Factor of Evolution.* New York: Garland Publishing, 1972.

Kurzweil, Ray. *The Singularity Is Near: When Humans Transcend Biology.* Oxford, UK: Oxford University Press, 2005.

Latour, Bruno. *Reassembling the Social: An Introduction to Actor-Network Theory.* Oxford, UK: Oxford University Press, 2005.

Linzey, Andrew, and Paul Barry Clarke, eds. *Animal Rights: A Historical Anthology.* New York: Columbia University Press, 2004.

Lorimer, Jamie. *Wildlife in the Anthropocene: Conservation after Nature.* Minneapolis: University of Minnesota Press, 2015.

Lovejoy, Arthur O. *The Great Chain of Being: A Study of the History of an Idea.* Cambridge, MA: Harvard University Press, 1978.

Mann, Michael. *The Sources of Social Power. Volume I: A History of Power from the Beginning to A.D. 1760.* Cambridge, UK: Cambridge University Press, 1986.

Marcus, Erik. *Meat Market: Animals, Ethics, and Money.* Boston: Brio Press, 2005.

Marzluff, John M. *Welcome to Subirdia: Sharing Our Neighborhoods with Wrens, Robins, Woodpeckers, and Other Wildlife.* New Haven, CT: Yale University Press, 2014.

Marzluff, John M., and Tony Angell. *In the Company of Crows and Ravens.* New Haven, CT: Yale University Press, 2005.

McCarter, Susan Foster. *Neolithic.* New York: Routledge, 2007.

McKibben, Bill. *Deep Economy: The Wealth of Communities and the Durable Future.* New York: Times Books, 2007.

———. *Eaarth: Making a Life on a Tough New Planet.* New York: Times Books, 2010.

Merleau-Ponty, Maurice. *Phenomenology of Perception.* Translated by Colin Smith. New York: Routledge, 1989.

———. *The Visible and the Invisible.* Edited by Claude Lefort. Translated by Alphonso Lingis. Evanston, IL: Northwestern University Press, 1968.

Morell, Virginia. *Animal Wise: The Thoughts and Emotions of Our Fellow Creatures.* New York: Crown Publishers, 2014.

Morgan, Michael L., ed. *Classics of Moral and Political Theory.* 3rd ed. Indianapolis, IN: Hackett Publishing, 2001.

Mouffe, Chantal. *The Return of the Political.* London: Verso, 1993.

Nagel, Thomas. *Mind and Cosmos: Why the Materialist Neo-Darwinian Conception of Nature Is Almost Certainly False.* Oxford, UK: Oxford University Press, 2012.

———. "What Is It like to Be a Bat?" *Philosophical Review* 83 (1974): 435–450.

Nagy, Kelsi, and Phillip David Johnson II, eds. *Trash Animals: How We Live with Nature's Filthy, Feral, Invasive, and Unwanted Species.* Minneapolis: University of Minnesota Press, 2013.

Newitz, Annalee. *Scatter, Adapt, and Remember: How Humans Will Survive a Mass Extinction.* New York: Doubleday, 2013.

Nibert, David. *Animal Rights/Human Rights: Entanglements of Oppression and Liberation.* Lanham, MD: Rowman and Littlefield Publishers, 2002.

Nietzsche, Friedrich. *The Gay Science.* Translated by Walter Kaufmann. New York: Vintage, 1974.

———. *On the Genealogy of Morality.* Edited by Keith Ansell-Pearson. Translated by Carol Diethe. Cambridge, UK: Cambridge University Press, 1994.

Nussbaum, Martha C. *Frontiers of Justice: Disability, Nationality, Species Membership.* Cambridge, MA: Belknap Press of Harvard University Press, 2006.

Osborne, Catherine. *Dumb Beasts and Dead Philosophers: Humanity and the Humane in Ancient Philosophy and Literature.* Oxford, UK: Clarendon Press, 2007.

Pachirat, Timothy. *Every Twelve Seconds: Industrialized Slaughter and the Politics of Sight.* New Haven, CT: Yale University Press, 2011.

Palmer, Clare. *Animal Ethics in Context.* New York: Columbia University Press, 2010.

Pearson, Keith Ansell. *Viroid Life: Perspectives in Nietzsche and the Transhuman Condition.* London: Routledge, 1997.

Peterson, Anna L. *Being Animal: Beasts and Boundaries in Nature Ethics.* New York: Columbia University Press, 2013.

Peterson, Dale. *The Moral Lives of Animals.* New York: Bloomsbury Press, 2011.

Purdy, Jedediah. *After Nature: A Politics for the Anthropocene.* Cambridge, MA: Harvard University Press, 2015.

Rawls, John. *Collected Papers.* Edited by Samuel Freeman. Cambridge, MA: Harvard University Press, 1999.

———. *Political Liberalism.* Exp. ed. New York: Columbia University Press, 2005.

———. *A Theory of Justice.* Rev. ed. Cambridge, MA: Belknap Press of Harvard University Press, 1999.

Richardson, John. *Nietzsche's New Darwinism.* Oxford, UK: Oxford University Press, 2005.

Richerson, Peter J., and Robert Boyd. *Not by Genes Alone: How Culture Transformed Human Evolution.* Chicago: University of Chicago Press: 2005.

Roman, Joe. *Listed: Dispatches from America's Endangered Species Act.* Cambridge, MA: Harvard University Press, 2011.

Rosa, Hartmut. *Social Acceleration: A New Theory of Modernity.* Translated by Jonathan Trejo-Mathys. New York: Columbia University Press, 2013.

Rousseau, Jean-Jacques. *Rousseau's Political Writings.* Edited by Aland Ritter and Julia Conway Bondanella. New York: Norton, 1988.

Rowlands, Mark. *Animal Rights: A Philosophical Defence.* New York: St. Martin's Press, 1998.

———. *Can Animals Be Moral?* Oxford, UK: Oxford University Press, 2012.

Rudy, Kathy. *Loving Animals: Toward a New Animal Advocacy.* Minneapolis: University of Minnesota Press, 2011.

Ruse, Michael. *Evolutionary Naturalism: Selected Essays.* London: Routledge, 1995.

Salisbury, Joyce E. *The Beast Within: Animals in the Middle Ages.* 2nd ed. London: Routledge, 2011.

Searle, John R. *Making the Social World: The Structure of Human Civilization.* Oxford, UK: Oxford University Press, 2010.

Singer, Peter. *Animal Liberation.* 2nd ed. New York: Random House, 1990.

———. *Practical Ethics.* 3rd ed. Cambridge, UK: Cambridge University Press, 2011.

Smith, Julie A., and Robert W. Mitchell, eds. *Experiencing Animal Minds: An Anthology of Animal-Human Encounters.* New York: Columbia University Press, 2012.

Smith, Laurence C. *The World in 2050: Four Forces Shaping Civilization's Northern Future.* New York: Dutton, 2010.

Snyder, Gary. *Earth Household.* New York: New Directions Books, 1969.

———. *A Place in Space: Ethics, Aesthetics, and Watersheds.* Berkeley: Counterpoint, 1995.

———. *The Practice of the Wild.* San Francisco: North Point Press, 1990.

———. *Turtle Island.* New York: New Directions Books, 1974.

Sorabji, Richard. *Animal Minds and Human Morals: The Origins of the Western Debate.* Ithaca, NY: Cornell University Press, 1993.

Sorenson, John, ed. *Critical Animal Studies: Thinking the Unthinkable.* Toronto: Canadian Scholars' Press, 2014.

Stamos, David N. *Evolution and the Big Questions: Sex, Race, Religion, and Other Matters.* Oxford, UK: Blackwell Publishing, 2008.

Steiner, Gary. *Animals and the Limits of Postmodernism.* New York: Columbia University Press, 2013.

———. *Animals and the Moral Community: Mental Life, Moral Status, and Kinship.* New York: Columbia University Press, 2008.

———. *Anthropocentrism and Its Discontents: The Moral Status of Animals in the History of Western Philosophy.* Pittsburgh, PA: University of Pittsburgh Press, 2005.

———. "Kathy Rudy's Feel-Good Ethics." *Humanimalia: A Journal of Human/Animal Interface Studies* 3, no. 2 (2012): 130–135.

Sterba, Jim. *Nature Wars: The Incredible Story of How Wildlife Comebacks Turned Backyards into Battlegrounds.* New York: Crown Publishers, 2012.

Sterelny, Kim. *Thought in a Hostile World: The Evolution of Human Cognition.* Oxford, UK: Blackwell Publishing, 2003.

Sunstein, Cass R., and Martha C. Nussbaum, eds. *Animal Rights: Current Debates and New Directions.* Oxford, UK: Oxford University Press, 2001.

Taylor, Charles. *Hegel.* Cambridge, UK: Cambridge University Press, 1975.

Taylor, Paul W. *Respect for Nature: A Theory of Environmental Ethics.* Princeton, NJ: Princeton University Press, 1986.

Thiele, Leslie Paul. *Environmentalism for a New Millennium: The Challenge of Coevolution.* Oxford, UK: Oxford University Press, 1999.

———. *Indra's Net and the Midas Touch: Living Sustainably in a Connected World.* Cambridge, MA: MIT Press, 2011.

———. *Timely Meditations: Martin Heidegger and Postmodern Politics.* Princeton, NJ: Princeton University Press, 1995.

Toulmin, Stephen. *Cosmopolis: The Hidden Agenda of Modernity.* New York: Free Press, 1990.

Uexküll, Jakob von. *A Foray into the Worlds of Animals and Humans: With a Theory of Meaning.* Translated by Joseph D. O'Neil. Minneapolis: University of Minnesota Press, 2010.

Villa, Dana R. *Arendt and Heidegger: The Fate of the Political.* Princeton, NJ: Princeton University Press, 1996.

Waal, Frans de. *The Age of Empathy: Nature's Lessons for a Kinder Society.* New York: Harmony Books, 2009.

———. *The Bonobo and the Atheist: In Search of Humanism among the Primates.* New York: Norton, 2013.

———. *Primates and Philosophers: How Morality Evolved.* Edited by Stephen Macedo and Josiah Ober. Princeton, NJ: Princeton University Press, 2006.

———. ed. *Tree of Origin: What Primate Behavior Can Tell Us about Human Social Evolution.* Cambridge, UK: Cambridge University Press, 2001.

Waal, Frans M. B. de, and Peter L. Tyack, eds. *Animal Social Complexity: Intelligence, Culture, and Individualized Societies.* Cambridge, MA: Harvard University Press, 2004.

Wadiwel, Dinesh Joseph. *The War against Animals.* Leiden, Netherlands: Brill Rodopi, 2015.

Ward, Peter. *The Flooded Earth: Our Future in a World without Ice Caps.* New York: Basic Books, 2010.

Willett, Cynthia. *Interspecies Ethics.* New York: Columbia University Press, 2014.

Wilson, Edward O. *Biophilia.* Cambridge, MA: Harvard University Press, 1984.

Wolch, Jennifer, and Jody Emel, eds. *Animal Geographies: Place, Politics, and Identity in the Nature-Culture Borderlands.* London: Verso, 1998.

Wolfe, Cary. *Animal Rites: American Culture, the Discourse of Species, and Posthumanist Theory.* Chicago: University of Chicago Press, 2003.

———. *Before the Law: Humans and Other Animals in a Biopolitical Frame.* Chicago: University of Chicago Press, 2013.

———. *What Is Posthumanism?* Minneapolis: University of Minnesota Press, 2010.

———. ed. *Zoontologies: The Question of the Animal.* Minneapolis: University of Minnesota Press, 2003.

Zalasiewicz, Jan. *The Earth after Us: What Legacy Will Humans Leave in the Rocks?* Oxford, UK: Oxford University Press, 2008.

Zalasiewicz, Jan, and Mark Williams. *The Goldilocks Planet: The Four Billion Year Story of Earth's Climate.* Oxford, UK: Oxford University Press, 2012.

Zalasiewicz, Jan, Mark Williams, Will Steffen, and Paul Crutzen. "The New World of the Anthropocene." *Environmental Science and Technology* 44, no. 7 (2010): 2228–2231.

# INDEX

WAYNE GABARDI is Professor of Political Theory and Honors Program Faculty member at Idaho State University. He is the author of *Negotiating Postmodernism*.